American Conservatism

American Conservatism

Thinking It, Teaching It

Paul Lyons

Vanderbilt University Press

Nashville

13 12 11 10 09 1 2 3 4 5

This book is printed on acid-free paper
made from 30% post-consumer recycled content.
Manufactured in the United States of America

Library of Congress Cataloging-in-Publication Data

Lyons, Paul, 1942–
American conservatism : thinking it, teaching it / Paul Lyons.
p. cm.
Includes bibliographical references and index.
ISBN 978-0-8265-1625-1 (cloth : alk. paper)
ISBN 978-0-8265-1626-8 (pbk. : alk. paper)
1. Conservatism—United States. 2. Conservatism—Study and teaching (Higher)—United States. I. Title.
JC573.2.U6L96 2009
320.520973—dc22
2008017705

for Maeve, may she remain bold,
for Liam, may he speak truth to power,
for Leo, may his laughter light up the world

Contents

Preface

American Conservatism: Thinking It, Teaching It is an attempt to demonstrate what academic scholars characteristically engage in but rarely discuss: the transformation of ideas into both scholarship and curricula. In an interview, the distinguished historian Lawrence W. Levine described the two desks in his office, one for his research, the other for his teaching. He wrote, "There is a very solid, integral connection between teaching and research. They are not separate entities, at least they haven't been in my life. They are not things that go on in bitter war between each other." Levine, like so many historians, worked out his thoughts in his classes; "teaching has been essential to me," he asserted.[1]

That is the framework within which I have approached this book. I want you, the reader, to understand how I began to be interested in the nature of American conservatism, how that interest translated into initial scholarship, how that developing expertise shaped my teaching in a variety of classes but especially a senior seminar called "American Conservatism," and how the teaching process, with my students contributing new insights and new questions, enriched my understanding of this subject. This is how many of us work—we go back and forth from ponderings to investigation to testing things out, to reflection and revision and, sometimes, rejection. I want you to get some sense of that process of academic work.

If I have a not-so-hidden agenda, it is to emphasize that most academics are, first and foremost, teachers. Even granted that institutions of higher learning, and not just the obvious research universities, reward and punish academics more for their scholarship than for their work in the classroom, I still wish to doggedly insist that we spend most of our time planning our courses, teaching our courses, and evaluating our students' performance in our courses, whether we teach 25 or 175 students per term, whether our course load is three a year, mostly graduate seminars, or ten a year at a community college. As such, it is essential to always keep in mind that during that portion of our waking hours devoted to work, we mostly teach. Teaching drives the story lines, the unanticipated questions, and the latent curiosity that characteristically leads to the research.

My interests in conservatism, especially its American variations, have deep roots in my intellectual development, much of which I discuss in the final chapter, "Is There an American Conservatism?" My third book, *New Left, New Right and the Legacy of the Sixties*, published in 1996, marked the first scholarly results of that interest, some of which was sparked by an extraordinary conference on American conservatism sponsored by Princeton University's history department.[2] What struck me was how rare it was for such matters to be incorporated into social science and humanities curricula. At that point, I had been teaching for almost thirty years.

As a teacher of the Vietnam War, I had always told my students that the most egregious and unforgivable mistake of American policy makers was their obliviousness to the nature of the enemy—they did not take the time to learn about the Vietnamese, their history, their culture. More recently we see a comparable ignorance regarding the Iraqis. As an unabashed person of the Left, I felt that something similar could be charged regarding American conservatism. I noticed that many of my students knew nothing beyond clichés about conservatism; this was true of those who self-identified as Right, those who claimed to be Left, and, of course, those—the majority—oblivious to politics. So I began my own investigations about American conservatism with this academic vacuum in mind.

Let me state, at the outset, what this book is and is not about. Whereas my seminar on American Conservatism covered all of its contributing streams—Burkean traditionalism, libertarianism, fusionism, the religious right, right-wing populism, and neoconservatism—the surrounding essays are more revealing of my point of view. I tend to view conservatism as fundamentally Burkean and, therefore, devote less time to conservatism's libertarian wing. As such, I am interested in how American conservatism violated its Burkean roots—thus my interest in seemingly marginal figures like Peter Viereck—but also I find conservatism in what has characteristically been defined as liberal—thus my emphasis on thinkers such as Hannah Arendt and Reinhold Niebuhr.

I hope that readers are not disappointed by my emphases as they proceed through the essays and the teacher log. What I seek is to contribute to the kind of vigorous and pointed dialogue that American conservatism, not to speak of liberalism, so sorely needs and so obviously deserves.

Acknowledgments

My first and most important acknowledgment must go to the group of students who inspired me to write this book in the hope that it would illuminate the importance of coming to grips with American conservatism. They were one of the best classes I have taught in over forty years—passionate, inquisitive, deeply ethical, and willing to go above and beyond even the most hopeful expectations I had at the outset.

I would also like to express the greatest appreciation for the Richard Stockton College of New Jersey, which has allowed me over almost thirty years to stretch myself in my teaching and to offer the widest range of courses that a professor could ever hope to make available to his students. They have never forced me to fit into conventional departmental boxes, instead allowing me to teach what in many institutions gets bottled up in curriculum committee bureaucracy and tunnel-vision thinking. In particular, I want to thank President Herman Saatkamp, Provost and Academic Vice-President David Carr, and a host of deans—Cheryl Kaus (Social and Behavioral Sciences), Robert Gregg (Arts and Humanities), Jan Colijn (General Studies), and Deborah Figart (Graduate Studies)—for their support.

My home school is Social and Behavioral Sciences. It is where I rely on the competence of a superb staff, starting with Assistant Dean Mary Beth Sherrier and including Nancy Reed, C. J. McClure, Patricia Pruitt, JoAnn Hulme, and Teresa Forbes.

There are individuals, colleagues, and friends who have been my sounding board, offering mostly gentle but never less than honest criticism of drafts of what became the chapters of this book. My colleague Rodger Jackson (Philosophy) has been most gracious and, indeed, most helpful in taking the time to read many versions of chapters. Alan Arcuri (Political Science) has given me valuable feedback on parts of the manuscript. And my former colleague and dear friend Joseph Walsh (Philosophy) has always provided me with the most astute and helpful criticism. I feel compelled to also thank Joe's better half, Helen Walsh, whose wise counsel has kept me on the right track for decades. My friend and colleague Dave Emmons (Criminal Justice), old Alinsky organizer and storyteller extraordinaire, has always served as a role model of a practicality rooted in ideals.

Outside of the College, my oldest friend Burton Weltman (William Patterson University, School of Education) has perhaps been my most challenging critic. Burt, I know this is not fully to your liking, but I just need to say that no one else keeps me more focused—and honest—than you. For that I am forever grateful. My good friend, poet Stephen Dunn, has always forced me to write with more precision and clarity. His criticisms of parts of this manuscript helped to make it significantly better. And to Jay Mandle and Joan Mandle, who have been central partners in my lifelong intellectual and ethical concerns, I can only say that I cannot imagine writing anything without immediately seeking out your most wise and always thoughtful counsel. I am also indebted to Josh Markel and Eva Gold, whose conversations and manuscript feedback have been invaluable.

I want to make a special expression of gratitude to Michael Ames, editor of Vanderbilt University Press, for doing more than anyone to improve this manuscript. Michael has served as my editor for many years and consequently knows how I think and how I write better than anyone else. Sometimes I bridled at his criticisms and suggestions, but he was *almost* always right.

Finally, there is family. My children, stepdaughter Jennifer Zelnick and stepson Nathaniel Zelnick, and their respective spouses, Max O'Donnell and Zoe Beckerman, plus my son, Max Lyons, have all in their own ways inspired me to make my modest contributions to an understanding of the world we live in and the world we bequeath to their children. And then there is my wife, Mary Hardwick, always and ever my most thorough reader and critic. That you have stayed with me through all of my scholarly obsessions these thirty-five years—well, bless you!

I would like to add a deep and affectionate thank you to all of the teachers who have inspired me to think that the classroom remains the bedrock of the best scholarship: Ruth Litzke of Weequahic High School; Warren Susman, Eugene Genovese, Richard Maxwell Brown, and John Cammett of the Rutgers History Department; Phil Lichtenberg; Dennis Brunn; Martin Rein of the Bryn Mawr Graduate School of Social Work and Social Research; and Harold Feldman.

American Conservatism

INTRODUCTION

What Is American Conservatism?

I begin with my dissatisfaction with the ways in which American conservatism has been defined and represented over the past half century. Perhaps there is something in the American water that distills and sanitizes conservative ideas and sensibilities, transforming them from their quintessential caution into a Reaganite "Morning in America," just as we turned Freudian psychoanalysis into the power of positive thinking. Perhaps Louis Hartz was right that a political philosophy grounded in a dour view of human nature cannot take root in a culture committed to "the pursuit of happiness."[1] At the core of conservatism is Edmund Burke and the notion that imperfection is congenital, that change must be pursued with sobriety and caution, that the human animal is flawed and prone to irrationality. Instead we seem to have invented an indigenous "conservatism" that apes the very worst of social Darwinism and laissez-faire ideology. My discontents have been exacerbated by the striking ignorance of both my conservative and liberal students concerning the mode of thought the former embraces and the latter eschews. As such I seek to help both, as well as those less ideologically committed, engage in a long-delayed conversation about traditional values.

The beginning of my own story can be set during both my undergraduate and graduate education at Rutgers, when I found myself inspired by several studies by the historian William Appleman Williams: *The Tragedy of American Diplomacy*, *The Contours of American History*, and *The Great Evasion*. Williams, an Annapolis graduate and founding spirit of what used to be called the revisionist school of U.S. foreign policy, expressed considerable respect for the perspectives of conservatives such as John Quincy Adams and Herbert Hoover. Several of my own graduate school mentors, most especially Warren Susman and

Gene Genovese, shared the view that Burkean, traditionalist conservatives understood the limitations of an unfettered capitalism, including its tendency to destroy community, threaten individuality, and subvert old-fashioned values. Thus I began my own academic career believing that radicals and conservatives had more in common than either had with mainstream—or what we then called "corporate"—liberals.[2]

I was profoundly wrong on this last prejudice, not so much because I overvalued conservatism, but because I undervalued liberalism and was not yet prepared to question the weaknesses of my own New Left neo-Marxism. At one point I found myself attracted to Daniel Bell's self-definition; he understood himself to be a socialist regarding the economy, a liberal in terms of politics, and a conservative concerning the culture.[3] Why was I drawn to this formulation? First of all, I continued to find capitalism falling short in its ability to eliminate in a larger context of affluence the worst forms of human suffering. To my eyes, this was and remains disgraceful, to tolerate unnecessary suffering when society has the capacity to lift all people to a level of basic security in education, housing, food, clothing, and health. In that regard, the Rawlsian notion of "fairness" strikes me as the barebones of political ethics.[4] Increasingly I have shrunk my utopian expectations regarding socialism to a welfare state bottom line within which there remain rich people, most folks are middle income, and poverty, at long last, is eliminated.

Bell's political liberalism made and makes sense to me because it addressed what all too many Marxists denigrated as mere bourgeois liberties. In fact those liberties of expression, religion, and assembly must be the core of any decent social order. Without choice, the ability to challenge the state, the corporation, and, yes, the trade union, freedom rings false. The social democrats who created the journal *Dissent* have, to their credit, always understand this central fact, that socialism without democracy is a fraud whereas democracy without socialism still offers human possibility.

My understanding of Bell's cultural conservatism was driven by the distance I felt from what, for lack of a better term, may be called "Woodstock Nation." I was taken aback by the self-destructive and infantile elements within the counterculture. The notion that the new socialist man (or woman) was in essence Peter Pan repelled me, possibly because I had appropriated the most compelling insights of psychoanalysis, especially Freud's understanding of the trade-offs required in sustaining civilization, his keen awareness of the irrational and of aggression in human behavior, and his sense that we always are close to the precipice, always at risk of a descent into barbarism.[5]

Part of my interest in conservatism rests on a long-term fascination with the relation between political ideology and views of human nature. Historically, the Left has tended to resist what one might call Hobbesian or Freudian emphases on the aggressive aspects of human behavior, thinking that a concession that human beings are irrational or sinful subverts any claim to a postcapitalist, harmonious social order. Early in my graduate studies, I came to question this resistance, initially in my studies of New England Puritanism and the first of the great awakenings at the dawn of the revolutionary era. I came to realize that many of the evangelical ministers preaching resistance to British tyranny castigated their colonial parishioners as sinners in their lust for British imported luxuries. But they were *equally* sinners, and thus equal to the revivalists. It is possible to believe in equality without holding to a romantic or a radically environmentalist view of human nature.[6]

Such a perspective, for me, was reinforced by Freud, who offered intriguing advice to radicals:

> The commandment "Love thy neighbor as thyself," is the strongest defense against human aggressiveness and an excellent example of the unpsychological proceedings of the cultural super-ego. The commandment is impossible to fulfill. . . . What a potent obstacle to civilization aggressiveness must be, if the defense against it can cause as much unhappiness as aggressiveness itself! "Natural" ethics, as it is called, has nothing to offer here except the narcissistic satisfaction of being able to think oneself better than others. At this point the ethics based on religion introduces its promises of a better life. But so long as virtue is not rewarded here on earth, ethics will, I fancy, preach in vain. I too think that it is quite certain that a real change in the relations of human beings to possessions would be of more help in this direction than any ethical commands; but the recognition of this fact among socialists has been obscured and made useless for practical purposes by a fresh idealistic misconception of human nature.[7]

For a number of years, I taught a seminar, "Marx and Freud," to explore the ways in which Freud's cautions might be reconciled with Marx's vision.

I was also influenced by the work of the British radical Stanley Moore, who made a persuasive case that the utopian quest for liberation from scarcity, the goal of a communist stage where the law of value was no more, was prone to totalitarianism, that there could be nothing beyond what Marx called the socialist stage within which inequalities and market mechanisms still existed.[8] Needless to say, I had serious reservations about the more visionary claims of the counterculture and its New Age heirs.

On the other hand, I didn't agree with those cultural conservatives who sought to roll back the challenges of second-wave feminism or of the gay and lesbian movements. I did share, however, their concerns about the family, breaking with many of my radical friends in finding compelling Daniel Patrick Moynihan's argument that the rising proportion of female-headed households in the African American community suggested an alarming crisis. I wasn't a cultural conservative, but I did believe that if liberals and radicals didn't face disturbing secular trends, if they buried their heads, ostrichlike, in the sand, they risked marginalization and truly merited contempt.[9]

As I entered my personal second half century and the turn into the twenty-first century, I found myself having a difficult time defining my own political position. I don't think this was unique among those of my generation who invested in the social movements associated with the 1960s. But over a period of years I have come to certain tentative conclusions that shape if not define my politics. First of all, I remain proud of my involvement in those sixties movements, such as civil rights, peace work, and inclusion. But I recognize the self-righteousness of parts of those movements and have become essentially pragmatic, both in philosophy and by temperament. My criterion tends to be, Does it work? Does it do no harm? With that in mind, I have placed part of idealism on a shelf for possible future use—at this moment in human history, the possibilities for socialism have disappeared in light of communist tyrannies and economic inefficiencies. There is no extant socialist society. Those claimants, most particularly Fidel Castro's Cuba, are unable to persuade me that any society run by one man for close to fifty years, even granted educational and health-care accomplishments and even considering the stupidities of the U.S. economic boycott, is worthy of support, not to speak of imitation. Recent left-wing romanticizing of the Venezuelan populist authoritarian Hugo Chavez leaves me despondent about the capacity of radicals to learn from history.

In the West, there has been a serious crisis of the welfare state, affecting both socialist and social-democratic parties. In the post–World War II decades, social democracy produced the freest and most prosperous societies in the history of the world. But they rested on a too-confident notion of economic growth, the assumption that Keynesian interventions had resolved the economic cycle. In the 1970s, this confidence was shattered when inflation and unemployment returned with a vengeance. International competition, the rise of the East Asian economies, and the ability to outsource production made it more difficult for labor demands to be addressed through price increases. When push came to shove, even though Western European nations sought to sustain solidaristic agreements about the welfare state, at least to a greater extent than the United States and the United Kingdom under Reagan and Thatcher, social-democratic and liberal assumptions about the inexorability of mixed economies faltered, became defensive.

In this sense, I would suggest that part of the seeming success of conservatism rests on the moral, political, and philosophical crisis of the Left, both in the social-democratic welfare state and in the Marxist promise of a classless society. In the second half of the twentieth century, those on the Left suffered a crisis of confidence: Could a capitalist economy sustain and nurture the elimination of poverty and insecurity and, at the same time, insure the economic growth upon which such welfare benefits rested? Was the Marxist dream of a postcapitalist order not only dysfunctional in terms of economic inefficiencies but morally problematical in terms of totalitarian nightmares, for example, Stalinism, gulags, Khmer Rouge killing fields, Maoist fanaticism? Part of the conservative ascendancy is inexplicable without factoring in the loss of confidence among liberals that capitalism and democracy can be reconciled and the related terror among radicals that socialism and democracy cannot coexist.

Here is where a critical examination of conservatism can be of value. Conservatives like Hayek had long expressed concerns about the threats to liberty spawned by the big government programs of social democrats and liberals.[10] The latter groups too often blew off such criticisms as extremist or archaic; for better or worse, the result was a blindness to the limitations of the welfare state. The neoconservatives were the most astute, at least in their earliest expressions, in declaring "the law of unintended consequences," that is, the risk of making things worse despite the best of intentions. Libertarian conservatives correctly pointed out the values of the marketplace, especially its efficiencies in the matching of consumer demand with producer supply. I came to value what I began to call "cockroach" capitalism, the nook-and-cranny businesses—small shops and stores, restaurants, bakeries, hardware stores, laundromats, bars—that central planning could not anticipate. Indeed, as I absorbed this lesson, I came to recognize that one of the gravest immoralities of the Left was its contempt for what it castigated as the "petit-bourgeoisie." There seemed to be no decent, free society that could function without such a group of small-scale entrepreneurs. Fortunately, some of our best non-Marxian radical critics, Jane Jacobs and Paul Goodman, fully understand such a need. The economist Alec Nove pointed the way many years ago when he sought to analyze "the economics of feasible socialism," that is, the ways in which the particulars—the scale of an enterprise—should drive the organizational form of that enterprise. In brief, petty enterprise, cooperatives, state ownership, degrees of participation, and factors of expertise were pragmatic and empirical, not theological, questions.[11]

As I reflected on the meaning of American conservatism, I was not moving toward it, insofar as I found it deeply limiting in analytic suppleness and human compassion. But I did feel that some conversation between radical, liberal, and conservative traditions was required to move away from predictable and counterproductive polemics and toward something that works. I was tired of the various dogmas, either libertarian or Marxist, about one-size-fits-all solutions. Wasn't it clear that some enterprises, for instance, health care, required different organizational forms, different structures of reward, than, for example, information sciences or military operations or the restaurant business? Increasingly, I found myself impatient with those who were unwilling to come to grips with the soft spots within their respective ideologies.

In the heyday of what Geoffrey Hodgson called "the liberal consensus," essentially the period from the New Deal through 1968, there was a lament concerning the absence of any substantive conservative intellectual tradition in the United States.[12] Both the literary critic Lionel Trilling and the consensus historian Louis Hartz suggested that the culture would be the richer if challenged by thoughtful conservatives. Neither considered the repressive and demagogic presence of McCarthyism to be genuinely conservative, nor did they find any intellectual substance in the conventional apologetics of the corporate order. Yes, there were conservatives, but none with compelling ideas. As Trilling noted, "In the United States . . . liberalism is not only the dominant but even the sole intellectual tradition. For it is the plain fact that nowadays there are no conservative or reactionary ideas in general circulation."[13]

Most scholars of an American conservatism share a narrative that cites its European roots, its various American strands, and its revitalization during the 1950s and 1960s. Most of the credit goes to William F. Buckley and his establishment of the *National Review* and then proceeds to the short-term disasters and long-term achievements of the Goldwater movement within the Republican Party. The dominant narrative also sets these developments within a crisis of liberalism marked by the most traumatic events of the 1960s, particularly the war in Vietnam; the cultural challenges regarding race, gender, and sexual preference; and the economic downturns that delegitimized the Keynesian paradigm.

Scholars proceed to analyze the traditionalist-libertarian tensions within the conservative movement, the rise of the neoconservatives, and the emergence of a politicized religious right among many fundamentalists and evangelicals. The successes of these various strands and traditions, marked by a remarkable institutional flowering, led to what most accept as the Reagan Revolution of the 1980s.[14] While the significance of that rightward turn came under some scrutiny in the administrations of George H. W. Bush and, more sharply, Bill Clinton, the reelection of George W. Bush seemed to have revitalized the sense of conservative ascendancy. One measure of a cultural hegemony is that whereas many proclaim themselves as conservatives, few can fight their way past the powerful prejudice against the "L" word, which has become a political liability.

But, as the notion of a conservative ascendancy, which peaked with the reelection of George W. Bush in 2004, has faltered in the face of what many observers—and not only on the Left—are considering to be possibly the most incompetent and destructive administration in American history, there is need for some perspective and, indeed, considerable humility. Hegel's dawn of Minerva, the cunning of history, the surprises that seem to inevitably be held in store for those who are foolish enough to anticipate the future, suggests caution. Indeed, as I examine the ideological and cultural landscape of the early twenty-first century in these United States, I see very little that sustains the notion of a conservative ascendancy. Of course, there are powerful forces, which define themselves as conservative, controlling the White House, the Congress, and, increasingly, the courts. And there is the cultural apparatus that impressively includes the *Wall Street Journal*, *Weekly Standard*, the Fox News network, the talk-radio ideologues, and such influential columnists as George F. Will, David Brooks, and Charles Krauthammer. But are they, by any historical definition, conservative? What do we mean when we call them conservative? My own inclination is to argue that over the past half century or so, an opportunity was missed to create a viable conservative intellectual and political tradition. In its place, I will suggest, we have experienced the growth of a business ideology grounded less in conservatism than in narrowly defined self-interest. Second, we have experienced the lesser successes of an idealistic libertarian movement characteristically caught up in contradictory moments. And, finally, we have been taken aback by the remarkable emergence of a religiously driven ideology that for the most part directly and systematically stands in opposition to virtually all of the values of conservatism. At all times, a business ideology, from the days of Mark Hanna to Tom DeLay's K Street Project, has been a driving force in what passes for conservatism. Even that ideology is rent with tensions, between its Wall Street and Main Street components, between its more sophisticated corporate forces and its local Chamber of Commerce elements.

William Appleman Williams offered a useful way to think about the arguments within the business class, what he defined as "interest" versus "class" consciousness. The former reflected Main Street, bottom-line narrowness, and short-term interests in profit maximization. The latter, which Williams hoped to see expanding within the corporate sector, took a longer-range approach, with a focus on the broad interests of the capitalist system as a whole. Thus, the class-conscious businessperson could accommodate unions as partners, could recognize the stability produced by a healthy and satisfied workforce, could accept that short-term greed subverted long-term rewards. With the economic crises of the 1970s and since, the West has seen the fragility of such class-conscious strategies; it has suffered the pains driven by a regressive interest-consciousness.[15]

I don't wish to deny the importance of libertarianism, what many accurately call a nineteenth-century Manchester liberalism. It is a powerful force, represented by such productive think tanks as the Cato Institute. It is certainly a major factor in the antitax ideology of those such as Grover Norquist and the Club for Growth. But I choose to place it on the margin of my analysis because I do not find it conservative in any meaningful sense of the term and, perhaps equally importantly, because I do not find that it has much to offer in helping us make sense of the institutional dynamics our economy and polity confront. At the risk of violating my call for humility, let me define libertarianism as fundamentally at odds with the complexities of modern institutional life, for instance, multinational corporations, globalization, environmental risks, and a fundamental interdependence that can only scarcely be illuminated by a worldview based on a radical individualism. That is not to say libertarianism cannot provide valuable criticism of the risks of bigness—governmental, corporate, party. Indeed, our polity is strengthened by the single-minded, if limited, focus of libertarianism on the individual and his or her liberties. But it is not of much assistance in addressing issues ranging from the HIV/AIDS epidemic to global warming to the impact of Wal-Mart on local communities. As such, I value its contributions but view it as an inherently limited ideology unable to offer a comprehensive model of a good society.

The American right wing can be distinguished from its European cousins by examining other groups in the United States going by the name of conservatism, especially a defensive religious movement framed by Christian fundamentalism and evangelism grounded in fearful responses to the forces of both modernization and modernity. In this most Protestant culture, a politicization of fundamentalism and evangelism, initially sparked by the perceived threats posed by the theory of evolution but perhaps even more challenged by the new literary analyses that historicized the Bible, reached critical mass with the even more frightening subversions associated with the 1960s—the removal of prayer from the schools, profanity, sexual revolution, feminism, gay and lesbian rights, family erosion, *Roe v. Wade*. I don't wish to underestimate the ways in which the religious right makes life difficult for those it deems as deviant or sinful. But I do want to point to its inherent weaknesses and failures.

Some observers are perplexed by the tendency of many cultural conservatives to complain incessantly about the continuing dominance of liberalism, for example, attacks on the mainstream media, on Hollywood. After all, liberal critics contend, they run the White House, Congress until very recently, the courts, talk radio. Why do they act as if they are the beleaguered minority, always the persecuted rather than the persecutors? Part of the answer is that despite political successes, cultural conservatives accurately perceive that they are losing the culture war, that over time the nation is becoming more and more inclusive, more open to women, more open to minorities, more accepting of gays and lesbians, more culturally relativist, more inclined to make consistent the deeply held creed of equal opportunity, more likely to judge individuals by their works and not their identities. This is not to suggest that we are past bigotries. Yes, racism is still out there, as is homophobia, sexism, hostility toward Arabs and Muslims and "illegal" immigrants. But there seems to be an inexorable expansion of the arc of inclusion, especially if we measure it by what has transpired over the past forty years. Indeed, the sixties remain the villain for cultural conservatives precisely because we see a growing openness, despite some regressions, over time. For example, conservatives, who only a few years ago defined all homosexual relations as immoral, now fall back to defend civil unions in their futile efforts to deny marital rights to gays and lesbians. Is there anyone out there who doesn't assume that within the next twenty or so years we will embrace gay marriage?

It is useful to examine the religious right as a part of the right-wing populism that, to me, has been the heartland of conservative strength over the past forty years. Whether one examines such influences as Albert Jay Nock and his sense of being a superfluous man in an egalitarian age, José Ortega y Gasset and his fear and contempt for the masses, or the Anglo-Catholic Toryism personified by the young dandy William F. Buckley Jr., it is apparent that what seemed to embody conservatism prior to the Goldwater movement was elitist, antipopulist, and, for the most part, as the *National Review* proclaimed in its first issue, standing in the face of history, with little hope of being more than a voice in the wilderness.[16] Pre-1960s conservatives tended to mistrust all forms of democracy, especially mass social movements.

The McCarthyist movement made successful appeals to a more diverse mix of middle- and working-class constituents, now including Catholics and immigrant-stock ethnics, who were inclined to blame the failure of the United States to shape the postwar world—especially in Catholic Eastern Europe—on external and internal communists and their dupes. It was a breakthrough compared with the nativism of the second Klan, and it was able to peel off some of those who had benefited from the New Deal but who now were worried about "their" homes and schools and taxes being used for "the unworthy poor," especially those who were not white.[17] The new right-wing populism evoked by McCarthyism contained a more potent mix than the older anti-Catholic, anti-Semitic nativist tradition.

Both libertarian and traditionalist forms of conservatism sought some distance from extremism and from the image of "nuttiness," thus the campaigns to marginalize Ayn Rand and Joseph Welch.[18] The liberal consensus, circa 1960, seemed so immovable, so invincible, during an era when the notion of "tax and spend" seemed decisively a formula for ongoing hegemony. Not until the 1960s fissure in liberalism did conservatives find an opportunity to effectively challenge for leadership. And that challenge *required* that an elite intellectual movement become populist.

The key marker for that challenge was Kevin Phillips's *The Emerg-*

ing Republican Majority, which made the right-wing populist case for a coalition built around Sunbelt suburbanites and Frostbelt ethnics, disaffected by the civil rights revolution, the rise of black power, rising taxes, rising crime, rising rates of welfare, declining families, and challenges to patriotism—Nixon's great silent majority.[19] Such a new majority was prefigured by the George Wallace campaigns of 1964 and 1968 and by the troops who rallied to Goldwater in 1964 and stayed around to build a movement.

This new majority rested on the collapse of liberalism. The golden age of American capitalism soured into the stagflation of the 1970s, opening opportunities for Republican conservatives to get past images of Hoovervilles and to make a case that the Democrats were now the party of economic failure. They also could skillfully make the case that the most radical challenges of the 1960s—racial and gender equality, gay and lesbian rights, environmental concerns, views of patriotism that include dissent as an indicator of love of country—defined liberalism and the Democratic Party.

After one processes through all of the foolishness and strategic and tactical blunders made by liberal Democrats, it remains clear that the challenges linked to the Left, liberal and radical, were so powerful, so demanding, and so traumatic that even the most skillful movement would have paid a major political price. Liberals were asking Americans, many of them barely treading water, to change along a whole series of cultural and psychological fronts: race, gender, sexuality, morality, family, food. And, importantly, there was ever and always the charge that those not changing fast enough were—take your pick—racists, sexists, homophobes, threats to the earth, imperialists, fascists.

This is where the populism of the Right played such an essential role. Imagine one of Kevin Phillips's voters—either a white Southern good old boy or girl, or that Macomb County, Michigan, blue-collar ethnic—Italian or Polish Catholic. Liberals demand that he or she change—or else! Some liberals don't even believe it is possible. There had always been a degree of elitism on the Left, evidenced by the celebration of the expertise of the Fabians and the notion of the "best and the brightest"; the cultural images of Stanley Kowalski, Ralph Kramden, and Archie Bunker had infected older notions of a plebeian salt of the earth. Many plebeian voters sensed that they were being held in contempt by liberals—limousine liberals if you will—and those voters began to hear hosannas directed at them by conservative elitists newly discovering the virtues of mass man. Voila! I can recall attending a Philadelphia meeting organized to oppose the right-wing populist police commissioner and mayor Frank Rizzo; the literature highlighted his bananalike nose and his school dropout status, scarcely aware how such anti-Italian and antiplebeian stereotypes reinforced Rizzo's claim to be the people's candidate.[20] I can recall Tom Hayden of the SDS telling me during an antiwar organizing session in 1967 that if white middle-class suburbanites were not yet against the Vietnam War, they were hopeless and ethically deficient.

Such a quickness to write off a variety of constituencies—middle and working class, urban and suburban—created self-fulfilling prophecies. Part of conservatism's strength, up to the present, has been its celebration of those it seeks to organize. Indeed, some of this strategy has been cynical, but more significantly, it has been able to depend all too often on liberal blindnesses to the hidden injuries of class and liberal and radical ambivalence about affluence. Right-wing populist shock jocks like Rush Limbaugh and Bill O'Reilly have feasted upon such examples, real and distorted, of liberal elitism, building on a tradition with roots in Joe McCarthy and George Wallace.

There was a moment in the late 1960s and early 1970s when it seemed that the United States was on the verge of giving birth to a genuinely conservative intellectual movement, spawned by reaction against the excesses associated with the 1960s but even more significantly grounded in the responses by a critical set of intellectuals in the postwar period to the implications of the horrors of the twentieth century: two terrible world wars, the rise of both fascism and Stalinist communism, the horrors of Auschwitz and other modern genocides, and the threats rising from the existence and use of nuclear weapons.

What interests me are the failures of that neoconservative moment or, to put it less strangely, its transformation into something called *neocon* but nevertheless having little connection to a tradition which began with the thoughts of Edmund Burke. As one interrogates the present Bush administration, sustained by pure business greed, religious fervor, and neoconservative bellicosity, one finds precious little that can be called conservative, neo- or any other version. As a culture we remain close to Trilling's distinction between conservative ideas and conservative impulses that "express themselves not in ideas but only in action or in irritable mental gestures which seek to resemble ideas."[21]

In his 1979 study, *The Neoconservatives*, Peter Steinfels offers "a rough notion of what a genuine American conservatism might look like." He states, "An American Conservatism would be devoted to liberalism—but a liberalism of the harder, more fearful sort. Pessimistic about human nature, skeptical about the outcome of political innovation, distrustful of direct democracy . . . it would defend the principles of liberalism less as vehicles for betterment than as bulwarks against folly . . . [it] would add to the limiting structures of liberalism Burke's advocacy of gradual change and historical continuity . . . [and] the avoidance of the sad fate prominently displayed, of nations which have given themselves over to utopian fevers."[22] Peter Clecak distinguished between temperamental conservatism that "degenerates easily into irritable reaction"; libertarian, or liberal, conservatism; and philosophical conservatism. He linked the philosophical kind to figures like Russell Kirk, Robert Nisbet, Richard Weaver, and Peter Viereck, and grounded it in Edmund Burke's reflections on the French Revolution.[23]

Thus, the quintessential question remains: what happened to neoconservatism? We need to understand how the potential birth of conservatism—long seen as missing from American intellectual, cultural, and political life—lost its initial focus and became, in many ways, its opposite. We need to address the more fundamental, Hartzian question of whether there is a place for conservatism within this quintessentially Lockean, liberal political culture.

Let me conclude by noting that the conservative Republican strength remains the weaknesses of their adversaries. Despite the failures of George W. Bush, despite the fact that a younger generation is leaning Democratic and that the Democrats have been building a fifteen-point margin over Republicans in recent polls, there remains the fact that conservatives assert pride in an identity that their political behavior often contradicts, whereas liberals still tend to hide behind euphemisms like "progressive" or "moderate," avoiding the "L" word at all costs. Until this evasion is addressed and resolved, there is not likely to be a sea change from conservative to liberal in American politics.

Liberals need to reconfigure their accomplishments and their failures. The Kerry campaign, like many before it, embodied the problem. Kerry wrapped himself in the flag of his military service but ran away from what brought him to political prominence—his testimony before the Senate Foreign Relations Committee calling for an end to the war in Vietnam, and the return of his fellow GIs from an immoral war. It is not just Kerry and his awkwardness, his nuanced responses that allowed him to be branded a "flip-flopper," his delayed reaction to the demagogic Swiftboat ads. It is that, since the 1960s, liberals have been paralyzed by a crisis in confidence driven by the relative failures of Keynesian interventions in the economy; by the divisiveness within the party over identity, values, and national security; and by the ways in which all of these tensions have been highlighted by parallels among our Western European allies.

During the 1960s, liberals came under attack from the Left and the Right. The Left, more properly the New Left, argued that what they called "corporate liberalism" had abandoned egalitarian and redistributionist ideals for a piece of the action offered by sophisticated corporate leaders, for instance, union benefits but no questioning of the profit motive, bureaucratization at the cost of "participatory democracy," alienation, and a fatalistic embrace of what Paul Goodman called "growing up absurd."[24] At their core, these criticisms, while harsh and total, were valid even if they were scarcely addressed, not to speak of resolved, by New Leftists too quickly enamored with Third World revolutionary models. The right made analogous critiques: the eclipse of community, the imperial presidency, the oppressiveness of the federal bureaucracy, the risks to individuality, the risks of secularization. Both Left and Right drew on communitarian and individualist, even antinomian, traditions. And neither was able to recognize that the "vital center" of liberalism, at its best, offered the best possibility to address and remedy these most difficult issues and questions.

The conservatives appropriately asked liberals to reconsider the values of the market mechanism as a source of democratic power—the people decide. They asked for more modesty in figuring out ways to redress grievances such as residential segregation other than with court-imposed busing, for recognition that there was indeed a deepening crisis within the African American family, that there was indeed a rising problem of violent crime not reducible to racism or poverty, that there were legitimate concerns about national loyalty and obligation that had been sometimes denigrated by the countercultural forces of the sixties.

From the Left, there is the nub of the Kerry evasion—why not stand up as proudly for one's dissent from the war as for one's service in that war? Just consider what might have happened if the instant the Swift-boat ads came out, John Kerry had called a press conference and stated: "I am proud that I served my country in uniform in Vietnam; I am as proud that when I returned from service, I spoke out to end the war. And, may I ask, what was my opponent proud of in that period of his life?" End of issue. Kerry's ambivalence, his political paralysis, reflects a very real dilemma for liberals. On the one hand, they need to recognize that the challenges associated with the social movements of the 1960s—civil rights, feminism, environmentalism, a patriotism committed to peace, gay and lesbian rights, other forms of inclusion—came hard and fast and faced inevitable resistance from white mainstream people. From an anthropological view, it would be most unusual if everyday people not at Berkeley or Madison or Harvard Square, mostly concerned with making a living and raising their families, could immediately or even in a short period of time integrate these fundamental challenges into their behaviors and their consciousness. Keep in mind how deep racial prejudice runs; how profound it is historically to seek equality for women both in the workplace and, with more difficulty, within the family; how powerful homophobia has been within our culture; how much of our civilization has rested on the notion that nature is available for conquest, domination. Now consider how much has changed over the past thirty to forty years in each instance. But those pushing the envelope, carrying the message, making the demands, have paid an inevitable price. A price well worth it, I should add, but one that punished the messenger. Even a liberal message of inclusion and environmental care sensitive to the lives of those affected would have generated resentments for at least a generation.

What liberals need is a way to affirm all that they—and their radical allies—have accomplished in making our society more inclusive, more fair, more just, without the busybodiness, the righteousness, and the snobbery that has, unfortunately, sometimes accompanied the message. If you think this is not a problem, spend a little time on any campus with a liberal and radical voice and watch how the activists, in a whole variety of ways, some gross, some subtle, communicate their contempt to those students who seem to reject any responsibility for environmental threats or for racial, sexual, or lifestyle prejudice. After all, many of the activists have been the minority, the nerds if you will in their high schools, marginalized by those who tend to run such institutions—the jocks, the social crowd, the preppies. Such resentments replicate themselves through the lives of many activists, making it hard for them to persuade those whom they still resent for earlier injuries. Those such as Bill Gates may be able to fulfill a kind of "revolt of the nerds"; political activists cannot. They must find ways to tap into the deep reservoirs of egalitarianism that once were the bread and butter of all left-of-center movements.

Liberalism and any chance for a revived radicalism will need to get past such resentments and make the case built on what they have contributed and on where they have fallen short. That will require a recognition of the relevance of insights and criticisms from both the Left and the Right. Liberals need conservatives to be more true to their mission; I would only add that they also need radicalism to insure that they do not ignore the forest for the trees, do not lose a necessary impatience with the slowness of change, do not become complacent while there is a single human being in our nation and in the world who unnecessarily, needlessly, immorally goes to sleep at night hungry, without proper shelter, insecure, at risk of disease rooted in poverty.

And American conservatives need to find their own ways, grounded in their own insights and traditions, to address the same moral issues without succumbing to apologetics for business greed, religious dogmatism, or abstract paeans to liberty oblivious to human suffering. They will be tempted to rally behind some version of a right-wing populism that, in mobilizing the forces of exclusion—against immigrants, gays, Muslims?—denies conservatism's integrity. But let us hope that the promise of a genuine "soulcraft" will revive in efforts to enrich the American polity with conservatism's truths.

I began this essay with my own political and philosophical journey as a chastened but still determined activist with roots in the social movements of the 1960s. I continue to struggle with questions that have framed my life for close to half a century:

> Can a society maintain ideals without a utopian vision?
> Are utopian ideals inherently prone to totalitarian nightmare?
> Can a vital-center liberalism complete the mission of the welfare state—responsible wealth, a vast middle class, elimination of poverty—without succumbing to bureaucratic strangulation and erosion of individual liberties?
> Can American soil nurture and sustain a traditionalist conservatism that tempers all tendencies of planners and reformers to ride roughshod over the habits and values of its citizens?

I would be a bit more optimistic if such questions were, at the least, asked, even if not fully resolved.

PART I

Teaching Conservatism

What follows is based on a teaching log I kept during the spring term of 2006. As I was inaugurating my seminar on American conservatism that term, I thought it might be useful to keep a running internal conversation about how the course unfolded. In the past, I had found some value in such a disciplined approach to teaching. For one, it forced me to gather my thoughts after every session when they were fresh in my mind and when my feelings about what had transpired were less diluted by reflection. On a few occasions, I was not able to get to my word processor immediately after class; the worst was that on a few occasions I wrote my thoughts the following day. But in almost all instances, the log was written within hours of leaving the classroom.

My students were required to participate in an electronic computer conference within a system called Web Board. Each week I directed them to consider a question related to the work we were doing in the seminar or to assigned readings. Some of their comments are incorporated into the log. Also included is a syllabus for the seminar, officially GIS 4628 American Conservatism: Senior Seminar.

Finally, I have added later reflections, in italics, to give the reader some sense of how a course stays with a teacher long after the course ends. I have also deleted some portions of the log when I thought the comments were either pedestrian or redundant and have framed the log with headings to provide them with some shape. Finally, I include an attempt to define this contradictory cultural phenomenon called American conservatism. Please regard it as a work in progress.

CHAPTER 1

Teaching Log: Starting Out

In the Beginning

January 17

Examining my initial comments, I am reinforced in my sense of how important beginnings are. Students are amazingly observant—they pay attention to what we wear, to whether we got a haircut, and to our idiosyncratic gestures; they approach the classroom as student guerrillas who need to scope out the more powerful figure in the front of the room, who need to figure out what they need to do to survive. This doesn't necessarily make them cynical or even manipulative; this guerrilla sense is often mixed with wonder and hopeful expectation. But it is always careful.

On my part, I try to empathize with that resistance to what I offer without succumbing to it. I enter every new class, even those I have taught many times, full of butterflies, encountering a bunch of strangers who for assorted reasons have registered for my class. Usually, the nervousness is gone within minutes of the class beginning.

I was more wired than usual, as it was not only a new term but a new course, and one I think of as more ambitious than others insofar as I see it as the core of a new book. We did the usual stuff—syllabus, basic information about me (office hours, e-mail, phone) and them (major, e-mail or phone). I wanted to give them a sense of the "why" of the course. So I started with procedures—three papers, electronic conferencing with weekly entries, attendance, and all that—but focused mostly on demeanor, the tone of what I expect from them and from me.

Most of them seemed "there," listening, positive body language, lots of questions, and even some discussion at the outset once I had talked about both the rules of behavior and why I decided to teach the course. Let me start with the latter since it leads inexorably to the former. I have noticed how few colleges teach courses on conservatism, American or otherwise. Yes, there are courses in politics, history, and philosophy that have sections devoted to conservative thinkers and movements, but few actual courses. Even those that exist focus mostly on right-wing extremism: the Klan, American Nazis, militias, anti-abortion militants, skinheads, racist groups. More importantly, I noticed that many nonconservative academics seem oblivious to conservatism except as a target of scorn, ridicule, and contempt. One colleague states that he has no interest in teaching this stuff because students get it all the time from our culture; he only teaches what he believes to be truth, which is indisputably on the left. Others just have such a negative view of anything conservative that they can't imagine dealing with it as other than pathology or human greed.

I told my class that I thought it was important to make sense of a movement and point of view (actually, as we'll see, points of view) that many argue have dominated the American political landscape for maybe thirty-five years. What is conservatism? Where did it come from? What are its variations, its contradictions, its tensions? Its strengths? Its future? I spoke of how student conservatives often know little of what they claim to be their point of view; liberals and radicals even less beyond pejoratives. And most nonpoliticals might mention Rush Limbaugh or Bill O'Reilly but have no more than an inkling of what it's all about.

When I asked the class to tell me what, at the end of the term, would disappoint them—a technique I've used with success on several occasions—there was a torrent of comments, initially from more conservative students, telling me, as they noted in passing how liberal Stockton was, how most of their liberal professors blow their comments off and treat them unfairly. I acknowledged their experience without agreeing with David Horowitz's polemic that colleges are intolerant places run by liberals and radicals in need of legislative remedy. I talked a bit about Horowitz, suggesting that his claims to integrity were compromised by his one-sidedness. Yes, there are liberal profs who are intolerant of conservative students, but then why doesn't Horowitz discuss political correctness at Bob Jones or Brigham Young or hundreds of religious institutions or many Southern or Rocky Mountain colleges where you are at risk if you are left of center? My gut feeling is that liberals are more tolerant than conservatives, but that may be my bias.

But what I wanted to do was to model modesty, humility, and tentativeness without sacrificing passion and directness. I told them I chose a history written by a conservative and an anthology organized by one so that they could have multiple points of view different from my own. We had an interesting discussion of whether profs influence their students; I told them that I didn't trust disciples, that I'm not impressed by students who become activists, right or left, because they are influenced by a prof. What matters is how they act over a lifetime and, to me, that requires a more critical thinker, not someone who becomes transformed and energized but only for six months or six years. As an old sixties activist I had seen too many burnt out, sold-out young people, passionate Maoists who are now investment bankers. Of course, that's an old saw and a cliché. In fact, my own research has demonstrated that most activists find a way to make a lifetime of their commitments, living in the world but not of it. But I think that the class got a sense of my approach, including my own curiosity.

So we'll start on Thursday with the readings from Edmund Burke, essays by Richard Weaver and Russell Kirk. I laid out the early framework: traditionalist and libertarian strands, later augmented by neoconservatism and the religious right. A good start, good feelings as we closed off, like we're at the start of an intriguing adventure. I told them that I was writing a book about the course and let them know that, with protection of their privacy, they would be part of it.

Edmund Burke

January 19

I worked with special diligence to prepare for this first substantive class—going over the Burke selection in particular several times, as well as the pieces by Richard Weaver and Russell Kirk, although I anticipated, it turns our accurately, that we wouldn't get to the latter. My concern pedagogically was how to address both the historical context within which Burke wrote his reflections and the writing itself. This is characteristically an issue at the beginning of a course, especially one that has no prerequisites. Some of the students are political science, history, philosophy, and literature majors with some experience in Western and American thought and textual analysis, but others come in with little background and consequently struggle with the meaty readings. My approach is to frame the issues: European history, the roles of church and state, the dynamics of feudalism and the rise of monarchies, the importance of the scientific revolution, and, finally, the bare basics of both the French Revolution and the Glorious Revolution of 1688. And I do this with sufficient time to engage Burke's words. I always worry about losing—or boring—the less-experienced student. I asked for initial reactions to the approximately forty pages of readings in Burke; one student told of her frustration, another of his boredom. This was good in that I knew many others were raring to go with what they found in the text. But I took a little time to discuss empathetically how such readings can be difficult for students who have little experience with noncontemporary commentary. I wanted to set a tone: I understand but will push you to get beyond the claim of boredom, to reach within to focus on why so many people consider this guy—Burke—so important. Most feedback was positive although, again, events will tell. I was less happy with how much of Burke we covered, but I was pleased with the sections brought out by students and with the concluding reading and discussion of Burke's statement about the social contract in which he includes the living as well as those who have passed and those yet to be born. It's really a passage of enormous poetic power:

> Society is indeed a contract. Subordinate contracts for objects of mere occasional interest may be dissolved at pleasure—but the state ought not to be considered as nothing better than a partnership agreement in a trade of pepper or coffee, calico or tobacco, or some other such low concern, to be taken for a little temporary interest, and to be dissolved by the fancy of the parties. [No worshiper of bourgeois values here!] It is to be looked on with other reverence; because it is not a partnership in things subservient only to the gross animal existence of a temporary and perishable nature. It is a partnership in science; a partnership in all art; a partnership in every virtue, and in all perfection. As the ends of such a partnership cannot be obtained in many generations, it becomes a partnership not only between those who are living, but between those who are living, those who are dead, and those who are to be born. Each contract of each particular state is but a clause in the great primeval contract of eternal society, linking the lower with the higher natures, connecting the visible and invisible world, according to a fixed compact sanctioned by the inviolable oath which holds all physical and all moral natures, each in their own appointed place.

With a caveat about democracy and my own essentially naturalistic bent, such wisdom belongs in any and all ideologies worth respect.

The students were zeroed in and understood how this differed from Locke; we discussed how the Burkean tradition was ambivalent about dimensions of capitalism, about what Marx called the cash nexus, about materialism, as well as how Burke valued his own version of diversity—slices of monarchy, aristocracy and its code of chivalry, and Whig predominance. At the close I asked them to consider how this traditionalist version of the social contract distinguished the English from Native Americans in deals over land. Who owns the land? Is it alienable? What rights do one's ancestors and one's heirs have? Can it be sold?

I tried to model multiple points of view, asking one of my more liberal students, Kate, to consider why she was so impatient with Burke's molasses-slow model of change. We discussed his skill in placing himself at the center and the idea of moderate Whiggish change as an alternate to reaction and revolution. We also discussed the excitement the intelligentsia felt in being the first to imagine that they could exceed the accomplishments of the classics, the power of the scientific revolution and its political parallels.

Making Adjustments, Serendipitous Happenings

January 20

I've been reading my students' Web Board logs, about half of them so far. Lots of enthusiasm; two useful criticisms. One, that I need to keep the language simple. Two, that I need to let the students go at it more. On the latter, I work a great deal, but on the former, sometimes, in my enthusiasm about an idea, I forget that I need to translate complexities, especially for the rookies. On the latter, I felt the need to offer background on the history without which Burke makes no sense; that might have been necessary, but at the same time I want to keep an eye on lecturing too much.

Interesting how much feedback I get in the hallways. Stockton is, for the most part, one long main street of connected building units. As you stroll along from class to the library, or cafeteria to the office, you run into colleagues. Often what should have been a three-minute walk turns into fifteen minutes or more—three, four, or five conversations. It's one of the things I love about the college. It includes the "hello, how are ya" with janitors and workmen and secretaries, but it also includes students who, of course, make up the bulk of the pedestrian traffic. Students from several years back, students from last term, and my newest students. There are some past students who either through shyness or hostility pay me no mind—usually they are the ones who didn't do well, whom I knew to be unhappy during the course. But what I see these past few days are some of my American Conservatism students offering big hellos and, in a few cases, stopping to tell me how much they're enjoying the first classes, asking particular questions, or making comments about Burke or some other point made in class. I've never seen a study of out-of-class behavior as a measure of teaching effectiveness. I've always envied my colleague Bill Daly, who seems to get stopped in the hallways by dozens of students with the biggest, fullest hellos. Given that I've always argued that real learning takes place out of the classroom, in the hallways and in one's office, I'm struck by how little we know about this phenomenon.

I want to highlight this out-of-classroom phenomenon of hallway banter. The best of our residential liberal-arts colleges create an environment within which faculty and students can regularly, normally bump into one another—in the quad, along pathways, at benches, in the eating areas and the library, but also at the local bar, cleaners, supermarket. Much learning takes place outside of classrooms, both during conversations between faculty and students and, perhaps more importantly, among students, those all-night bull sessions over beer that I recall from my college years, arguing about the meaning of life, about God, about behaviorism versus psychoanalysis, about whether Jackson Pollock should be taken seriously, about anything and everything. The real curriculum is what saturates a student's life, creates that very life of the mind that those of us fortunate enough to have shared that extraordinary experience carry with us, in our bloodstream, within our central nervous system, for all of our days. The issue is how to translate such environments, characteristically limited to the elite institutions, to the theaters where most professors perform.

Nonelite colleges have a more difficult time establishing such learning environments, given that many of their students do not live on campus and most of them are rushing off to their twenty- to forty-hour-a-week jobs at the local mall. In such a rushed and less leisurely setting, what happens in the hallways and cafeterias matters more. I've never seen a study of how such interactions affect learning, but my own experience makes me wish that someone would do such an investigation.

Russell Kirk: The Dilemmas of Postwar Thought

January 24

What an extraordinary class! Our task was to thoroughly discuss and analyze Richard Weaver, Russell Kirk, and, hopefully, Albert Jay Nock. We never got to Nock and barely started Kirk. The first hour or so went wonderfully—students were prepared to make points about Weaver, whom many of them favored. Interestingly, both openly left and right students tended to read into him what was at best only there by inference or, to be unkind, in the mind of the student. So one mission of this course is to help them focus on the text, to respect it, to interrogate it before drawing any inferences from it. Toward that end we had lively and wide-ranging discussions that I focused on a series of questions: What's wrong? When did things go wrong? Who went wrong? They needed some assistance with William of Occam and his razor that made the "evil decision" which started the turn toward everything from the scientific method to rationalism, empiricism, Darwin, Marx, positivism, and pragmatism. The students seemed interested in the theme of essence and existence, in the notions of transcendence and of universals, in legal realism. Their backgrounds are meager; even the conservative students who claim to have some knowledge coming in seem to be thin on basic concepts and historical framework. But the discussion took off when a few students pointed to Weaver's critique of his own times: "the deep anxiety, the extraordinary prevalence of neurosis, which makes our age unique." They were moved: "The typical modern has the look of the hunted." They commented on disintegration, hatred, fear, powerlessness. Jack noted, "It's amazing that he saw that way back then." I had to place them in the postwar era that Weaver inhabited, one that I have been studying a great deal lately, influenced by Ira Katznelson's *Desolation and Enlightenment*, a study of how thinkers such as Hannah Arendt and Reinhold Niebuhr sought to sustain the Enlightenment project in the face of the horrors of totalitarianism, genocide, and fears of nuclear annihilation. I wanted them to see that Weaver shared deep concern with many nonconservative thinkers; indeed, I wanted them to see that the best way to make sense of the postwar period is to recognize how profoundly shaken most intellectuals were by the fact of evil. We discussed Weaver's claim that "hysterical optimism will prevail until the world again admits the existence of tragedy, and it cannot admit the existence of tragedy until it again distinguishes between good and evil."

Above is a good example of how what I was reading at the time shaped my interventions in the seminar. As other essays in this book indicate, I have been deeply influenced in my approach to modern American conservatism by Katznelson's remarkable analysis of the impact of twentieth-century trauma on postwar thought. At this moment I had the opportunity, unplanned, to indicate how radical, liberal, and conservative thinkers were grappling with the same dilemma: how to make sense of the pervasiveness of barbarism—Holocaust, total war, Stalinism—without succumbing to cynicism or despair. Certain themes run through monographs and courses; they interlace the narrative and are fully integral to making sense of whatever story is being told. Katznelson's account still seems to me to be a starting point for framing post–World War II political culture.

BEING DIVERTED: THE "WAR ON CHRISTMAS"

We began to discuss Russell Kirk, beginning with his six canons of conservatism—the first being "belief that a divine intent rules society as well as conscience" and that "political problems, at bottom, are religious and moral problems." After a few questions, one and then another and then a third of my conservative students opened up with lots of emotion about what they perceive, I imagine courtesy of Bill O'Reilly, as a war on Christians and Christmas. It came fast and was becoming furious; we're not ready for this one yet. Within my model, we need to work our way through traditionalism, libertarianism, and fusionism; then set them in political terms in relationship to Goldwater, Wallace, Reagan, and Nixon; then proceed to factor in neoconservatism and the religious right—and then we can talk about an alleged war on Christians. It was my first real test, emotionally. My impulse was to quickly and sharply challenge the notion, both in terms of the commercial concessions of the O'Reilly thrust and on its own terms, empirically. And I was rising to the bait, wanting to just say that the idea was ridiculous. But I used the format of the course to fend off my desire. I did suggest that the issue was fair game on our computer conference, so long as the discussion was respectful. So I'll see what comes up there this next week. It's looking at this point that all or most of my conservative students hold deep religious views. We're too early in the game for conclusions, but I want to respect those views without patronizing them, that is, to push them to be cogent, logical, historical, consistent. What may help me is my feeling that many of the conservative students are so pleased with the existence of such a course that I have an advantage so far in terms of their willingness to engage.

COMPUTER CONFERENCING ON "THE WAR ON CHRISTMAS"

Marc:

> Christianity in my view is constantly being attack. Whether or not you believe in O'Reilly's "War on Christmas," Christian holidays and beliefs are definitely being marginalized for the practice of "political correctness." Try to find a card that said Merry Christmas. If they existed I didn't see them.

Janet countered:

> I am going to be as honest as I can here, I enjoy debating religion and religious values, but the pretext for this conversation is a little upsetting to me. I almost wish we didn't have to talk about this one at all. America, yes, clearly a religious nation. However, I am uneasy about connecting religion with whether or not a sign on a super Wal-Mart says Merry Christmas or Happy Holidays. Where exactly does it say "thou shalt not shop at a store that doesn't clearly display the signs of American commercialism" in the Bible. Just wondering.
>
> Really, does it matter what the sign at Wal-Mart says? I know I can't get away from this and I'm sorry, but does anyone else see this as really not the issue at all? If you are a Christian, then be a Christian and go to church and pray and celebrate Jesus and all of it. Fill your home and your life with love and around Christmas buy a tree and put up some lights. No one is going to stop you or blame you for that. I would think someone would want to put more effort into practicing their beliefs and less into caring about what others are doing.

But Kris disagreed:

> I believe that we are mostly a Christian nation. I also feel that Christianity is constantly being attacked lately. It is almost as if it is a "bad" thing to be Christian or celebrate anything that stands for the Christian religion.

> Funny how I never see anyone attacking any other religion, such as the Jewish who celebrate Hanukah and Passover. I never hear the ACLU (American Civil Liberties Union), who is a major contributor against the attack on Christianity, saying that you can't say "Happy Hanukah" or that you can't have a menorah placed somewhere where it might "upset" people. I am not saying that it is the way it should be. I think that we should all be able to celebrate our faith and our faith's celebration without offending anyone. In my opinion anyone who has a problem with a Christmas tree or someone saying "Merry Christmas" needs [to] relax. Faith and belief in God or a higher power is good for the soul and our nation. If you don't want to participate no one is forcing you to.

Last word goes to Geraldine:

> This may sound dumb, but I never took part to notice that individuals around us were attacking the Christians, until just recently. I was taken by surprise when my cousin who is in high school told me that students were being suspended for saying "Merry Christmas" to each other which I thought was absolutely ridiculous. First, you are not permitted to say "One Nation Under God" and now you are forbidden to say Merry Christmas. Not for nothing, but we say Merry Christmas for a reason, and it is not meant to be hurtful towards any other religion and people of other religions should not view it as hurtful either. I agree with Janet, why should it matter what the sign says at Wal-Mart and whatever religion you believe in you should not stop believing because a group says to. Also, like Janet said, can someone expand on the Muslim issue because I do not think that they are treated with that much respect? Can someone expand on what the ACLU is. I have never heard of this group?

I've included these comments because they point to how the classroom invariably throws a monkey wrench into a teacher's game plan. In this instance, I was totally unprepared for the topic and tried to refrain from voicing my visceral response of ridiculing the very idea that in this most Christian of nations there could be a war—even a skirmish!—on Christmas. I didn't want to signal an impatience or a contempt for what some of them felt to be a serious issue. So I let it play out but used the existence of the computer conference to close off classroom discussion.

It is always difficult to draw the line between indulging student foolishness and respecting student voice. What may have helped me in this instance was the fact that I was fascinated by their arguments and found myself interested in hearing how they justified what seemed to me to be absurd allegations. Perhaps that's what I should have said sometime during the classroom or conferencing discussions. But it was early in the term and I wanted more time to pass before taking that kind of risk. Timing matters a great deal in classes; I can say uncomfortable truths later in the term after having earned student trust and respect. But at early moments, especially when there are bases for mistrust—existential, racial, ideological—I am more likely to listen, prod, and wait.

The Inevitable First Flat Moment

January 26

I came out of class for the first time feeling less buoyant; I'm not sure why at this moment. In most ways, it was a productive class. We started with all of the basics, which Kirk helpfully organized into categories: the canons of conservative thought, the canons of anticonservative thought, the problems conservatives need to address in the present climate. Then we spent a few minutes discussing Nock, focusing on his argument that a loss of power by the public means a gain of power for the state—in a zero-sum context—with the development of government (either the version promoted by Native Americans or the Founding Fathers) consistent with social power to the extent that it does not, à la Marx, act as the robber of citizens' property. Maybe I lectured too much, but they seemed a little rammy in the last half hour, with the most aggressive conservatives laid-back. Perhaps I'm wrong, but a few seemed to be stepping away from participation. Others were right there, with lots of questions and comments. The most interesting were about state, government, and public power, with some consideration of the Katrina example. We had a good consideration of the Founding Fathers that came from one of my most religious conservatives, Dick—the student who first complained about the war on Christians—who added that Andrew Jackson, who I was presenting as a key step toward democracy in contrast to the Founding Fathers, had driven Indians out on the Trail of Tears. That allowed me to juxtapose Jackson—whom I detest—with John Quincy Adams, the last of the patrician gentlemen, who sought to protect the Indians from the settlers. We discussed a voting franchise based on virtue (church membership, rebirth) with one based on property (students always chuckle at my lame joke that this explains why New Jersey has freeholders, whom I call freeloaders). We discussed some differences between Hamilton and Jefferson in terms of governmental power and hierarchy—all this came out of Kirk's canon, which values order and hierarchy—and I gave them a profile of how politics operated in the Revolutionary Era—among the better sort, the middlin' sort, and the lower sort, that is, the rabble, the mob. I didn't make note but tucked away one issue for later—the religious views of the Founders—but stressed what older conservatives used to highlight—that the Founders believed in a republic but not in democracy.

Toward the end of the session, we discussed 1946 and Robert Taft, but here I felt that intensity disappeared. Perhaps it's my expectations, especially for a class that so far has been really *there*. My dad loved Al Jolson, who kept the lights in the theater on so he could see the audience's eyes. When I teach I have the same demand, that I make eye contact with each and every student—if all but one are attentive, I'm not satisfied. Crazy, yes. But it's how I've taught for forty years. In this class I had more than one distraction. So I left class asking myself if the students were just tired or if I was off, and I determined that the next session would restore the level of involvement I expect.

I've been impressed with how many of my colleagues share this utterly unreasonable expectation to reach each and every student. At the same time, I am always in wonder and amazement when I pass a classroom whose door is open to see a professor lecturing in the front of the room while more than a few students in the back doze off or read the student newspaper. As my comments in the following class session indicate, my approach is to not ignore even the appearance of fakery. Students have all too much experience with classes in which all parties are just going through the motions. I try to make my comments empathetic; "Hey, last class really stunk. Such things happen—why do you think this time?" And, amazingly, they often tell me what they, at least, thought and felt in that last session. At the very least, they feel that I'm paying attention.

Let me also note here that in these first weeks, several colleagues have asked me about the course. Two have asked if I would send them the syllabus. One is quite liberal, the other I don't know well enough—my sense from both of these cases, as well as from a few other comments, is that there's some interest, some curiosity, even some befuddlement at the fact that I am teaching this course. Given that most of my colleagues perceive me as among the faculty radical activists, that makes sense. Mostly I am enjoying it all, a bit bemused, and most curious about how this experiment is going to work out.

I'm already noticing a range of behaviors—some conservative students seem wary, angry, resentful, as if they're the aggrieved party to anything from happy holidays to affirmative action. Others seem innocent, idealistic. It is much like the range within the Left, Old and New. I used to suggest that one could divide the Left into those who are lovers and those who need an enemy, something to hate to allow for the capacity to love. I never have trusted the latter; I suspect similar dynamics are true on the Right. Is it more so? I have no idea other than my prejudice that the Right is more screwed up. But I don't wish to prejudge my own students, nor to just recapitulate old stereotypes from the fifties of authoritarian personality and of all-too-convenient oversimplification.

When a Class Becomes a Class

Below are the logs from a few seminars during which the class jelled as a class. In a good class, when the teacher is having an off day, the class sustains the energy and momentum. They carry you. In a less-successful class, you can have several lively classes in a row, but the moment you are off, they regress to apathy and passivity. This seminar began with its unique chemistry: more than a normal number of high participants, unusual motivation in the subject matter. But there is always a testing out, a normal and understandable mistrust, a waiting, before students embrace the course. Once that happens, there will be slack times, but the norm will be that wonderful mix of seriousness and camaraderie that all teachers recognize as a good class.

January 30, 2006

I was blown away over the weekend when I discovered that, tucked within the directed topics on our Web Board computer conference, there was a strand started by students on social class, within which the most articulate conservatives and liberals exchanged thoughts, respectfully, about how they viewed the concept. One conservative, Karl, raised questions about the existence of social class, especially in America; others, including conservatives, critiqued him. Lots of nonsense of course, but also impressive and nuanced understanding about the relationship between equality of opportunity and equality of outcomes, between income and wealth, about social science tools (the student didn't reference Weber's ideal types, but understood the notion quite well). I'll help them to frame it better, but it's wonderful to open up a port that reveals students actually learning at their own initiative. There are times when I need to just stay out of their way—a hard lesson for a professor!

January 31

We spent lots of time analyzing Hayek's views and placed them within the context of the 1940s. Participation continues to be robust, perhaps two-thirds joining in, albeit with maybe eight to ten students dominating. Most of them found Hayek to be as difficult as Burke; they're really inexperienced with anything but contemporary, slangy, easy-listening prose. But they were able to see Hayek's fundamental concern that fascism was a potential future for all modern nations because of the illusion, "the unintended consequence" (a point brought out by Janet, my most astute liberal from a previous class, addressing that neoconservative law) of well-meaning liberals and social-democrats who choose statist, socialistic solutions that inevitably yield totalitarianism. We didn't discuss his romantic and distorted view of the past, which claims almost all accomplishment—cultural, political, scientific—for the champions of liberty, as if the polis, the church in the High Middle Ages, the Italian city-state republics, and the early nation-states inclined toward free markets. But we did a fairly useful overview of what those who Hayek criticizes actually believed. I laid out the vision of the welfare state championed by liberals and social-democrats, a mixed economy, a pragmatic blurring of models, still capitalist but restrained. I then contrasted this model with laissez-faire and statist models. They were listening, although there's more to address in this regard ahead—that promiscuous use of "socialistic" for any governmental intervention. Then we considered Frank Meyer critiquing both Kirk's traditionalism—a temperament, not a principle—and Murray Rothbard's "libertine" libertarianism. The latter will roll over into Thursday.

I complimented them early on about the thoughtfulness and respect for one another with which they have been engaging the issue of social class on Web Board. I filled in some factual issues—when "under God" was included in the Pledge of Allegiance, how to usefully define class as opposed to caste, old money versus new money, the origins of the celebration of Christmas as consumer festival. This time I gave them a break, given the tiredness that seemed to roll in during the last half-hour of last Thursday's class. This time around, we were still cookin' at the close.

I'm feeling good about our building blocks, the layers of traditionalism and libertarianism, and look forward to the next units when we inject more American history—McCarthyism, the Cold War, Goldwater.

February 2, 2006

In the best courses, even in good ones, successful ones, there is usually a moment, one class, when things click, when you as the teacher know, deeply and profoundly, that you have made a connection with the students in your class that will carry through the rest of the term. That happened this morning. I've been at this craft for forty years and it remains thrilling to experience that moment. It is comparable to the best of sports contests, when two evenly matched teams go at it, ratcheting up the quality to stratospheric levels, comparable to those best moments in research, when either you find some gem in the archival records that defines your thesis or when your writing becomes automatic and you become totally wrapped in the narrative flow, not fully realizing how four or five hours have passed.

This class began today with the assignment of the first paper—on fusionism—the handing out of an Ayn Rand selection from *The Virtue of Selfishness*, and a short discussion of her life and work. Then we began a lively, focused discussion carried over from Tuesday about the different takes on libertarianism by Frank Meyer and Murray Rothbard. Rothbard's principled libertarianism, castigated as libertine by Meyer, is attractive to many of my students, including some of the liberals, because his style is modest and direct and his argument seems consistent—any state intervention is coercive, from taxation to the military draft, from censorship to drug laws. Meyer, on the other hand, argues that liberty must be a means but not an end, that it must serve the good, the quest for virtue. Rothbard unashamedly counters that libertarianism isn't concerned with "what a person *does* with his or her life," which he sees as "vital and important but . . . simply irrelevant to libertarianism" (263). The class came alive in our discussion of Rothbard's notion that given the mix of good and evil in all humans, that with limited government "bad men can do least harm." I suggested that liberals and radicals historically have tended to lean toward the goodness of man, whereas traditionalists have favored notions of sin, evil, aggression, irrationality.

We took a break with me posing a question for them: libertarian conservatives see the essential choice as between independence and dependence. How do we factor in interdependence? When we returned from the break we did some fancy footwork around this issue, which seemed to disturb some of my conservatives. But they responded admirably. Indeed, the conversation shifted, even digressed—with my full permission—toward issues of work. I used the examples of Chernobyl and global warming, but also put them through a kind of exercise—unplanned—of why our class begins at 8:30 A.M. and ends at 10:20 A.M. I wanted them to understand how our modern division of labor and organizational and logistical needs mandate—in schools, in businesses, in factories—a coordination of time, a quantification and a disciplining of time. I told them about E. P. Thompson, the great British historian of the English working class, who studies the ways in which premodern peasants comfortable with qualitative time—for instance, sunrise, morning, dawn—had difficulties adjusting to their first days working in a factory. What did it mean to be there at 8:00 A.M. sharp? Somehow this led us to a consideration, without using the term, of alienation from work and school, and what makes such experiences fulfilling. My most conservative student, or perhaps my most interesting conservative, Karl, a history major, spoke of learning the trade of masonry, how well it paid, how pleasing the work could be. I told them of *One Day in the Life of Ivan Denisovitch* by Solzhenitsyn, where within the horror of the gulag Ivan experienced real fulfillment, real satisfaction in building a brick wall, pleasure in the skill, in the usefulness of the result, in the camaraderie of his fellow workers.

I've done this in other classes with similar results, but I'm always impressed with the ability of students to recognize and discuss astutely the constraints of work and school. How many people you know would stay at their present employment if they hit the jackpot in the New Jersey lottery? And, how many of your fellow students would take an offer of a counterfeit diploma if they were assured that it was absolutely secure from detection? I later noted as they proceeded, with me just rapt, listening, how the discussion had little to do with our isms, conservative or liberal, how such ideologies too often get in the way of pragmatic problem solving, how I often thought we'd be better off just shelving such loyalties to focus just on what works. We ended up discussing, both personally and analytically, community colleges, fast-food jobs, the middle-class demand for college rather than craft training, working for someone else, bureaucracy, and the Jeffersonian ideal of property-owning farmers and planters and maybe some artisans, an ideal subverted by a corporate order.

They were very complimentary to me, although that is not, unless I'm more vulnerable to flattery than I suppose, what makes me see this day as special. Some of them talked of how in our class they feel able to participate openly and comfortably. Of course that's good. But when the class ended, my conservative history major Karl took aside a student Sarah who, in complimenting me, had had some negative things to say about another instructor. He urged her to give the prof more of a chance, that he had found that this professor was open to being challenged and graded him fairly despite sharp differences with Karl. Other students were still talking about our issues—interdependence, work satisfaction—as they exited.

One thing that convinces me of a breakthrough is that I could sense that both my most conservative and especially my most liberal students were experiencing one another as individuals, contradictory and distinct individuals. That conservative guy was no longer just the predictable gun nut or religious fanatic but that guy who seemed really interested in construction work and was trying to be fair about a professor easy to dump on. I certainly don't expect everything to be a lovefest from here on in, but this humanization will make it more difficult for any of them to stereotype the other, to presume to know what their ideological opposite is thinking and feeling. That's not a small accomplishment!

A Liberal Screed

Willie, quiet in class but perhaps my most radical and provocative student, just tossed in the following on Web Board:

> Here are some things President Bush might forget to include in tonight's State of the Union Address, which are also indicators of the current State of the Union.
>
> You will NOT see:
>
> - Faces of those who will be pushed aside because of the devastating and immoral cuts to the federal budget
> - Photos of 2,300+ U.S. coffins flown back from Iraq

- A chart showing the 250% increase in terrorist attacks since 2000 and the 550% increase in deaths by terrorists
- Posters showing no-bid contracts for Halliburton for the rebuilding of Iraq
- A ticking display showing the $400+ billion deficit
- A billionaire sitting beside the first lady, smiling broadly because of the administration-led and Congress-passed tax cuts that benefit only a handful of ultra-wealthy
- An Exxon-Mobil executive holding up a sign saying "Thank you, Mr. President and Congress for refusing to bring up price gouging—we raked in the biggest quarterly profit in the history of the world."
- "Brownie" (President Bush's pet name for former FEMA director Mike Brown) sitting in the balcony smiling broadly beside a grateful Ninth Ward New Orleans resident, proud of our government policies that put people first.
- Photos of U.S. secret prisons showing humane treatment of its detainees.
- Scientists applauding the U.S. for its refusal to join in the worldwide effort to stop greenhouse gases, even though the U.S. is the world's biggest polluter.

Whittaker Chambers: American Hero

February 7

Well, I wouldn't call it a letdown, but a little deflation—both understandable and to be expected—after last Thursday's excitement. Actually, the first half of the class was excellent, a vigorous discussion of Whittaker Chambers based on a selection from *Witness*. Interestingly, all of the participants, especially my most liberal students, really were moved by Chambers. First, he is quite eloquent and it is difficult to not recognize his earnestness. Students pointed to the moral power of his argument, a cosmic battle between good and evil, two faiths, one God-centered, one human-centered. Most of them also recognized that Chambers didn't trash communists as lowlifes; indeed, he suggested, obviously with himself as a model, that idealists became communists for the most moral of reasons. My liberal/left students were particularly taken by that; it surprised them. I didn't get enough response to the probe of how less-religious folks might respond to Chambers's dualism—where did they fit? Much of the rest of the first hour centered on two themes I urged them to consider: First, I noted that Chambers seemed oblivious to politics—nothing on the working class, on unions, on social movements, even on party dynamics. I brought in my own first book, *Philadelphia Communists*, and told them a bit of how these Depression-era radicals came to the party and some of the specific issues that interested me—their friendships, marriages, kids, ethnicities, ways of dealing with frustrations. None of this seemed to interest Chambers. Second, I asked where liberals or social-democrats fit within Chambers's dualism. It was clear that they were subsumed by the human-centered communist heresy, the alternative faith in Chambers's sense. I suggested that New Deal and post–New Deal liberals might see it differently. One of my conservative students, Milton, stated that he always saw liberalism as a form of communism; we engaged in this for a while, returning to the definition of a welfare state I had presented last week. I "hear" some thought going on in the room that is still percolating, gestating; many of my students are struggling with this other way of seeing liberalism as in the middle, as a moderate path between extremities, equally opposed to fascism and communism, but also to laissez-faire capitalism. Many of my conservatives have difficulty not seeing any use of the state not related to defense or police functions to be socialistic or communistic. And of course that was Hayek's point.

In any case, we exhausted ourselves and I called for a needed break after filling in some of the biography of Chambers, including the Hiss hearings and trials. After the break I felt the need to work with them on what McCarthyism or, as I argued, the Second Red Scare, did—and how it related to the Cold War. We were best when focusing on the distinction between a thought and an act, how membership in a Communist or Communist-related organization became grounds to not hire, to fire, or to bring criminal charges against. I challenged them with the situation of a teacher who belonged to a Nazi or Klan organization. Did one have to demonstrate unprofessional conduct in the classroom? Was mere affiliation, a First Amendment right, sufficient to be punitive? They seemed to see the moral dilemma. But they just ran out of gas and, as sometimes happens, I was late to notice. I felt that I lost them in the last ten minutes; I was trying to do too much—Truman Doctrine, Chinese Revolution, actual spy cases, attorney general's list. So as a result—I should learn my lesson about cramming—we dribbled to the end.

After class, two of my most conservative students, Darren and Kris, told me that they had never questioned the notion that liberalism was a step toward communism and that they wanted to read my book on communists since I seemed to be interested in the everyday life of radical activists.

The above discussion about Chambers reflected my own transformed view of this most complicated figure. I came of political age like most of those left of center assuming that Chambers was a pathological liar and degenerate for making false accusations against Alger Hiss. When I actually read Chambers's Witness *and then Sam Tanenhaus's biography of Chambers, I was surprised to discover that he was a rather compelling if sad figure but hardly the vicious stereotype perpetrated by the Left. He was often eloquent, deeply moral, and very human. Of course, he was also very wrong, at least to my mind, in his astoundingly abstract portrayal of communism and communists and in his view of the world as divided between the godly and the ungodly. Not for the first time, I found that those on my side of the ideological divide could be just as unfair as others.*

As a result of those reflections and of teaching about Chambers in this seminar, I included him as one of my "American Heroes" in a National Council for the Humanities–New Jersey Council for the Humanities seminar series for public school teachers I taught in the spring of 2007. My "Heroes" in the seminar on McCarthyism also included Arthur Miller, Lillian Hellman, and Zero Mostel; heroes are all flawed but can remain heroic if they demonstrate courage at their moments of truth.

Peter Viereck

February 9

Today we had our first student presentation with a focus on the upcoming take-home exam/essay due in a week. Nick presented on Peter Viereck. He came to see me yesterday, somewhat nervous but quite prepared and surprisingly agile for one with little experience in history or politics (he's a business major). He was clear on Viereck's background—his father's notoriety as a pro-Nazi propagandist—and his central ideas, forcefully Burkean, about the place of the New Deal within the American tradition, the ways in which McCarthyism gave conservatism a bad name, and, most tellingly, the ways in which conservatives and liberals share a common tradition of constitutionalism, commitments to liberty and democracy in opposition to both fascism and communism, and, in essential ways, laissez-faire capitalism of a social-Darwinian sensibility. Our discussion centered on Viereck's road not traveled, an alternative kind of conservatism that the fusionists—Meyer, Buckley, the *National Review* group—spurned as bogus, indeed, as a threat to the creation of a genuine conservatism. As such, Viereck was more an enemy, a threat to fusionism, than either Hayek or Kirk, or Rothbard.

As will be clear in the following essays, I have come to view the excommunication of Peter Viereck as a central defining moment in the failure of a Burkean, traditionalist conservatism to take hold on the Right. In addition, Viereck's alliance with figures like Richard Hofstadter and Daniel Bell suggests to me that an intertwining of liberalism and conservatism defines what has been called consensus, or vital-center, or Cold War liberalism.

The Cold War

We saved the discussion of the McCarthyist loyalties of Buckley and Bozell for next week. After a short break—I'm trying to maximize the intensities of the second hour—I took charge with a framework for understanding the differences between what I called fusion-conservatives, Cold War liberals, and progressives/radicals on the Cold War. There had been several references to Yalta and Poland and Berlin and Potsdam, and to liberal appeasement, especially in the Edwards history; I felt that the class needed a clearer sense of the arguments. They seemed responsive. I started with the shared view among both conservatives and liberals that we were the good guys and the communists were a real, dangerous enemy. The progressives—for example, Henry Wallace in 1948—were more prone to see some shared responsibility in who was to blame. The key difference between liberals and conservatives is that liberals contextualize communism—"the communists"—with the anchor of the nation-state, recognizing the variations between Soviet and Chinese and Yugoslav communists. Then we went through Yalta, the loss of China, and the controversy over the Soviet A-bomb in 1949 before juxtaposing the conservative liberation/rollback model with Kennan's containment. I emphasized that the conservatives tended toward the notion that foreign policy disappointments were ever and always rooted in failures by liberals, indeed, that if the United States asserted its will, given its resources, there were no barriers to a communist-free world. I wanted them to engage the issue of the limits of power and to begin the longer-term conversation about the accomplishments and limitations of containment. I didn't yet discuss my own view that Kennan and his allies, like Viereck, were the "true" conservatives. And I didn't have enough time to discuss the progressive view other than to note that it saw carrots as more effective than sticks. I used the *Patton* film, which every white male seems to have seen, often more than once, to point to the unrealistic nature of a certain kind of militancy. What would it mean to have invaded the Soviet Union in mid-1945, to just get on with it? How did one factor in the Red Army, its critical victory at Stalingrad, its occupation of Eastern Europe, our war weariness, even the mutinous feelings of our GIs wanting to get home after three to four years of war?

I want, at some point, to continue a discussion of whether the United States, that is, our top foreign-policy advisors and actors, exaggerated the power and, consequently, the threat posed by the Soviets. Certainly the United States served a valuable purpose in bolstering Western Europe such that it could become a group of stable capitalist democracies of the welfare-state variety.

Ayn Rand I

February 13

I spent some of the weekend rereading Ayn Rand, especially her essay on selfishness and the much-discussed John Galt speech in *Atlas Shrugged.* When I was seventeen, I had been a Rand devotee, gobbling up *The Fountainhead* and *Atlas Shrugged.* This enthusiasm had lasted about half a year. Rand's idealism, her atheism attracted me then. Now I can barely get through the text; it is so turgid, repetitive, indeed ridiculous. In the late 1950s and early 1960s, there was a longing for something better, finer, more inspirational than the Age of Ike and Mamie, the era defined, perhaps unfairly, by the work of Reisman, Whyte, Packard, and C. Wright Mills. Conformity, grayness, buttoned-down shirts, skinny ties, crew cuts, pensions, little houses made of ticky-tacky à la Malvina Reynolds. Such concerns spawned the Beat rebellion, the cult of James Dean, the excitement about Brando, the best of foreign cinema, interests in existentialism, Salinger. How many like me found a thrill in the nobility of Rand's heroic characters? It couldn't last, at least for me—unlike Alan Greenspan—as I began to become an historian. After all, Rand made one of her heroines a railroad magnate, a symbol of laissez-faire capitalism despite the overwhelming state role in subsidizing such mass transportation. I wonder if any of my students will find inspiration in Rand's prose. And I would love to find out how many were like me, seekers for inspiration who passed through a Randian phase on their way to SDS, civil rights, and the peace movements

Buckley, Fusionism, and the Antichrist

February 14

Another extraordinary class, although in this case more in terms of inappropriate behavior. The class started with a review and expansion of discussion on the Cold War and the golden age of American capitalism, the latter theme stressed to highlight one reason conservatism made so small a dent in the 1950s and early 1960s. We migrated to a discussion of the basis of that growth, including military spending and the rise in effective consumer demand in part driven by Social Security benefits and union wages. But most of the conversation centered on the importance of what I have always jokingly called "SHMA"—the suburb/highway/mall/auto complex—that is, the ways in which the GI Bill and the 1956 Federal Highway Act stimulated a new residential and work environment that required mass ownership of cars. Of course I stressed the federal subsidies upon which this prosperity was based, but we mostly got into the Wal-Mart issue. First, a student asked what I meant by suburb. That's part of my shtick, originally in a community organization course within which I had students divide by whether they grew up in small towns, cities, or suburbs. The discussion of development, that is, the conversion of farmland into suburban community, led to consideration of the mom-and-pop shop, which led to Wal-Mart. I suggested that they consider the dilemma articulated, I believe, by Marvin Meyers in *The Jacksonian Persuasion*, that the characteristic American sought to preserve the past and affirm traditional moral values while at the same time seeking to fulfill the American dream of material success. I noted the well-worn argument that capitalism is an inherently revolutionary, subversive force that converts all phenomena into a cash nexus (Marx), into market value. It is always best pedagogically when a notion immediately connects to students' experience. And these children of suburbs, many of whose parents and grandparents have told them of the small towns and farms from which they came, understood the dilemma, although some of my conservatives, especially Karl, insisted on defending Sam Walton for making lots of money. I joined them in noting that even if one argued that Sam was a son of a bitch, he was one among many competitors, distinguishable not by his nastiness but by his efficiency.

Of course I related this Wal-Mart discussion to their papers—considering to what extent fusionism successfully bridged the tensions between traditionalist and libertarian conservatism through anticommunism. The latter wasn't relevant but the tensions were. That set off a discussion of Buckley's *National Review* statement of principles. Our first consideration was of his contempt for middle-of-the-roadism. One of my most conservative students, Jack, affirmed his own distaste, to put it mildly, of such fudging. He got emotional in stating his repugnance for such moderation. I was surprised when one of my more liberal students, Janet, expressed her surprise that others didn't see Buckley as criticizing fusionism itself for being middle-of-the-road. In this sense she was dead wrong, but her argument was interesting, that the contradictions between libertarian and traditional views were so deep that any effort to bridge them was sure to fail and, she felt Buckley thought, was deserving to fail. I suggested that there were two forms of moderation, one strictly opportunistic—the Bill Clinton variety, at times—the other the essence of politics, the ability to compromise, to make deals, to succeed in the legislative arena. I challenged my conservative as to whether his view simply was principled, noble, but not at all politically serious. Just as an amusing aside, when several conservative students mentioned Hillary Clinton as an example of the worst kind of opportunism, I referred to her as "the Antichrist"—much laughter all around. Sometimes when you just casually bring out deeply felt feelings into the open, there's an ability to laugh at oneself. We'll return to that theme at another moment for sure.

As I reread the above, I think of the concerns I had about Hillary Clinton's race for the 2008 Democratic nomination and then the presidency. I worried that if she was successful, or seemed to be approaching her goals, she would be assassinated. It wasn't just her much-discussed unfavorables in the polls (50% in June 2007); it was the intensity with which people opposed her, as perhaps reflected in the not-so-joking association with the Antichrist. Of course, much of it was a deeply rooted rage about feminism and women; some of it was a mostly misplaced view of Senator Clinton as embodying the spirit of the 1960s social movements. As a historian, I think of the hostility directed at Jane Addams during World War I and at Jane Fonda in terms of Vietnam.

Political Incorrectness: Classroom Boundaries

February 15

This is the first time this term that I have been so inundated with committee meetings and such that I have had to wait to get back to this log. Most of academic life is a blessing; sometimes I'm amazed that I get paid for doing this, doing what I love. When class discussion turns to work, I always ask my students if they or people they know would stay at their jobs if they won the New Jersey lottery big time. Almost all say that they'd quit. This is a useful marker for defining alienation, doing what is alien to you. And, of course, it is paralleled by students staying in school for reasons that are alien to their desires. Similarly, all academics hate wasted time with self-important administrators, having to deal with petty and occasionally vicious colleagues (the academy is more vicious than high finance precisely because so little is at stake), paperwork and more paperwork. For most of us it is relief to walk back into the classroom.

In this particular classroom, I found myself offering a brief biog of William F. Buckley Jr. I was well prepared having reread John Judis's definitive study. So I walked them through his family life, his early "bad boy" years at and after Yale, his most influential books, his role in the founding of *National Review*. Then, with maybe ten minutes remaining, I read to them marked-out sections in Judis's biography that pointed to Buckley's worst moments of narrow-mindedness, comments he made in the 1950s and early 1960s about civil rights in America and independence movements in Africa. The statements, sometimes flippant in that Buckley "squire of the manor" style, were at best patronizing, at worst, deeply racist, particularly one statement in which he suggests that Africans will be ready for self-determination when they stop eating one another. I wanted my class to come to grips with the burden conservatives carried in that period, being on the wrong side of history, still holding onto a kind of British arrogance about "wogs"—Colonel Blimp if you will. But one of my most conservative students, Dick, jumped in with support for Buckley's worst comment, responding with a smirk, with a knowing look about "those people," those Africans. If there is such a thing as a teaching moment, this was it. I stopped him and asked the class if it would be different if there were African American students in this class. They quickly saw my point, but one responded, "They'd beat the shit out of Dick." I countered by suggesting that it shouldn't be the obligation of black students to call Dick on his statement, but the obligation of whites to do so. There were a few quizzical looks as I explained the unfairness of expecting blacks—or Jews or women or gays or Catholics—to be obliged to defend themselves from inappropriate assault.

I was thinking on my feet, mostly trying to figure out how to chastise Dick without putting him too much on the spot, how to signal what's OK and not OK in my classroom without stifling legitimate commentary, how to, in effect, be politically correct without being stuffy, hypocritical, humorless, unwilling to engage on controversial issues. I have examined some of the literature that addresses the plight of so many African nations—the kleptocracies, the genocides, the ethnic wars, the waste of resources. I have rooted for the best of African leaders, anticipated that the resource-rich nations of Nigeria, South Africa, and Congo would have to be the linchpins of development. And I have thought a great deal about the reason why East Asia and now all of Asia is moving forward to rapid economic growth—with all the caveats about inequalities, environmental dangers, corruption, dictatorship—and Africa stagnates. Sometimes I think that it must be that Asian cultures, Asian imperial history, especially in China and India, sustained an identity that now provided the cultural capital for an Asian version of the work ethic. Africa seemingly has struggled more with the very creation of nation-states. When I consider Latin America and then the Islamic Middle East, I am more confused, in my relative ignorance of their respective histories.

I am sometimes taken aback by what we do not teach our students. Aside from the above-noted gaps in what we can reduce to the "great books," there are other appalling shortfalls, at least in many public institutions: the shortage of courses in what are probably the most salient developments of our times, the reemergence of China and India as players on the world stage, the increasing importance of Asia where almost two-thirds of the world's population lives; the minimal attention paid to world religions—my students are not only unable to demonstrate any accurate knowledge of Buddhism, Hinduism, or Islam, but they are also remarkably ignorant about their own religious backgrounds. Few can tell me what a Christian is, at least if I ask for comment on Catholics, Protestants, and Orthodox. Fewer can distinguish Presbyterians from Episcopalians, nor can they define evangelicals or fundamentalists, not to speak of Pentecostals. More heartening is that most of my students are motivated to learn about organized religions; our K–12 schools, afraid of offending almost anyone, do not teach them about the history of the very Judeo-Christian tradition they abstractly celebrate.

But I do know that leftists and well-meaning liberals too often respond to questions of African horror with the same old saw—its colonial and neocolonial factors. True but not enough to explain why Taiwan and South Korea and China have moved forward. And it just plays into conservative stereotypes that the Left always blames the West and the United States and never holds people of color, here or elsewhere, accountable. It is the macro version of what I will simplify as the attacks on Daniel Patrick Moynihan's study of the African American family. So I tried to make sure that in chastising Dick and indicating acceptable boundaries of discourse, I was simultaneously, and as strongly, modeling that raising questions about African nations is legitimate. How could I not, given my own point of view? Whether I was successful remains to be seen. Time will tell. But it was, I think, a useful beginning of a discussion I assumed we would engage when we got to George Wallace and the white backlash of the 1960s. I am debating whether to post a question on this issue on Web Board this week or to wait until we have more meat and potatoes on the plate such that we can do more than discuss without context or information. But I must admit that I left class pumped with the anticipation of that set of discussions and, hopefully I'm right, with some confidence that we started it well.

I don't think we as academics and teachers do a very good job teaching about race and racism. Some seems to be liberal guilt. Mostly it rests on the lack of confidence that one can present complicated situations, nuanced realities without risking being misinterpreted by colleagues and students.

Several years ago at a panel on racism I suggested that we begin by seeing if we could agree on four axioms, the first being that there is more racism in America than most white people were willing to admit. No controversies there. The second was that there has been considerable progress over the past forty years based on the civil rights revolution of the 1960s. More curious looks but no hostility. Then the third axiom, that there were some African Americans who see racism when it doesn't exist. At that point, the room became more agitated with some furrowed brows and raised eyebrows. The fourth axiom brought down the house: that given the above three axioms, it was presently more difficult to assess allegations of racism. Indeed, I added, there were now so many divergent voices within the African American community—a partial measure of the successes above noted—that no one could any more claim to represent "the black voice."

The panelist following me denounced my position, arguing that racism was as bad or worse than forty years ago, merely more hidden. Then the panel opened for questions from the audience. A black female undergraduate asked me how I would respond if she believed that I had said something racist in class and she came to complain to me. I told her that I would take her allegation very seriously, consider whether I thought it was valid, and give her my most honest response. She was dissatisfied, indeed offended by my response, as were many on the panel and in the audience. The student asked me why I wouldn't accept the validity of her allegation. I told her that I thought it would be harmful to her or any other student to allow an automatic acceptance of any allegation, that it risked corrupting her or anyone else in that it would allow for false charges to go unchallenged. I ended by suggesting that true respect included disagreement. I added that if not satisfied, a student always had the remedy of taking the allegation to my superiors.

The room erupted with anger at me, with one white colleague screaming at me that I was patronizing the student. I was disappointed and depressed by this display of what seemed to me to be wrong-headed, racially retrograde, and demagogic. I need to add that I was not angry at the student who raised the issue; she seemed honest and forthcoming, even in disagreement.

Most interesting is that over the next weeks several of my African American students asked me what had happened—there obviously had been a buzz in the hallways. This led to some fruitful conversation about how one determines the existence of racism. I also received several notes from white colleagues expressing admiration for what I had said but confessing that they were too cowardly to do the same. This depressed me even more than the hostile responses. Had we come to this—faculty, even tenured ones, afraid to speak their minds in fear of being charged with racism? Indeed, we had. One junior faculty member told me that he never goes near certain hot-button issues like affirmative action or underclass behavior because of his fear that it might put his job at risk.

As teachers we struggle with students who hold back from authentically discussing issues of prejudice, who go silent or simply echo agreement. It is hard work to achieve honest discussions; all students enter with bruises. One must establish a trusting environment for such discussions to be fruitful. Trust does not exist at the beginning of a class. I tell students that the handshake is an apt metaphor for our relations—I hold your hand, you hold mine—we trust one another but I also prevent you from hitting me in case that is your hidden desire. We trust and mistrust simultaneously. And then we can begin to have an honest dialogue.

I begin with a modest sense of how much influence I have with my students, especially regarding changes in their essential behavior regarding issues of social justice. Teachers are fortunate if we increase at the margin those who are willing to stand up for others. But human behavior being what it is, we remain burdened with the knowledge of how difficult it is to educate individuals to identify with all of the "others," to construct a global identity focused on human rights. Sigmund Freud, given the trauma of World War I, asserted not only that reason and enlightenment were fragile, but also that there was something in the existence of human intelligence which never allowed the darkness to be all-engulfing, and that this indistinguishable light of humane thought had a surprising persistence. Our goal as educators is to widen that ray of light, to assist a few more ordinary men and women to resist the extraordinarily evil and to stretch toward the extraordinarily good.

My own view is that the optimal way to help students respond to moral challenges is to help them understand the contradictory strands of heroism and knavery, the victimized and the victimizing, of many of our peoples. And we as educators need to understand and communicate the contextual nature of human behavior, its range and subtleties, and the contradictory ways that humans respond to moral challenges. As such, we teach humility before the wonder—the heroism, the cowardice, the insensitivities, the villainies—of our own natures, our own histories.

This might be called the double helix of all peoples, the intertwining of their burdens and their inspirations, their hidden shames and forgotten accomplishments, the recognition of which makes it more likely that they will be able to recognize the same complexity in others.

All of this has to begin with the obvious: that I am a white guy teaching about race and racism. No matter how you slice it, it makes a difference. It does help that I was born and bred in Newark and have some "cred" with my city kids (keep in mind that many of my African American students are middle class and suburban). I work very hard to break down the obvious stereotypes, including those blacks have of non-blacks. I want all of my students to recognize that each of us is simultaneously a member of an ethnic/racial/religious group, a human being, and a very distinct and unique individual. When we address social class and poverty, I want my students to understand the need to disaggregate poverty, to note three kinds of the poor: the temporary poor, the working poor, and the underclass poor. The first two groups share all of the values and behaviors of Americans, for example, the work ethic. They suffer from short-term crises, such as a husband and father splitting and not providing sufficient support, a worker facing a health problem without insurance, or people suffering from poor educations that limit their income potential to close to minimum wage, holding jobs with no benefits. It's only the latter category, sometimes linked to a "culture of poverty," certainly no more than one-fourth of those poor, who exhibit the self-destructive behaviors—substance abuse, bad work habits, impulsive control problems, criminal activities, abuse of women and children—that fall outside of societal norms. Most of my students of color have no difficulty in affirming that such behaviors exist; indeed, they often go farther than I am willing to go in ascribing such behaviors to the black poor. I rely a great deal on the work of William Julius Wilson, the extraordinary black sociologist, in teaching about the links between class and race, between behavior and opportunity and, especially, the need to address the most painful and least flattering aspects of black street life honestly and directly.

I tell all of my students to go beyond the snapshot to the motion picture. That guy drinking from a bottle in a paper bag in front of a bar—how did he get that way? I bring in the start of the motion picture, the differential chances of success already there in birthing rooms. How is it that I can stand in front of that room full of newborns and, based on race and social class, tell with a high degree of accuracy which babies will graduate from college, who will have a decent middle-class life, and who will end up in prison or dead before age thirty. That is criminal to me. No baby determines the well-being of its parents. But the odds are set very early. Now odds are not determinants; people beat the odds. But I remain angry and want my students to share that rage at the inherent injustices that await so many of our poor children.

Many of my African American—and increasingly, Latino—students are quite inspirational. Many, not most or all, come from difficult environments. Many have surmounted extraordinary barriers—broken families, crime-infested neighborhoods, drug experiences, lousy schools, early pregnancies and child-rearing, physical and sexual abuse—to make it to college. I hope that my pride in them, which includes pushing them to excel, prodding them to resist racial and often gender stereotypes, comes through in the classroom. I want that young woman who was offended by my comments at the panel discussion to hang in there, continue challenging me, but I also want more time to try to persuade her that there is respect in disagreement, that she will be best served by being taken seriously.

Ayn Rand II

February 16

Adam didn't show today for the Ayn Rand presentation. I had some concern, given that he started late, missed a few classes, and rarely participates. But he did say on Tuesday that he'd be ready. I anticipate that he will drop the course. Several students have expressed concern about their ability to do well in this course, their concern being crystallized by the due date of the first paper. Most of the class seems engaged, indeed, excited, enthusiastic—I look forward to starting their papers tonight. But there are some, maybe four or five, who seem lost. They either aren't interested in politics, as Sarah told me this morning, or they're weak in history, or they have great difficulty making sense of some of the readings. Today, for example, we were analyzing the text of Rand's essay on selfishness. Sarah made a comment based on a paragraph in which she surmised that Rand was against selfishness. When we went over the paragraph it was clear to almost everyone that Rand was criticizing those people who claim that selfishness is an evil: "Since nature does not provide man with an automatic form of survival, since he has to support his life by his own effort, the doctrine that concern with one's own interests is evil means that man's desire to live is evil—that man's life, as such, is evil. No doctrine could be more evil than that" (ix, *The Virtue of Selfishness*). That's a careless misinterpretation, but moreso one of inexperience. I hope I can pay more attention to those worried students, make a better effort to make sure that they understand the material, although not at the cost of rigor. It is an interdisciplinary senior seminar after all. But I've been here before, for example in my Vietnam War seminar, having to explain basics of geography and European history and politics that the course presupposes.

Back to the class: I tried to fill time, hoping that Aaron would merely be late; so I began with what I wanted to close with—the Eisenhower administration's policies regarding Hungary '56, the *Brown* decision, Sputnik, the missile gap, Castro and Cuba, U-2, with some mention of the CIA coups in Iran and Guatemala. I think I'm helping them understand that Cold War liberalism à la Kennedy was not squishy as some of them stereotype post-sixties liberalism. I'm always a little surprised at how I seem to many of my students to be pro-Eisenhower. Certainly I chastised him for the failure to use the bully pulpit after the *Brown* decision and for his CIA adventures to empower the Shah and the Guatemalan colonels. But there is a measuredness, a maturity in Ike that compels me—especially his resistance to the myth of the missile gap, his contempt for service rivalries and bloated military budgets, his opposition to a space race, his confidence in himself and in those he represented.

After a short break, we addressed Ayn Rand. I like the pattern we've established, of students making claims by referring to the text, which we then read and interrogate. My task is to make sure that interpretations are sound, nuanced, but mostly to let them engage one another productively. Most of the time this occurs. My interventions come when a point is raised or a question is asked that requires more than they can supply. Once in a while I jump the gun and *assume* that only I have the answer, but most of my interventions seem to fly. My first intervention involved Rand's atheism; I introduced my students to Feuerbach and added some of Freud to clarify the notion that, among these thinkers, religious faith—Rand's mysticism, Freud's oceanic feeling—is a form of alienation, the projection of humanity's accomplishments and being onto an abstracted and illusory deity. Then Jack, one of my most astute and deep-thinking conservatives, claimed that Rand's notion of selfishness paralleled that of Karl Marx. That led me to a minilecture on Marx's contempt for utopian socialists for their investment in altruism. I often use this formula to make my point: the "was," the "is," and the "can be," as opposed to the "should" or "ought to be." Marxian dialectics, to my understanding, rests on a historical materialism that sees movement from contradictions within social phenomena, the "can be" already existing within the "is," the future in the present. In that sense Marx saw the self-interest of the emerging proletariat as formed within the developing interdependence, the sociality of the factory, the office, the corporation or trust. So to Marx individual self-interest morphed into group self-interest, or what he called class consciousness, or more accurately, in Stanley Moore's notion, of interest consciousness.

Then, with about ten minutes remaining and much discussion of the John Galt speech in *Atlas Shrugged*, I introduced them to Thorstein Veblen and his distinction between engineers and capitalists, industry and business, using Dos Passos's *USA* for an example—Charley Anderson as tragic figure, the pilot, the engineer, the inventor succumbing to business mania, money-making. We all noted that Rand fused these two functions and roles. With that, we ended the class.

Some of the best things that happen in the classroom are serendipitous. In the seminar described above, I had no plan to discuss the utopian elements in Marx or to introduce my students to Thorstein Veblen. Nevertheless such moments are almost always the best for teaching—how do you teach thinking on your feet?

Other Classes, Similar Keys

February 17

The best of times for teachers is when what happens in one class synergizes (terrible word!) with what occurs in another. It is, of course, best when students make such connections; at such times, one feels that real learning, synthesis, is taking place. But it is also wonderful when the teacher has such an experience and brings it to students. That occurred today in my Ethnic and Minority Relations class. This has been a wonderful group, less advanced than the American Conservatism class, more sophomores, but it includes some grand nontraditionals, older women mostly—one guy—black and white, plus two of my best freshman seminarians from last term. The discussions have been lively and within the parameters I set for addressing controversial issues such as race and racism. Today was our first debate on whether hate speech should be allowed on college campuses, a debate driven by the rise of speech codes on some campuses in the nineties. The six students did well in their presentations, mostly tilting toward freedom of speech, and the follow-up discussion bringing in the rest of the class was lively and thoughtful. This is a group that has been clicking from the get-go, a real pleasure for me—I walk in and feel at home, with an immediate and ongoing rapport with most of the class.

Today, as we worked our way through the key issues—hostile work environments and the differences between classroom use, college-sponsored events, and access to college facilities for, for instance, a Klan meeting, I used my own experiences, as did many of them. I first turned to my thoughts and feelings when faced years ago with a Nazi rally. My ACLU loyalties focused me on the right of even Nazis to public space; my Jewish identity led me to admit that if present during such a rally, hearing hateful speech about killing Jews, I would intervene and beat up the speaker. The contradictoriness of values. The second point was using what occurred in my American Conservatism course discussed above. I explained what happened with the student's remarks on Buckley's quote and then explained my thought processes: to chastise the student, to reaffirm appropriate boundaries, to encourage that student and others to seek legitimate ways to raise controversial points, in this case, about failed states in Africa. My Ethnic and Minority Relations students seemed to get it.

I have found that students are appreciative when I talk about the craft of teaching, including one's worst decisions. I guess it humanizes as well as makes conscious that what we do includes strategy, tactics, serendipitous moments, elation, and depression, and that we, just like them, are affected by what we bring into the classroom from our personal lives. I don't believe in imposing obviously inappropriate dimensions of my private life on students, but I have found that it is almost always pedagogically valuable to relate an academic matter to a personal experience.

Barry Goldwater: The Issue of Bigness

February 21

Today one of my most interesting—that means bright—conservatives, Jack, made a well-prepared presentation on Barry Goldwater. Jack did well on the first paper but isn't a fluid writer, nor always a crystal-clear speaker. I say that because he is the most thinking-out-loud student in the class; sometimes he gets caught up in working through the themes and questions that seem to come to him in mid-sentence. So occasionally I have to stop him and say, "Jack, I'm not sure what you're saying; try to put it as simply as you can." It's not that he's wordy or pretentious; indeed, he's elemental and minimalist. But he sees complexities en route to a point. OK, in this case he was very well-organized and went through Goldwater's biography, his political history, and most of the key issues for discussion: states' rights, flat tax, anticommunism, Vietnam, civil rights, regulation, liberty, Social Security. After he finished, the class raised a number of points and I decided to let them go at one another with only facilitating interventions and a few provocative questions. It made for a rowdy class, with many sidebar discussions between students. Lots of passion and energy, which is why I chose to allow somewhat free rein. Perhaps the most striking was the tension between conservatives and liberals over the role of individual responsibility and situations beyond people's control. Conservatives see individual responsibilities as central, leading them to deny a federal role in old-age pensions, unemployment compensation, health care, concluding, "Why should I have to pay for them?" My more liberal students spoke of situations beyond people's control—depressions, capital flight, disasters like Katrina. As we proceeded the key issues became these: Why don't people save? How much is their lack of moral fiber? How much is their lack of income? How much is a systemic inducement centered in Madison Avenue, which encourages consumers to lust for goodies and spend beyond their means? I always like to discuss this, making the point that such an assault on old-fashioned values—a penny saved is a penny earned and such—comes not from Murphy Brown or secular humanists or the Clintons or hippies, but instead from the Fortune 500 and the advertising industry who need hungry and debt-accumulating consumers.

I pushed them to consider how changing economic, technological, and organizational environments, for instance, the rise of the corporation and multinationals, made arguments about individualism and local rights more problematic, indeed that such challenges gave birth to modern liberalism, not to speak of socialism. I wanted students to come to grips with the implications of bigness—big government, for sure, but big business as well. We didn't go there, but it would include big parties, as in bolshevized ones. Undue concentrations of power—economic, political, cultural—tend to corrupt, and tend to overwhelm individuals and small groups. They all, conservatives included, seemed to recognize this in terms of big money political campaigns, although we agreed that to monitor or control private spending, what George Will insists is a form of free speech, is easier said than done. Janet made one of the more astute observations, suggesting that libertarians are quite utopian in ways as bad or worse than those Burke et al. criticize on the Left.

I intentionally kept issues of civil rights and anticommunism at the margin of discussion, anticipating that they would be the center of our seminar on Thursday. That class will be more structured, more focused. But I don't want to put too much of a damper on the kind of free-flowing, animated discussion we had today, with side conversations erupting, talk continuing after class, students really engaging with one another over important issues. This class is turning out to be way too much fun!

It's three in the afternoon, and I just spent an hour talking with two of my conservative students, Dave and Marc, who stopped in to discuss their papers but really wanted to talk about class today. Both were "up," feeling that the discussion was excellent. The latter guy, Dave, a military veteran and libertarian, said it was the best and would be hard to top. I guess my own sense of being focused and working through essential information will always leave me less than elated at such a mess of a class, but it may be that more is learned by peers in such seeming chaos—students actually using their life experiences to make points about Social Security and health care and job opportunities—than when students diligently take pen to paper to follow the brilliant lecture of such as me.

COMPUTER CONFERENCING ON GOLDWATER

Karl captured the sentiments of many:

> . . . as much as I disagree with some of his points and especially his support of McCarthy, I believe he was an amazing figurehead in the conservative movement. He was a clear and poignant speaker, uncompromising and staying to the issues he considered to be most important. He was an unchanging and uncompromising figure and his skills as a politician are unmatched by most. He may have been a bit old-fashioned and not willing to sway his speeches for different crowds, but that just proves that he had an agenda and was going to stick to it regardless. He did not promise anything he wouldn't of delivered, therefore I think he was an important figure, even if you disagree with him entirely.

Trudy countered:

> I disliked him, he is racist and extremely blunt, to some that is a sign of admiration but to me it is not. Words can cause more damage than all the weapons in the world. Goldwater in my mind knew from the very beginning that he was not going to win the election.

Royce defended Goldwater:

> People are quick to criticize Goldwater and the Republicans as racist because of their states' rights views, especially regarding the civil rights amendments. While the truth remains that had the civil rights amendments not been passed, racial inequalities would have still existed to some degree, the heart of the matter lies in the fundamental differences between how liberals and conservatives see the function of government. It's not that Goldwater supported the repression of blacks, it was more a matter of the force of law regarding to social attitudes. Similar to the current Supreme Court's views on affirmative action, Goldwater saw more potential in creating TRUE racial equality through the will of the people rather than by force of law.

Janet added her two cents:

> What I have to say about Goldwater is a little different. I think it may be refreshing to talk about a candidate who had beliefs and stood up for them "uncompromisingly" as many have stated. However, Goldwater just doesn't do it for me.
>
> I guess it is hard for me to see Goldwater in a positive light, being that many of his "uncompromising values" I disagree with. Goldwater says that "a Conservative's first concern will always be: Are we maximizing freedom?" (214). I can't say that getting rid of the civil rights act and eliminating welfare seem to maximize freedom to me. And I am not saying that Goldwater is a racist, because I think we covered that nicely in class and dismissed any of those thoughts.
>
> I imagine that my main concern is practicality. I understand that Goldwater's argument for states' rights is his basis on a lot of issues. However, as a presidential candidate, are you really doing what is right for the country by stubbornly subscribing to these ideas? I say stubbornly because it is obvious to me that Goldwater knew not all states would willingly accept civil rights on their own.
>
> Feel free to agree/disagree, I would love a response.

February 23

I'm feeling flat; students were so high after Tuesday's class in which almost everyone was passionately engaged in discussion that I was reluctant to structure this class around Goldwater's foreign policy and then civil rights views, knowing full well that it would make things more lecturelike, less participatory. That's what I'm feeling. It was actually a good class with lots of questions and comments but also one in which I was feeding them a lot—mostly about U.S.–Cuba relations, the rise of Castro, the Bay of Pigs, the missile crisis, then Berlin and the Wall and a moment on Vietnam before shifting to the question of whether Goldwater's opposition to the Civil Rights Act of 1964 was inherently racist despite his own personal track record of opposition to bigotry.

The interesting moments included addressing Trudy's comments about her Cuban-American friends who hate Castro and who believe that most Cubans share their animosity. Here I had to address what most historians accept, that in the early years Fidel was enormously popular, that even now with economic stagnation and suffering he probably would win a free election, though at 55 percent or so, and that the Cuban-Americans are mostly European and affluent and not trusted by many of the darker, more African-descended and poorer Cubans who feel they have benefited from Castro's health and educational policies. I tried to frame all foreign policy discussion with the three viewpoints—conservative, Cold War liberal, and progressive/radical. In the latter case I emphasized the notion of distinguishing nationalism from communism in the context of Castro and Ho; examined the downside of the U.S. boycott, which allows Castro to blame his economic failures on us; and raised the issue of Finlandization in discussion of Germany and Austria—was a neutral but free, democratic, and prosperous nation better than a divided or tyrannized one? They seemed interested in this question that was new to them.

Finally, we addressed Goldwater's race issue, with my emphasis on the particulars, the experience of it—could he give a campaign speech in the Mississippi that gave him 87.3 percent of its vote without being aware that part of his base was racist? I spoke of meetings in that period where observers noted that a segment of the audience at a meeting or convention was openly bigoted. How did Goldwater handle this, as a man of at least some principle? Just as a distasteful part of politics? We know he refused to run one particularly provocative and mischievous TV ad because he worried that it played into prejudice. But he also had to know that he was instrumental in building a new GOP based on the South, which at least in part flowed from opposition to the civil rights revolution. Sometimes the best moments in class are when a historical situation can be transformed into a theatrical act or play or movie—I always envision such moments and try to help my students "see" historical drama as drama, in this case, getting into Goldwater's head, his psyche, his tension between ambition and ideals, ego and principle.

In any case, it was a useful segue to next week's discussion about George Wallace.

February 27

The recent computer conference comments on Web Board suggest strong enthusiasm for Barry Goldwater, not only because he is easier to read—one clear point—but because his clarity and idealism touch many students, especially but not only my declared conservatives. After reading their comments—one exception being my most liberal student, Janet—for the first time I feel some urge to correct them, to insure that they understand how destructive a Goldwater presidency would have been, especially in civil rights and foreign policy. But this compulsion needs to be calmed; it rests on a lack of confidence in my students' judgment—OK, maybe that must be addressed, over time. I can't assume that I can be in control, or want to be in control. It will be emotionally depressing if, at the end of the term, my conservatives are more locked in and some of my other students have been persuaded to become conservative. But if that's the case, that's going to be the case. I'd have to lump it. And hopefully think a little more deeply about the attractions of conservatism, which is another way of saying that I'd think a little more deeply about the lack of attractions of liberalism and radicalism.

George Wallace: Conservative?

February 28

I just got into my office (it's 11:00 A.M.; class ended at 10:20). Long discussion with Dave, one of my libertarians, who wanted to talk about William F. Buckley's "Cronkite-like" call for an end to the Iraq War. I had read the piece on the web earlier but decided not to bring it to class; instead I brought copies of George Will's book reviews in the Sunday *Times* of Bartlett's attack on Bush as a betrayer of conservatism and Jeffrey Hart's new book on the history of the *National Review.* We ended up talking about court appointments, Kerry, Congressional behavior. It's interesting how much there remain two rival realities at work—to Dave, Kerry bought in to North Vietnamese positions, the Republicans in Congress have been too soft and accommodating on court appointments. This is a very bright, inquisitive guy. I ended up suggesting that he consider how libertarian positions inexorably become instruments, used disingenuously, cynically by big-business and K Street project Republicans to cover their venality. Was I trying to convert him? Not really. I both like and respect this guy. But I do want him to think more rigorously about how libertarianism plays out in the real world. I look forward to his later report on the Cato Institute.

One of my concerns with the course, which increased as we proceeded and has deepened during the writing of this book, has been whether I am too cavalier about the importance of libertarianism. For one, I do not see it as conservatism, at least in the Burkean sense. But I am, more tellingly, disinterested in it as a relevant political philosophy and strategy in what I insist is an interdependent nation and world. As such, I find myself not taking it seriously. At the same time, I am fascinated by its power, both historically and contemporaneously. And, I must admit, I am distressed by how powerful it remains at the very heart of American identity as a barrier to beginning to address the very real potential catastrophes we face, for instance, global warming, nuclear annihilation.

Shortly after Dave left, Marc—one of my most enthusiastic conservatives—popped in, with similar questions and comments, but more about electoral politics, his passion. At the end of our conversation, he asked me, "I took your sixties course and thought I understood where you were coming from, but now I'm not so sure. What are you?" I love such a query! I answered that I am mostly comfortable calling myself a pragmatist, although certainly left of center.

In class, Dick took almost half an hour (the call is for ten to fifteen minutes) to present a kind of biography of George Wallace, only getting up to 1963–1964, his segregationist phase. Dick is from the South and resonates with loyalties and sentiments that make him sympathetic to Wallace. He seemed nervous insofar as he didn't want to affirm Wallace's obvious bigotry. Well, just as I wrote that, Marc stopped in again—he stops in regularly—to ask some questions, to apologize for cutting me off in his enthusiasm to make a point (I found it all wonderfully bemusing), and to chat. He talks a mile a minute; is clearly a modern conservative, is very well read, is committed to civil rights, is antiracist, loves taking philosophy courses, is a future lawyer who leans to the idea that the Warren

Court went too fast in its agenda, and, and, and. . . . Well, a half-hour later, and it's time for lunch. I'll get back to this class when time permits. What's clear is that many of my students, including, it seems, all of my conservatives, are thoroughly enjoying this seminar. As am I.

Dick got us started with a highly detailed profile of Wallace that allowed me to talk about Big Jim Folsom, Wallace's early sponsor and a racial moderate/populist whom Wallace criticized in the sixties, and also about the dynamics within white Southern politics—bourbon and populist, planter and farmer, cavalier and redneck—which required the elimination of the black vote to be comfortably engaged. Janet pointed out how impossible it had to be to sustain a states' rights position without recognizing how much it was indebted to racists. My conservatives split on this, some ferociously pro–civil rights and critical of any hint of bigotry, others taking a kind of Burkean view that it would all have been better if there had been no *Brown* decision and the South had had the time to gradually rectify Jim Crow. This forced a discussion of the conspiracy against civil rights activists during the freedom rides, Selma, Birmingham—the collusion of the police, the role of Bull Connor, the dirty-work duty of the Klan, the respectability of the White Citizens Councils, the few decent cops who refused to descend to terrorism.

We have more to cover on Thursday when Rick (the literature major leftist) discusses "his" Wallace. We started to consider Samuel Francis's article in the readings about Middle American Radicals (MARs), an early version of Nixon's great silent majority. I laid out the ways in which Wallace understood by 1964 that the nation was essentially Southern and that he could test the waters in the Democratic primaries—Wisconsin, Maryland, and Indiana—demonstrating considerable voter strength among what soon would be called ethnics. We discussed the Democratic Party New Deal coalition of "the people" against "the interests" and the Popular Front notion of economic royalists; then I offered the Wallace model of right-wing populism, which offered a new "common man" against a cultural elite from Harvard, Berkeley, Hollywood, of Washington bureaucrats and media types—busybodies all, aligned with an underclass associated with crime, welfare, busing, promiscuity. Time ran out but this analysis will be the heart of Thursday's class. It's the point at which the Republicans, the conservatives, figure out how to dominate. Darren offered, during our discussion, that Wallace could not possibly be considered a conservative. That questions remains at issue: conservative, right-wing populist?

COMPUTER CONFERENCING ON WALLACE

Marc, along with several other conservatives, was critical:

> Wallace, in my view, was not a conservative. He was one by choice. I like the fact that he changed his racial views, although I believe that he was always a true bigot. He was in favor of social programs and against government intervention. In considering that, I consider him a shrewd politician rather than a conservative.

Dave added, with a final kicker:

> George Wallace was nothing more than an opportunist and a hypocrite. On one hand he opposed desegregation on states' rights grounds but then on the other hand, he said that the federal government didn't do enough to help the state of Alabama. I realize that Southern Democrats are generally less liberal than those from the North, but George Wallace was no conservative. Hell, he endorsed Jimmy Carter in '76 after dropping out of the race. He may have espoused some conservative views, but that certainly doesn't make him a conservative.

Different Classes, Special Moments

March 1

It's interesting how different classes are. You know the moment you walk in, that first day, what the energy level is, how participatory or passive it will be. If you're a good teacher, you can deepen the live-wire class and get the quieter group going, at least with some regularity even if not all the time. But the differences remain. The conservatism class is live-wire, so is my ethnic minority relations class—questions, comments, students engaging with one another, a good and warm feeling when I enter the room, a welcoming that's quite personal—we like this guy, he's a good teacher, what will we learn about today? Strangely, my Vietnam War course is my most passive. I've taught this maybe twenty times and it is almost always full of energy and curiosity—how could it not be so? There have usually been four to six, and up to eight children of Vietnam vets registered who come with personal interest in learning about the war, then some war buffs, a few history and poli-sci majors—that's enough to carry most classes. But this time most of my class prefers to listen; there are a few more active ones, and I have no sense that the students are not interested, but they are resistant to participating. I hate to call on students but will on occasion. In this class, every session requires me to get my energy up to compensate for what seems to be their lethargy—although that may be based on my unreasonable expectations rather than their levels of interest. I say that because I've had many students who said nothing, seemed disinterested, and yet told me after the term ended or the following year how much they loved the class, how much they learned. So, go figure. In any case, I enjoy my conservatism and ethnic classes more in that they embrace me. That sounds like I'm quite needy, and, in a sense, I am. I want students to be passionately interested in class, to think about it before and after, to connect it to other classes and to show that interest and passion in the discussions. Fortunately, that occurs in most of my classes, but I have to admit that I expect it, demand it—albeit without sufficient success—in all of my classes. I don't feel guilty or less skilled, just let down a little. If most or all of my classes were like that, I'd have to think about leaving teaching, retiring.

March 2

First, yesterday was Stockton's Day of Scholarship, a day's worth of presentations emphasizing faculty-student collaboration. This event has been a disappointment up to now, with few faculty or students attending sessions. I've usually had four to six people at mine. But this year seems different. I was involved in two sessions, one with my students who did Red Cross training with me and then spent two weeks working with Katrina victims in New Orleans; the second with some of my conservatism students. Both sessions had audiences of about twenty-five or so. The Red Cross session was great—I simply introduced the three students—all social work majors—and then sat back with my coteacher Donni Allison and let them tell their stories. Aside from learning how to work forklifts, they all were impressed by the grittiness of local people, trying to reestablish their lives, especially in the Lower Ninth Ward—worst hit, most poor, most black. I was really proud of the students, who had given a similar talk a few weeks ago at a social work conference in Newark, where they were the hit of the day. Janet is one of them; she's one of the best social work students I've taught in many years and helps to make the conservatism course such an exciting experience for me. She's very bright, an accomplished academic but one who is also a "doer."

The conservatism group included her and four of my more conservative students—Karl, Dave, Marc, and Jack—all of whom spoke of how much the class meant to them. It was ego-gratifying to me, of course, but I was most pleased by their generosity toward one another, their willingness to take risks, to question. Marc said that he was no longer sure if he was a conservative—that should have made me feel good, but, in fact, that's really not my goal. I don't trust rebirths, religious or political; I prefer gradual questioning, deep ponderings. What I felt mostly was a pride in all of them; I said little but poked at some of my liberal colleagues in the audience with my motives in teaching the course—the shame of our institutions not helping our students understand this dominant political force of the past half century. And I concluded by noting that what got me going the most was how idealistic both my conservative and liberal students are. Most students have a gloss of indifference, of cynicism, of not caring about Iraq or Darfur or Katrina, of not reading newspapers. But I've always felt that students today are not much different from students of other eras, including the 1960s. We romanticize the sixties, of course; recognizing a more nuanced, contradictory sixties, however, is central to much of my own research. But we also exaggerate how conservative and/or apolitical today's students are—many seem to have a not-so-hidden idealism, a longing for a time when there were ideals and idealists—that's what leads so many to take my sixties course. Just a short discussion often reveals that longing just beneath the surface.

MORE WALLACE

Rick was well prepared for discussing Wallace. He picked up where Dick left off, focusing on Wallace's 1964 and 1972 campaigns, handing out data on his primary and election numbers. We somehow began to consider religion, I guess because we returned to the issue of Wallace's faith. Dick has been wonderful in this regard, describing his own upbringing in the South, how different it is from Jersey, how many people attend church, how central religion is in their lives. I used this to prep the class for our discussion of the religious right in two weeks. We discussed the meaning of evangelical, fundamentalist, and social gospel versions of Protestant Christianity. They seem very interested in all of this, especially in my use of Martin Luther King as an example of the social gospel. I spoke of black civil rights activists arriving Sunday mornings at church services in all-white congregations—what greater challenge to one's Christianity could exist than this challenge testing the notion that we are all God's children? Once again, students used their personal experiences to connect to the issues—one of my conservatives, Alex, spoke of the dilemma of marrying a Catholic; my born-again couple spoke of living together and the criticism they face from their own circles. I told the class how fortunate I was to have studied with Warren Susman, one of our most astute intellectual historians, who always emphasized how central Protestantism was to American identity and culture, how one could never underestimate how important religion was to Americans, especially in our most religious region, the South.

Then we took a break and returned to address what Wallace represented. I listed broad categories—nation, nature, gender, morality, race—and then issues—welfare, affirmative action, crime, profanity, hair, promiscuity, sex. I framed the discussion with the challenges embodied by the 1960s, noting that Newt Gingrich and other conservatives were correct in some ways in their sixties-bashing, blaming all problems on that decade. After all, it raised profound challenges which we still struggle with, which still define our culture, which we haven't resolved—in that sense we still live the sixties, it is not the past, but the present. What is the nature of patriotism, how does one demonstrate love of country? What is right and what is wrong? Is it OK to love the one you're with, to do your own thing, especially if it feels good, it is good? What's a man and what's a woman and how does the substitution of brain power for brawn power drive the challenges of gender? Is Nature to be conquered and exploited or to be nurtured in harmony? What can I eat? Throw out? Recycle? And can the races live together? And, of course the hot-button issues—riots, cursing. We juxtaposed Malcolm and King, nonviolent demonstrations of well-dressed people with kill-whitey, burn-baby-burn black power rioters. I wanted them to feel the ugliness of Wallace's message, but also how it tapped into the genuine confusion, frustration, and defensiveness, the basic bewilderment of what came to be called the white backlash of ethnics. A real good class.

CHAPTER 2

Teaching Log: The Stretch Drive

Neocons

March 7

Well, we finally had one of those days. I looked forward to a discussion of neoconservatism with Marty presenting, with Kate as possible follow-up on Bill Bennett, and with Sarah on Allan Bloom. Marty did a bang-up job on a difficult subject, but it was clear from the get-go that this was one weary group. Sometimes I forget that there are rhythms to courses. We are on vacation, spring break, next week; most of my students have exams and papers due this week. In fact I pushed back the second conservatism papers until after the break, not so much in order to give them relief as to examine more themes. But they just looked bleached, exhausted. When I noticed something was wrong, they spoke right up and told me of their burdens. We joked about it, I nudged them, but, alas, I did all the heavy lifting once Marty finished. It was all right—I gave them some framework for understanding the Trotskyist background, the Jewishness, the commitment to modernism, the reaction against the sixties, the role of Scoop Jackson, some of the media, the key articles, the core anticommunism. But this is difficult stuff, especially since few of my students have any background in what shaped the neocons. My conservative students at least have some awareness of Buckley and Goldwater, they know the TV and radio jocks—but not Daniel Bell on the cultural contradictions of capitalism, Nate Glazer on the law of unintended consequences, the role of Leo Strauss, the trajectories of Irving Kristol and Norman Podhoretz, Hilton Kramer's defense of modernism against postmodernism, or the role of the Committee on the Present Danger. I hope some of this stuck with them. Mercifully, I let them go a few minutes early; I really can't teach when it's obvious that we're just going through the motions. I made a good-faith effort; they understood and humored me. But this wasn't going to be a good day for learning. Hopefully they can get it together on Thursday—hopefully.

March 9, 2006

Today Kate made a top-notch presentation on Bill Bennett, former drug czar and virtucrat. She was, as usual, well prepared, vigorous, and passionate. Kate is a nontraditional student, one of my favorites, very bright, strong, opinionated, funny. She covered Bennett's professional and political biography—NEH, drug czar, education commish—and then focused on the controversies, for instance, beheading drug kingpins, his gambling addiction, his unfortunate comments recently about aborting black babies. I tried to make sure that the discussion included his strengths, the basis of his concerns about virtue and character, his early civil rights advocacy—I ended with his own story of when he stopped being a liberal—at Harvard Law when one of his advisees, a black student, told him that he couldn't join him for a bite because the table was limited to blacks only. But the class, including the conservatives, were astonished at his radio comments, although Jack noted that Bennett followed the abortion statement with a declaration that such a choice was totally unacceptable. But the class, urged on by Kate, felt that even to suggest such a policy was at best mischievous and ill-advised if not despicable.

We ended up talking a lot about the similarities between traditionalist conservatives, including neocons, and many liberals and radicals—Bennett's desire for the community to express its outrage over deviancy, Hillary Clinton's notion of it taking a village to raise a child, in both cases leaning toward the premodern notion of shaming over guilt, of the community being responsible for maintaining appropriate behavior. I wanted them to recognize the shared assumptions that sometimes link all but libertarians—the idea of the polis. This led to an interesting discussion of crime and punishment. There was too much of the mindless conservative "let's execute and stop coddling" versus the liberal "let's do a better job of rehabilitating," so I asked them to separate the moral from the pragmatic and empirical. What works? What are the consequences of capital punishment? Of residency laws covering sex offenders? Why is it that our most punitive states continue to have the highest rates of violent crime? Mostly I asked them to consider why the United

States has the highest rates of violent crime among advanced nations and the highest rates of incarceration as well. I told them that when I used to teach this stuff back in the early 1980s I would mourn that we were third in the world in incarceration rates trailing apartheid South Africa and the USSR—some company! Now I regret to note that we are number one. What I wanted them to think about was what works. Interestingly, my libertarians, especially Dave, suggested that the elimination of drug laws would go a long way to reducing incarceration rates. As they spoke, the more traditionalists—Milt and Jack—blanched, no, no, no. The class was back to vigorous and thoughtful conversations.

Then after a break I distributed a sheet on the developed conservative infrastructure of foundations, think tanks, lobby groups, and media that drove the successes of conservatism as a movement. In discussing Accuracy in Media and David Horowitz's popular culture organization, Darren made the point of parallel biases left and right, Fox and CNN and the like. I intervened and asked them to think about the inadequacy of that viewpoint. I told them how this replicated what so many New Leftists argued, that all culture is political, that the mainstream media is anti-Left, liberal, establishment. Of course there is some truth in this, but to reduce what our best media try to do, whether the *Times* or public TV, to politics denies professional integrity. The fact is that there are journalists who focus on professional standards of reporting. I got more polemical than usual in arguing that this politicizing was one of the most pernicious behaviors among conservatives, justifying ideologized news because there is the assumption that the other guy does it, and did it first. The problem is that good reporting is good reporting, period. Just as good scholarship is good scholarship—and add in dentistry and accounting if you choose. I was interested to find that several of my conservatives didn't know that the *Times* had conservative op-ed columnists, several had never heard of David Brooks or John Tierney or, indeed, William Safire. Obviously their media sources made it seem implausible that such MSM outlets would hire a conservative. I added that the *Wall Street Journal* had a forcefully conservative editorial policy but that its reporters were not part of that ideological bent and in fact were good professionals.

This is an issue that continued to arise within the seminar. Of all the developments emerging out of the rise of conservatism, perhaps the one that most disturbs me is the ideologizing of all thought. I must admit that the Left, including postmodernism, has contributed to this reduc-

tionism, but I was taken aback by how deeply it shapes how my students gather information. Conservative students seem to limit their quest for information and analysis to aggressively right-wing media and have a contempt for all outlets that can be labeled as liberal or leftist. This is a sad and dangerous phenomenon.

Allan Bloom

March 21

Back from a wonderful week in the UK, still feeling some jetlag plus some resistance to returning to my normal work life. But today's seminar worked well. Sarah gave an uneven but brave presentation of Allan Bloom; this was one of the more difficult topics given the inexperience of most students—including Sarah—with thinkers such as Bloom. I followed up with a framework of understanding that began with the ways in which neocons came out of three streams—Trotskyist, Straussian, and antisixties—with Bloom drinking at the latter two. Only one student, Marc, a political science major, knew anything about Strauss, so I had to fill in many gaps, focusing on how Strauss's and Bloom's views differed from libertarian and religious forms of conservatism in several ways: their views of natural reason, virtue, and the polis; their criticism of modernism and postmodernism as forms of relativism and, inevitably, as forms of nihilism. Then I discussed Bloom's life story, important in that I see it as central to his emergence as a best-selling writer in 1987 with *The Closing of the American Mind.* My colleague Dave Emmons had a class with Bloom at Yale in the early 1960s when Bloom was visiting from Cornell; Dave describes Bloom as a brilliant, charismatic lecturer, dazzling his students with his erudition, his passion of text, his focus on textual analysis. I talked of his romance with those post–GI Bill undergraduates, upwardly mobile, working-class and middle-class kids thrilled to be introduced to the life of the mind, to drink in the classics, to be aided by the embodiment of that cerebral life. That Bloom seduced his students, intellectually and, sometimes, erotically, had to be noted. Some of the class had difficulty with that, mostly because of their immaturity, the tendency of many youth to still be uncomfortable with a serious discussion of homosexuality. I didn't want to focus on any hypocritical aspects of Bloom's behavior, nor to play into any sense of the prurient. What I wanted them to understand was that Bloom wouldn't share their notion of perversity; he would see his behavior, his sexuality, his epicurean tastes, his passions in every sense of the term, as consistent with his notion of virtue, of living a polis life. In that sense he is closer to those on the left; I called him a kind of secular humanist, tweaking my religious conservatives a bit. Some asked if his book would have been as successful if people knew of his sexual behavior; I suggested that it certainly would have lessened his appeal to some traditionalists, especially the religious right.

It was a lively and thoughtful discussion for the most part, although I think the class still remains fuzzy on the nature of the neoconservatives. But then we moved on to Willie's report on the religious right, which will continue into Thursday's seminar. Willie is one of my favorite students—he usually strolls in a bit late but not too late, sits off on the side, but seems among the most attentive of my students. Plus, his comments are always thoughtful, sometimes funny, and, while strongly stated, not said in an arrogant manner. He's one of my liberals. When he began to lay out his argument, first on the blackboard and then in his slow, almost drawled but precise manner, I realized that he was gay. He did say that, but he prefaced his comments by noting that he would be approaching the religious right as an active member of the progressive religious community, adding that he was involved in several church-based gay organizations. I was impressed with the way he laid out differences between fundamentalist and modernist churches; gave some of the history of conflicts over the ERA, abortion, feminism and gay rights; and then offered a clear, concise overview of the most important religious right organizations—Moral Majority, Christian Coalition, Focus on the Family, Family Research Council. There were lots of questions. One allowed for a useful distinction between fundamentalism and evangelism. Willie stated that he considered himself evangelical except that the good news he was offering differed from that of the religious right. He has a manner of expression that seemed to earn him the respect of the class. Finally, they're intellectual snobs in the best sense of that phrase and recognize Willie as one of them despite what they might think about his sexual identity.

Next class before we get to antifeminism, I want to spend more time laying out the journey that led religious conservatives from a rejection of politics to an affirmation of it. This should segue well into the responses to second-wave feminism. Meanwhile, I'm still trying to get back into a rhythm of teaching; my experience carries me through and carries my students as well, but it's too much on automatic. Hopefully in a few days . . .

COMPUTER CONFERENCING ON NEOCONSERVATIVES

The most astute comment on neoconservatives and fundamentalists came from Janet, a liberal but certainly among the seminar's most thoughtful members:

> I think that neoconservatives were indispensable to what we now see as the conservative movement. I have absolutely no problem arguing that position and did so in our last paper. In reality, I believe neoconservatives do mirror some conservative values, but fall short of what I see as a "true" conservative. Neocons come close to conservatives in their traditional sense. They are Burkean in that they were unhappy with the rapid changes of the '60s, and would have preferred them to be slower and calmer. They are respectful of traditions, showing most in their study of intellectual works, belief in meritocracy, and creation of the law of unintended consequences. Where neocons differ, and where I think most conservatives would be upset with them, is their views on government. Many neocons were New Dealers, and also supporters of the welfare state. Neocons may have felt disillusioned by the Great Society plan for the welfare state, but nevertheless, they were supportive of federal government interventions in the past. I think this sets them apart vastly from what a "true" conservative would opt for.
>
> Like it or not, neoconservatives are included under the conservative umbrella. They have added a depth to the conservative movement (and Republican Party for that matter) that was missing prior to their intellectual contributions. I think it would be silly for the Right to alienate this group who self-diagnose as part of the conservative movement.
>
> Honestly, I have more to say about neoconservatives than fundamentalists. But, when it all pans out I do not see fundamentalists as conservatives. I would like to think that there is more to a political ideology (conservative or not) than just the idea of traditional values and god. I don't see being a Christian a precursor to being conservative, or being a conservative a precursor to being Christian. I think there is plenty of room for Christians on the Left side of politics (as Warren so nicely points out). I think that fundamentalists find themselves identifying more with conservatives because they are a group that actually uses the idea of being based in religion in order to get fundamentalists as their constituents.

Conservative Professors at Liberal Colleges

March 22

Yesterday I had a long talk with Casey Rizzo, a colleague whom I want to come into the conservatism seminar to speak about what it is like being a conservative academic in a liberal environment. The first issue was this: how did I know or surmise that Casey was a conservative? I had never had a discussion with her in the past; she's recently tenured, our paths have rarely crossed. But I had heard in the hallway gossip, which so shapes the information flow at a college, that she was on the right; so I took a chance. She affirmed that yes, she was a Republican—which is not what I asked. But she added that she was culturally moderate, economically conservative, and hawkish on foreign policy—what I would call a New Jersey Republican—Kean, Whitman.

I am always interested in the politics of the children of the immigrant generation of the turn of the twentieth century—the Italians, the Poles, the Jews, the Irish—in part because much of the turn toward conservatism since mid-century rests on the shift of such folks from New Deal Democrat to conservative or Reagan Republicans. There's an interesting argument that goes on among scholars about what drove that change: friends like the historian Tom Sugrue argue that the roots of such shifts, especially linked to racism, go back at least to the 1940s, well before "white backlash" became the going phrase, well before the more confrontational side of black politics came to the fore—riots, black power. Others see more fault with the Democrats shifting toward identity politics, away from a class-based politics, symbolized by the marginalizing of urban machines and labor representatives under the McGovern rules of the 1972 Democratic Convention. I think Sugrue is certainly correct in arguing for serious difficulties well before the mid-1960s, but I also argue that there has been a blindness on the left—liberal and radical—which often took the form of a contempt for what blue-collar and lower-middle-class whites, the ethnics, were going through, from deindustrialization to all of the challenges associated with the 1960s movements—challenges to family authority, to traditional views of patriotism and morality, and so on. As such, I am always interested in the kind of profiles that scholars like Jonathan Reider have evoked, in his case, in Italian and Jewish Canarsie.

In any case, I explained why I'm teaching the course and why I'm interested in having a conservative colleague speak to my students. She was willing, seemingly persuaded that I was genuinely curious about her views. Casey proceeded to give me innumerable examples of what it is like to feel isolated and disrespected—from the more routine everyday of seeing anti-Bush cartoons and posters outside the offices of so many of her colleagues, to conversations where colleagues seemed oblivious to how she might feel when they vented against Republicans. One liberal colleague told her to just come back at such comments—stand up, be brave! And, indeed, Casey is no shrinking violet; she is feisty and stubborn—and bright. But she told me that in her first term here she had a knock-down, drag-out argument with a senior and very left colleague, that she was told flat out that her tenurability rested on making some compromises with her ideology. And yet here she is—tenured and promoted. Why? In part because she is very good at what she does—she turns out publications and is a good teacher and does college service well—but also because there are lots of colleagues on the left who take seriously their commitments to academic freedom, to real diversity—or, simply, to fairness.

And yet later in the day I ran into a more liberal colleague and mentioned that I had had a talk with Casey; he quickly and brusquely expressed impatience with Casey's defense of free-market economic policies and suggested her politics was grounded in her parents' influence—surmising that she still lived with her parents, which is not the case. What I heard, for the most part, was a denial of legitimacy to conservatism, a sense that it was inconceivable for any sane and intelligent person to honestly and thoughtfully come to conservative conclusions. In some ways I learned more in this latter encounter, which took two minutes, than in the more than an hour that I spent with Casey.

Conservatism, Feminism, and Gender

March 23

Today we finished our consideration of the religious right and then devoted much of the seminar to feminism/antifeminism. I filled in our consideration of the Christian right with discussion of several topics: the key Supreme Court decisions (prayer in the schools, *Roe v. Wade*); the IRS decision to examine private academies, which started after 1953 to assess their violations of civil rights; and the Conference on Families, which played such a large role in the hostility to Jimmy Carter among "betrayed" evangelicals. We also touched on the factors that helped to bring Carter down—stagflation, the Iranian hostages, the Soviet invasion of Afghanistan. There's still more to consider when we get to Reagan in the next weeks, but I wanted to leave lots of room for Janet to present on antifeminism. I wasn't disappointed.

Janet had stopped in yesterday for some help in preparing her presentation. I helped her in framing feminism, how it evolved, the significant variations within it. Today she did a solid job in discussing origins and early history, but really took off in laying out a rich variety of people critical of feminism, from Daphne Patai to Christina Hoff Somers to Cathy Young to Midge Decter to Phyllis Schlafly. Janet is one of my all-time favorite students, partly because she is bright and highly motivated, but more because she literally sparkles with enthusiasm for life. She can be funny and funky and during her presentation stayed organized and focused. She liked Patai, who is a liberal feminist with serious criticisms of the conformism within women's studies; Janet was fair-minded about the libertarian Young and the neocon Decter; she hated Somers for being excessive and partisan; and Schlafly, well, Janet tried to be balanced but clearly disliked everything about her.

We ended up talking a lot about how the industrial revolution transformed gender relations—the link between home and work that drove most of human history based on agriculture was broken and the housewife was born, to stay home while her husband went off to either office or factory, to have fewer children to the point of having much of the remainder of her longer life with an empty nest, to have been allowed extensive education without the encouragement of putting it to use—all creating the contradictory context for second-wave feminism. The most interesting moment to me is when Milt stated that, as a fundamentalist, he believed that the man should be the head of the household and the wife subordinate, but that that didn't justify mistreatment or abuse or disrespect to the woman. One of my liberal students, Kate, worked very hard to restrain herself from going at Milt, but my sense is that most of the class understood that Milt was speaking honestly and without any arrogance or self-righteousness. As such, they heard him out, didn't agree with him, but showed respect for his point of view.

We talked a lot about the battle between nature and nurture, and I suggested that it was a dumb-because-false dichotomy—that despite a woman dunking in a recent March Madness game, men would, on the average, remain faster and quicker than women in sports and that there were consequences to our biological asymmetries. Everyone seemed to agree that we waste lots of time arguing either side exclusively, although I worked hard to get them to understand why feminists in the early days were so adamant in arguing for social construction. We ended with my own emphasis that the industrial revolution and all that has built on it increasingly makes brainpower trump brawn power, thus reducing the work advantages men historically possessed. One of the difficult things in a class like this is how little time we have to concentrate on what could use much more analysis and discussion. But they were "there"—participating, talking about their own job experiences, talking about the extent to which shopping was part of a social construction of gender, feeling amazed that when I was their age the help-wanted section of newspapers divided between male and female job opportunities.

Lastly, we had our first day of bad attendance. One-third were out; that hasn't happened before. I run seminar lightly; I have a seating chart that I used quietly to check who is in class. My rule is that if you miss you are obliged to let me know why as soon as possible. I have no sense that this was more than an aberration, a quirk—some very active students were out, but I'll mention it next week (we only meet once because there is an advising day on Tuesday with all classes cancelled) to see if there is any problem of mid- to later term drift. More likely a mix of illness and personal factors came into play. One of the best things about this seminar is that I rarely consider such things as attendance because there is such enthusiasm that gives a feeling of choice—we're here because we want to be here, because we enjoy the class; we look forward to coming.

We also talked about the issue of washing one's dirty laundry in public—the tendency for oppressed groups to resist discussing deficiencies within their group with outsiders in fear that it will be used against them. My friend Joan Mandle, who ran a women's studies program and center at Colgate University, discusses this extensively and bravely in one of her books. I had just addressed this at a conference on diversity at Oxford University during spring break. Most of the participants, including many African Americans, seemed to accept my argument that it is both unethical and politically unwise to suppress unpleasant truths, for example, the crisis in the black family, since one's adversaries will inevitably latch onto such realities for their own ideological purposes. Better to look it in the eye, explain it, and, hopefully, work to resolve it. But I know that some were less pleased with my consideration of underclass pathologies, the phenomenon of "acting white," and the like. What always bothers me most is the cowardice of too many of my left-of-center colleagues, who avoid controversial issues regarding race or gender in fear that they will be attacked by others—this is the core truth within the notion of being politically correct. My own experience is that being honest and respectful is always the best policy; otherwise, one treats people as children, as incapable of handling the truth, or at least a claim of truth. Indeed, my own experience, alas, is that my students are more able to recognize contradictory truths than are my colleagues.

Ideologues and Pragmatists

March 30

I'm thinking about an essay for this planned book on the following: the need for transformations in conservatism, liberalism, and radicalism; the ways in which each ideological tradition is serving its respective constituents and loyalists badly; the ways in which this nation really needs a more rigorous and robust conservatism—clearly the incompetence and recklessness of the Bush administration makes this more than apparent, as does the developing and fascinating intramural brawls among conservatives.

But it is also apparent that liberalism remains in deep trouble, still haunted and sometimes paralyzed by its postsixties decline, a kind of crisis of confidence as measured by the evasion of self-descriptions, the pejorative use of the "L" word. And radicalism, essentially Marx-based traditions and movements, well, they're in desperate need of a cold shower of self-reflection—is it possible to imagine a postcapitalist economy, polity, and culture that doesn't succumb to dictatorship, economic inefficiencies, or cultural orthodoxies? Peter Clecak addressed this triad many years ago in a significantly different historical moment, but I want to return to it to argue that we would truly need a vigorous debate among and between the best of our traditions—Burkean, libertarian, social-democratic, socialist, green—a debate that begins with simple rules: no red-baiting from the Right, no brown-baiting from the Left, no assumption that the Center is by definition wiser or more mature or more practical. OK, now I feel energized for class!

Well, it was a wonderful morning after all. Things started slow, a few folks were late, the first report on the American Enterprise Institute was adequate but not sparkling—Geraldine, who is one of the quieter members of the class, was clearly nervous and very soft-spoken. Dave followed with a short but focused report on Cato; he is a forceful libertarian who, upon questioning, agreed that he might support a Libertarian over a Republican in the next presidentials. In the discussion that followed I asked the class, especially those with libertarian leanings, to address two major concerns usually raised by nonlibertarians: environment and big business. First, how could libertarian principles be applied in such a way as to insure a safe environment, especially regarding global warming? Second, in what ways does libertarianism, including the essay we read by Milton Friedman, address the impact of large-scale enterprise upon liberty and democracy?

We addressed the environmental issue first, and the class seemed reignited with energy and purpose. Jack, from the back of the room, remained unconvinced that the case has been made for global warming and held to a position of waiting, keeping hands off. Janet and Darren came back at him, soon joined by Willie, arguing that the evidence was clear enough to require intervention. I poked at Willie for making a conservative argument, that is, that it was wiser to be cautious if the evidence was strong but not conclusive, since the consequence of doing nothing was so severe. As we approached break time, I asked Jack and Dave if it was reasonable to assume that their position rested on a mistrust of the experts, framing the discussion with our already establishment view that conservative success rested on replacing the liberal binary of the people versus the Fortune 500, with the people versus the New Class. I wanted to push them in terms of how important they found the evidence or even potential evidence. Willie agreed that if the evidence was persuasive to him, he would agree to controls; Jack remained adamant that there was no evidence that could persuade him to impose controls over an individual's property rights. That actually moved the argument forward by virtue of its absolutism.

It was interesting to hear several of my liberals (actually radicals) voice zero-sum notions of economic growth, notions of what I explained to them was Marx's initial take of absolute immiseration, that is to say, the capitalists get richer, the proletariat gets poorer, and then its replacement with the notion of relative immiseration, that economic growth allows the rich to get richer as the poor get less poor or even become affluent. Was this globally possible? How could we weigh the evidence now available regarding India, China, the four tigers of East Asia? I told them that the night before I had had this discussion with my son Max, who was pessimistic about the capacity of development, especially in India and China, to be sustained in terms of water, air, soil, energy. We agreed that our differences—my assumption that there were possibilities for development to temper, to make the kinds of environmental adjustments made by Western nations, and his assumption that this was not possible—could not be resolved by the available evidence. It came down to our basic, existential predisposition—half full versus half empty, optimism versus pessimism.

It was a delirious conversation with about half the class totally engaged—in word, in body language, in intensity. We looked at the dilemma of libertarian responses to bigness in capitalism. Karl spoke passionately against tossing moral charges at entrepreneurs who outsourced to secure lower wages, Dick spoke contemptuously about George Soros and Teddy Kennedy for saying one thing and doing another, in Kennedy's case opposing windmills on the Cape. I suggested that we needed to move away from a focus on the individual hypocrisies of those we opposed, left or right, since it tended to be a way to avoid taking adversaries seriously. Then I switched the challenge to my left-of-center students, using Friedman's text to ask whether any postcapitalist arguments could remain credible in the face of Stalinism and its economic inefficiencies. My kids on the left want to believe that there are possibilities out there, but they seem so fixated on an antiglobalization model that presupposes that the non-Western world is getting fucked over by neoliberalism that they have difficulty recognizing the accomplishments of capitalism and the gains being made in what once was called the underdeveloped world. I felt a bit like a ringmaster trying to keep all three rings challenged, tossing questions to eliminate any self-satisfaction, any ideological smugness, any sense of certainty. When class ended, discussion continued out into the hallway for fifteen or twenty minutes until I broke it off to sit down and put these thoughts on paper. I remain impressed with the intellectual and ethical honesty of so many of my seminarians, with how well they seem to engage with one another, to now kid one another, to really listen.

During the class, Sarah, my only nontraditional liberal, asked my personal opinion on where the world is headed, following a brief discussion of Francis Fukuyama's new book criticizing neoconservatives on Iraq. I laid out, more forcefully than I had at any time in the past, my view that the Bush administration was the very worst, the least competent, the most reckless I have experienced and that I felt that it would take generations to even begin to remedy what they have wrought. Then

I added what I discussed above about the comparative failures of conservatism, liberalism, and radicalism. And I advocated the kind of pragmatism that has been my comfort zone for a while. Don't obsess over the moral purpose of something, just ask what are the consequences of any action or policy. The worst thing about ideologues, left and right, is that they lock in to formulaic solutions to all problems—characteristically, the market for conservatives, planning for liberals and radicals. One of the studies that has influenced me greatly is Alec Nove's *The Economics of Feasible Socialism*, which took a situational approach to economic organizational questions—what works in specific settings, at specific times.

Ronald Reagan

April 3

I've been thinking a lot about how to best prepare for discussing Ronald Reagan this week. We did look at him in terms of his emergence in 1964 and 1966, but this will be a full week's examination. I'll try to have the class focus on domestic issues on Tuesday and foreign policy on Thursday, but that may not be possible given that I can't predict how the two student reports will go. My own take is to credit Reagan with a restored optimism in the nation and with showing flexibility in negotiating an elimination of intermediate range missiles with Gorbachev. But on economic matters, race, class, gender, AIDS, Central America, Iran and Iraq, Israel-Palestine-Lebanon, deficits and debt, illegalities that showed a contempt for Congress—to just get started—I find him to be a seriously deficient chief executive. Perhaps the key issue will be around the common assumption that Reagan won the Cold War. I have never bought this argument, which seems to me to be patently ideological and based on circumstance and a set of assumptions asserted but rarely examined. I look forward to seeing how my seminarians engage with this clearly "great" president, great in the sense that his impact and influence has so shaped the past quarter century.

Since the course ended, I have read John Patrick Diggins's intriguing if perverse biography Ronald Reagan: Fate, Freedom, and the Making of History, *which makes the case that Reagan was an Emersonian libertarian whose heroes included Tom Paine. I find it most interesting to approach Reagan as a representative figure in the transformation of conservatism into a populist movement and in its embracing of a utopian foreign policy.*

April 4, 2006

Alex wasn't ready to present today—she will be on Thursday, and Trudy was absent. So thank goodness I had prepared a rather ambitious layout on Reagan: preceding events that contributed to his history, for example, the Panama Canal treaty battles, the hostage crisis, stagflation; the election itself; domestic policies; foreign policies. I was amazed at the length of issues, many still with us, many still driving our national and global politics, mostly for the worse I should add.

I began the class by giving back their papers, which were fairly good. Several very bright students, fortunately a sprinkling of both liberals and conservatives; many more decent, workmanlike efforts; very few stinkers. That always unsettles a class for at least ten minutes following, as students try to decipher my handwriting, compare grades, either feel wonderful or resentful or envious or relieved, or a little bit of all of that. Then I told them that addressing Reagan forced me to pay attention to my teaching approach, especially as it related to issues of partisanship and objectivity. I began with the claim that Reagan should be considered one of our most influential presidents and, in that sense, a great one. I added that I believed that the consequences of his policies were mostly damaging to our culture, our economy, our international position. But I also added that what he accomplished was a revival of the American spirit, which was depressed by the series of traumas in the 1970s: Vietnam, Watergate, stagflation, and the late seventies events in Afghanistan, Poland, and Iran. I told them that I recalled an argument two of my colleagues had when I first arrived at the college twenty-six years ago. One veteran colleague, one of our best instructors, says that he lays out a variety of interpretations, ways of framing issues and events, and keeps his own views to himself, believing that this grants to the students more responsibility for coming to resolve. Another colleague, more leftist, also a fairly good teacher, countered that this was a bit self-deceptive in that our points of view always are revealed and, even more importantly, he explained that he felt no desire to present points of view he detested—they already got enough coverage as is, why add to it?—and instead focused on what he saw as the truth. I identified with parts of both positions, sharing with the former a commitment to multiple perspectives, but sharing with the latter a belief that one has a responsibility to honestly state what one considers to be the truth. So regarding Reagan, that's what I did and will continue to do—present the differing interpretations of his legacy while at the same time offering my own conclusions and, of course, how I arrived at those conclusions.

The class itself was OK, but more lecture than makes me happy in a seminar. But once again the discussion flooded out into the hallways, in this case for almost an hour, as some of my conservatives wanted to discuss a variety of issues: Was George W. really a conservative? What was the appropriate response to communist states? How did this differ from responses to other repressive governments? Is Rumsfeld like McNamara? The best discussion both during and after class had to do with Reagan's nature—his clear set of principles, combined with his political astuteness, mixed with his lack of curiosity and his tendency to prefer anecdotal stories to data-driven analysis. Did he know about Iran-Contra? Did he understand that the contras were not, strictly speaking, freedom fighters? Did he understand that most people on welfare were not the welfare queens he chronically described as entering their Cadillacs with liquor purchased from their food stamps? Is George W. a Reaganite?

I suggested that our foreign policy has been a struggle between competitive values: the old Wilsonian, now neocon vision of a city on a hill committed to liberty and democracy; the conventional Fortune 500, big business interest in profit maximization globally; the political and military-strategic interest in balance of power or hegemonic advantage. We discussed how Reagan could support Marcos or the Shah or the contras or the South African apartheid regime or the Afghan mujahideen by seeing all of them as opponents of communism and therefore, in some sense, on the side of freedom. My own view is that he was never cynical but rather saw the world simply and firmly, a right-wing idealist protected from several realities by his celebrity, his privilege, and his style of thinking. Marc just interrupted this log with a few questions and comments about Reagan, so now I'm back to close up shop for the day. Thursday's class should be very interesting.

April 6

Another one of those extraordinary seminars. Alex started it off with a solid if workmanlike presentation on Reagan. When she finished I suggested that we focus our discussion around the following questions that drive much of the evaluation of Reagan's legacy: Did he win the

Cold War? Did he generate an economic boom? Did his policies harm the poor? We almost immediately got off on a discussion of higher education that began when Karl commented on the resentments he holds toward those who receive work-study for college but who respond lackadaisically. That set off a brouhaha by two of my female students, one very liberal—Kate—but the other usually quiet and decidedly apolitical—Sarah—voicing concerns. Darren added that he resented students who feel they have a right to a college education. Sarah exploded, "I'm a working mom with three kids—without the government I wouldn't be able to go to school, and I'd be on welfare and you'd all blame me for it. I thank God that the federal government helps me out and I resent anything that questions my right to that help—I don't know what I'd do without it." She was angry, crying, a little surprised with her own vehemence—and visibility. Darren thought he was being attacked and responded, at first, defensively: "I don't like being attacked for saying what I honestly believe, and if you knew about my life—I won't go there—well, I just think too many people think they have a right to college and I don't agree." Others got in on the discussion, which was heated and deeply charged. I worked hard—my social worker skills—to help Sarah and Darren understand one another and, as a result, for all to see underlying themes. I talked about the pain I was hearing all around, which was a theme within the course—conservative students often asserting pride in being independent, at some sacrifice; several liberals noting how much they struggled to juggle school, work, and family. I spoke of my experiences teaching group dynamics, during which, given enough time, virtually all students brought forth some deep pain, deep anguish from their respective lives—even that seemingly rich suburban kid, who had a younger brother with cerebral palsy, or the handsome jock whose mom died of cancer, and so on. I wanted the class to understand how widely these personal hurts were shared but the ways they seemed to create barriers between people, especially given initial stereotypes, in our case, conservative and liberal.

As a teacher of social policy, I tell students that there are inherent trade-offs depending on one's goals: if for example you want to include all those deserving, you will necessarily give to those undeserving; if, like Reagan, you seek to restrict to the "truly needy," you will necessarily exclude some of the truly needy by virtue of the careful, intrusive approach that will lead some to say, "I'd rather forego the benefit than go through that humiliation of my honesty being challenged and my dignity denied." The class seemed to understand this. I then extended the discussion to how it works in college aid, our initial beef. If you limit benefits to the poorest students, you will exclude many needy working-class ones who are likely to resent their exclusion and who will notice bad behavior among those lucky enough to receive the benefit. So it becomes in policy terms particularism or universalism, whether one discusses scholarship aid or health care. The more who receive, the more costly, the more wasteful, but also the more popular. I focused on the working kid from a family making forty to sixty thou, ineligible for aid, resenting those who were eligible, especially if color came into play. We also discussed the quality of higher education, the increasing elitism of the most elite schools, and the overall question that drives so much of our differences—what is the public interest, what should be supported as a public service? I asked my libertarians to consider where they drew the line. I had to close off the discussion as time was narrowing and we still had to address Reagan's foreign policies.

The second half, actually third, of the class focused on Nicaragua, Iran-Contra and the fall of the Soviets, with stops at Lebanon, Grenada, and Panama. I suggested that Reagan's idealism played a fascinating role in his receptivity to Gorbachev at Reykjavik, causing his advisors to draw him back; that he genuinely hated the MAD strategy that had dominated policy since the nuclear age; that he saw a solution in the problematic Strategic Defense Initiative—Star Wars—but bought into a drawdown with Gorbachev. I also suggested—more next week I suspect—that the fall of the Soviets was more internally driven, particularly by rising costs, than driven by Reagan's policies. The question that has interested me for some time is when Soviet leaders and cadre lost confidence in communism. This wasn't true under Khrushchev, who genuinely believed that he would bury the West with a superior planned economy. But some time under Brezhnev, the rot set in, cynicism triumphed, and it was only a matter of time for the system to implode. It was Gorbachev's great accomplishment, at the cost of his political career, to facilitate this nonviolent process, something no one predicted. As such, I contend that Kennan was the most prescient, in arguing that containment of an inherently irrational system would force it back on its own resources, its own contradictions, and thus toward an eventual collapse. We ran out of time but interest remained high, and, after a little hallway chat, I had to run to a meeting. One measure of how much I enjoy this class is how much I didn't want to leave the hallway group.

COMPUTER CONFERENCING ON REAGAN

Dave, my libertarian, reflected the dominant view, but included his criticisms as well:

> Ronald Reagan was the greatest president in my lifetime. I have absolutely no qualms saying that. He wasn't perfect, though. Despite the fact that he is, in large part, responsible for my political beliefs, there are a few things that truly disappoint me about him. The first is Lebanon. That was absolutely shameful. The second was the Iran-Contra scandal. Constitutional issues aside, it was morally reprehensible. We were playing both sides of the Iraq/Iran War, which isn't that big a deal except for the fact that Iran was responsible for the murders of 241 U.S. Marines in Lebanon, a few more soldiers in Berlin, and there was that little matter of invading American soil when they took over our embassy and held U.S. citizens hostage for 444 days. How's that for a run-on sentence? Both of those concerned Iran. We had no problems bombing Libya but Iran has gone unpunished for twenty-five plus years. We should have bombed them back to the Stone Age. Anyway, the third transgression was the illegal immigrant amnesty in 1986, I think.
>
> No, he wasn't perfect but he was a better man than anyone else to hold the office since.

Kate, ever liberal, countered:

> His crap about the "truly needy" was just garbage and put many people in jeopardy for many years. . . . The Reagan years were as distasteful to me as the Vietnam and Nixon years.
>
> Reagan's foreign policy didn't singlehandedly solve the Iran hostages, or tear down the wall, all by himself. There were years of diplomacy, other factors in the world, and politicians before him that played some of the parts; he just was lucky enough to be president when it happened.

Marc made an astute rejoinder:

> Politics is a game of rhetoric. Reagan realized this and was able to capitalize on this concept with his quick wit and humor. Politicians need this ability to be successful in their careers. They have to be able to show their programs/goals/agenda to large masses of people and make them

> believe in the programs that they want to institute. Reagan in this respect was an effective politician. America needed boosts of confidence and the assurance that we are the best country in the world, which unlike President Carter, President Reagan was able to provide. He will always be attributed as the president that stopped communism, rightly or wrongly, and would always be an icon of the conservative movement. Iran-Contra would always be his "failure," but compared with everything else, he was still able to be the most effective president in the past sixty years.

And Darren topped even that with:

> To me—Reagan was the most memorable president of my life! He was larger then life. When I listen to his famous speeches, like the Brandenburg Gate speech, I still get misty eyed. As I have gotten older, I have become aware that he was not all good, but then who is?
>
> So, while there were "bad" moments to his presidency and while he was not perfect, few are. With all his faults, Reagan will always be the vision I have in my mind when I think of what we NEED in a president . . . strong, stalwart, righteous, passionate, and compassionate (although homosexuals, working poor, and immigrants might disagree the strongest with that last one).

Janet got frustrated with the celebration, albeit with some honest efforts to be balanced:

> So, I guess I'll be the one to take the heat—I hate Reagan. Yes. I've said it.

She followed with a litany of his failures, especially in Central America and regarding the poor. Dave cut to the chase in his response:

> That's exactly how I felt during the Klinton [*sic*] years.

Conservatism and Liberalism

April 10

I can feel the rapid closing of the term, perhaps because I am off to Atlanta for a conference that forced me to cancel Thursday's seminar and then I noticed that there will be only two more weeks to go. In the past few weeks, I have started to anticipate some of the writing I will seek to accomplish during the summer and fall. One thought has been my sense that the three major ideological systems available—conservatism, liberalism, socialism (perhaps more accurately these days postcapitalism)—have not been serving the nation well. What do I mean? Well, as should be clear by now, I find the conservative ascendancy to be a tragedy. In short, conservatives believe that they know the answers and seem incapable of the kind of self-reflection that might make for a compelling vision and strategy. It is not just the present crack-up generated by W.'s failures, the internal squabbling over debt and deficit, big-government conservatism, foreign-policy catastrophes, and so on. It is my firm conviction that there really is no legitimate conservatism out there. I sensed this before beginning the seminar, before swimming on much of the literature. Perhaps I began to sense the problem while reading George Will's *Statecraft as Soulcraft*. Back in the 1970s, when he was becoming the most compelling voice among conservative journalists, Will laid out a thoughtful model of a Burkean traditionalism, respectful of individual liberties within an organic metaphor of community, nation, religion. And yet we have watched him become an only occasional, episodically wise counselor; we have seen him flack for the Reagans, hold to an absurd notion of campaign spending as free speech despite the social and moral costs, and take shamelessly partisan positions, especially in the Clinton years, as he became a celebrity pundit. There is no conservatism, to answer Lionel Trilling, no meaningful, Burkean voice—measured, wise, cautious. Consider whether any of those descriptions fit Bill Frist viewing a video to confidently proclaim that Terri Schiavo is a living, breathing, feeling, thinking human being; consider Tom DeLay and the K Street Project; consider the Bush doctrines of unilateralism, preemptive attack, monarchical powers, legitimating torture—consider the irrelevancy of libertarianism as a portrait of an extraordinarily interdependent and global community, the reactionary and repressive dimensions of the religious right, the flat-out procorporate hogs-at-the-trough policies of those who claim to be conservatives. The neocons, or thinkers like Peter Viereck, made good faith efforts, came the closest to constructing a genuine conservatism, but the neocons were consumed by their hatreds, their resentments—Viereck was simply ignored.

The liberals, well, they don't seem to believe in what they say or do. They don't call themselves liberal, maybe progressive or, better, moderate, centrist. They can't seem to take pride in what they accomplished to make this a better, fairer, freer society: civil rights, women's rights, environmental protection. Instead, they play defense, hug the center without seriously engaging in an analysis of what modifications experience mandates. Indeed, there is a need for a new liberalism, perhaps what Bill Clinton meant by New Democrats. But it is not the cynical triangulation that often passes for a new view; it is not the backing up, the embarrassment about one's record. Liberals need to face up to the legitimate criticisms from the Right and the Left—unintended consequences, the role of the market and the state, problems of neoliberals internationally. But they need to reassert the centrality of the notion of the public interest, something the neocons initially understood but abandoned. Who stands for the public interest in an era of globalization, global warming, capital flight, declining unionization? Here in New Jersey, a capable liberal Democratic governor is proposing cutbacks in services, public services, to move toward a sane, sensible budget. The issue is framed as one of excessive public pensions, excessive health-care costs. The reality is that this scenario, repeated in state after state, allows public schools to deteriorate—or raises unacceptably high property taxes, allows public colleges to begin to imitate the costs of private ones. This is because conservatives have succeeded in casting the notion of public services, the public interest, as suspect—too much, too high, too corrupt. This isn't conservatism; it is simply Grover Norquist's murdering of public resources, the privatization of the nation—schools, army, politics. Liberals need to step back and become aware of how defensive their approach has become. Corzine, a decent and smart man, is afraid to suggest raising taxes, equitable taxes, a graduated income tax for example, which is presently unconstitutional in New Jersey, to restore the income taxes Christy Whitman cut many years ago. Who gets hurt from these policies of strangulation?—the parents of college students, the students themselves in terms of rising debt.

What the above suggests is that we need a more liberal conservatism and a more conservative liberalism. And, indeed, a rigorous radicalism, one that at the very least hold up a vision of the good society, the beloved community of Dr. King and John Lewis, of the social gospel, one which demands that if we maintain a capitalist economy as the most sensible, workable constellation of interests, that it at the very least use its capacity for creating enormous wealth to eliminate the unnecessary suffering of all citizens, nationally and globally. And we need to do all this while taking seriously risks of totalitarianism that mark the history of leftism, respecting but not worshipping market mechanisms, holding a transformed sense that life is essentially tragic and requires a healthy awareness of the human capacity to do evil. A mouthful, my Monday morning vent.

Such venting has its uses. In many ways, it lays out my essential argument about the inadequacies of our present ideological conflicts. Letting it rip is not always the wisest strategy, but it works as first draft.

More Venting: Does It Make a Difference?

April 11

It was a decent but flat class, perhaps because I wasn't feeling well. We started with a report on black conservatives by one of my most religious conservatives, Milt. He did an adequate job but made some factual errors grounded in some of his sources. In any case, we then proceeded to discuss whether social welfare interventions caused or exacerbated black poverty and social dysfunction with regard to family, crime, drugs. I tried to push the discussion to a few themes: the role of deindustrialization in reducing opportunity for non-college-educated blacks who migrated North for exactly such jobs; the ways in which liberals for too long denied the self-destructive dimensions of black behavior that conservatives would then address to their advantage; and a related theme, the ways in which the civil rights revolution liberated conservatives from being on the wrong side of history and freed them to focus on post–civil rights issues around which there was less consensus, such as affirmative action, busing, welfare. Most of my conservatives, with one important exception, tended to blame liberals for sidetracking what they presume to be black progress via bootstraps. I had to do a brief overview of the respective roles of Booker T. Washington and Du Bois, then point to the ways in which self-help strategies often were joined with black nationalist politics. But the key in the discussion became the issue of what it means to be working poor. Is it OK to tolerate a work environment in which work yields an income of around $10,000 a year as opposed to $8,000 in welfare? My conservatives believe that the elimination of much of the $8,000 option has been beneficial to poor blacks; I pushed them on what it means to be working poor and, of course, poked at them regarding minimum wages, EITC (earned income tax credit), and unionization. They're remarkably naive; my impression is that they have very little contact with blacks, especially those struggling near the bottom. Many of them tilt toward a faith-based alternative to sustain their religious faith and conservative humanism, that is, they want to help the needy but oppose government coercion through taxes. My liberals were fairly quiet; only Kate actively intervened to empathize with what welfare moms confront in the everyday. The others—Rick and Janet, who are organizing a die-in for Darfur tomorrow—seemed preoccupied with that event.

The second half of the class we had a report from Maggie on Newt Gingrich, which was based on mostly pro-Gingrich stuff except for his personal life, which Maggie handed around on a sheet but didn't want to discuss. It is difficult to discuss Newt in a half hour, other than to note his role in the polemicizing of Washington, his moral hypocrisies, his energy, his rise, fall, and more recent partial revival, his high tech and history interests, his battles with Tom DeLay. I felt that we barely scratched the surface. That's probably why I left the class feeling dissatisfied. Perhaps when we return next week and discuss Pat Buchanan, the media jocks, and the first Bush administration, especially the Persian Gulf War, I can help my seminarians make some sense of the post-Reagan era, at least through Clinton. If I do the course again, I'll need to consider whether I want to leave more time for these past twenty-plus years. Right now, I'm exhausted, hoarse, feeling weak, and preparing to run off to Atlanta for a conference tomorrow.

I'm feeling unusually bleak this afternoon. Again, illness drives it, but an unwelcome thought betrays feelings I prefer not to acknowledge. I'm feeling that I've had no effect on my conservative students. Now of course my better self didn't seek to persuade them of the wrongness of their ways; it didn't see itself as proselytizing at all. Indeed, that is precisely what I abhor. Nevertheless, there is a part of me—this is true in all courses I have taught—that expects, against all reason, my students will buy in to my point of view, will be persuaded that my interpretations are convincing. Is it, fundamentally, to be loved? I don't think so, since my conservatives seem to genuinely enjoy the class and show considerable affection toward me. It isn't that I realistically expect to convert students on a dime. Even if I could, I don't trust that at all. I do have faith in the force of human reason, particularly, I guess, when it's emanating from my brain, my lips. And in this climate of what seems to me to be Bush lunacy—invading Iran for crissakes! A world so out of kilter that all the king's horses and all the king's men may not be able to put it together again, or at least not for a generation or two. And as such, it's hard to see the staunch commitment of students to anything from Mitt Romney to the overturning of the Seventeenth Amendment, which called for the direct election of senators—mentioned in class today; I'm unable to get past the childishness of libertarian selfishness, the resistance to the patently obvious interdependence of the culture, of our nation, of the world, the inherent sociality of culture, of language, of morality, of responsibility, the absurdity of biblical fundamentalism, the insensitivity of notions of the United States of America as a Christian nation—I guess this is venting day for me—puke it out, laddy, you've obviously been holding it in all these months. OK, I guess there are limits to my capacity for open-mindedness, for empathy. I still love these kids, all of them, and have enjoyed, obscenely enjoyed teaching them, learning from them, pushing them, provoking them, forcing them to think more systematically, more analytically, more logically. But at this moment I'm overwhelmed by the catastrophe our world faces and by the incompetence and arrogance and corruption and stupidity that seems like a laser beaming into the epicenter of this present administration. But when I step back and grab a breath, I return to my essential pedagogical position, the ethics, if you will, upon which I stand, which is that the impact I have on students is long term and somewhat unfathomable, that it's a wager that I can, at the margin and within a lifetime, have a slight influence in helping my students figure out how to make sense of the world they inhabit and do so ethically, passionately, analytically.

I remember I. F. Stone, Izzy, coming to Temple University in 1969, speaking before an audience of ultraleftists, temporarily—so it turned out—drunk on revolutionary rhetoric—power to the people, Ho, Ho, Ho Chi Minh, Che posters, red bandannas. They had contempt for Stone, the old Jeffersonian democrat who had had such a profound influence on me and other New Leftists, putting out his weekly, providing so many of us with the essential information we needed to make sense of the Vietnam War, especially in its early phases. The new lefties demanded to know what Stone was doing to further the revolution. He smiled, stuck his thumbs in his suspenders, and told them that he considered himself to be like an old *pischer*, pissing on a large, seemingly impregnable rock. He pisched and he pisched. And it looked like nothing happened. But after years, decades, a lifetime of such pisching, he noticed a very slight indentation in the rock. The students weren't impressed, but I was. And now I need a drink.

The existential terror of this particular teacher: meaninglessness, futility, appearances without substance, going through the motions, being played the fool by a mocking universe committed only to teasing and empty promises. It can't be just a job. I know it will be time to retire if I ever have such feelings over time.

Ann Coulter and Treasonous Liberals

April 18

I think I've become more polemical, or at least combative, in these last weeks. We started today quietly, with me giving a minilecture on the key issues and events of the presidency of George H. W. Bush—Persian Gulf, Cold War, Panama, Americans with Disabilities Act, "read my lips" and then tax increases, his family background. The key issue we discussed was whether he was a conservative and whether he was an effective president. On both counts, my conservatives voted negative; others tended to stay on the sidelines of this one. I did stress the benefits of his tax shift and ended with the important issues still surrounding the Persian Gulf War and Desert Storm—the signals we gave to Saddam giving him the impression that he had a green light to invade Kuwait, the split within the nation up until the war started, the decision not to invade and conquer Iraq after a quick, decisive war, the failed uprisings of Kurds and Shi'ites and of our culpability in encouraging them to think we'd help, the Saudi decision to bring in U.S. troops and reject bin Laden's offer, which sparked the beginnings of Al Qaeda and took us toward 9/11.

But the fireworks started, as expected, with Marc's report on Ann Coulter. His report was fairly straightforward and contained, but what followed was raucous. I certainly pushed the envelope on this one. I had actually read Coulter, or at least her book *Treason*; as such I wanted the class, especially the conservatives among them, to address the issue of whether she was a conservative. My right-wingers all affirmed her credentials, albeit admitting that she went over the top. But there was little accurate discussion of what she actually said. Some called her a libertarian; one of my religious guys, Dick, often the first to speak from the gut, admitted that she was simply hot. Most accepted that she was somewhat of an opportunist or sensationalist, but softened that with the claim that this gave her more access to the public she wanted to provoke and, of course, make money from. I pushed further—how could one defend her insofar as she consistently demonizes all liberals as traitors—and I made it personal: "She's calling me a traitor." Is there any more dangerous, less conservative thing one could do? Can one be a libertarian and call Joe

McCarthy an American hero? My most thoughtful conservative, Jack, admitted that when she vents on the air, when she goes after her left-wing targets, he cheers, feeling emotionally at one with her. After class, Janet expressed dismay and disappointment that he—and others, but especially Jack—could resonate with Coulter and her views. I was struck by how strongly most of my conservative seminarians defended Coulter by citing, to them, the equally unfair, slanderous views of people like Al Franken. But I was unwilling to see equivalence, suggesting that calling Bill O'Reilly a liar was not on the same moral plane as calling all liberals traitors. Do liberals call all conservatives racists? We began the course with the notion that if they do, this was unfair and inappropriate. Conservatives resent not being respected by liberals, yet they seem to deny respect to liberals. This is contradictory and fraught with dangers.

Then Clark reported on Fox News, a very solid overview of Rupert Murdoch, his media empire, and the successes of Fox News on cable. The discussion that followed focused on questions I raised: Is it a good thing for there to be ideologized media, whether conservative or liberal? Can journalism be objective? The Coulter discussion folded into this one. Many saw media and journalism as inherently biased. I provoked the class by saying that they were all postmodernists, denying objectivity, reminding them of all the conservatives we studied—Allan Bloom, Richard Weaver, Russell Kirk, among others—who argued that it was liberalism, the Enlightenment, nominalism, that denied transcendent truths and objectivity, and, in privileging a relativism, set the world on a catastrophic plunge toward totalitarianism.

Thursday we continue with discussions of Rush Limbaugh and Bill O'Reilly and will use whatever time remaining to discuss the Clinton years. I want to think about how I'm feeling at this point. Because I'm tending to put things together, looking forward to the essays I want to write over the next year, because my point of view seems to be jelling, I worry that I'm becoming more impatient with my conservatives. I did close the class reaffirming that what I like the most about teaching the class are the passions, the idealism both the Left and the Right bring to the seminar. But I wonder if that was a kind of sop, given how hard I rode them on the contradictions of their views. At this point, I'm wanting to get onto this issue of the postwar coming to grips with evil, with the Holocaust, totalitarianism, and total war. Following Ira Katznelson, there seem to be three dominant responses: the Marxist, especially the Frankfurt School, which sees essential problems in the Enlightenment project vis-à-vis its bourgeois categories, its instrumentalism, its conformism, what Marcuse might define as a totalitarianism in disguise, one-dimensionality; the Straussian/conservative, which blames the Enlightenment for all twentieth-century horrors in its espousal of non-transcendent truths, its essential relativism; and the sobered liberalism Katznelson honors—Arendt, Polanyi, Hofstadter, Niebuhr. This is what I want to explore. And given that the conference in Atlanta reinforced my sense of the astounding incompetence and arrogance of this present Bush administration, I want to make sure that I am fair-minded as we approach the last sessions.

Right-Wing Talk Radio

April 20

I'm not sure where to begin. It's 2:10, class ended at 10:20 and I haven't had a chance yet to put down my thoughts. Class included two reports, one on Rush Limbaugh, the other on Bill O'Reilly; we also discussed broadly the Clinton years. After class about half a dozen of the conservatives—Jack, Marc, Karl, Dave, Dick—kept me busy for more than an hour with extensions of class discussion. Then after my run and lunch, one of them, Dave, a libertarian and army vet, stopped by to show me one of his projects and to talk more about everything from Che Guevara to Tora Bora. Now I'm weary if exhilarated, needing to get a blood test and frustrated that I won't be able to get all of my thoughts down fresh about today. Surprisingly, this is the first time this term that I haven't been able to get thoughts down close to the bone. So, I'm leaving it here, but will return to what transpired today ASAP.

April 21

Add to the above that I came home to a wife with a 103-degree temperature, a visit to the emergency room, and canceling two get-togethers because of the need to go to NYC this weekend to help out my step-daughter, who is moving to Boston and needs to take a look at a house, with our two granddaughters. Whew!

Well, what remains most salient from yesterday is the remarkable energy and passion of most of the seminar. Dave, who came to see me later in the day, asked, "Why do so many rich white kids worship Che Guevara?" That proved to be an interesting conversation, which included the romanticizing of right-wing African leaders by American conservatives, a consideration of suburban boredom, a tempering of Dave's exaggeration, for example, "Che was responsible for many deaths in Cuba," an overview of the Cuban Revolution, a discussion of the hilarious visit by Allen Ginsberg and other Beats to Cuba in 1959 and Ginsberg's expulsion for solicitation of male prostitutes.

In the seminar, I was impressed by the nuanced presentations by Darren and Kris on O'Reilly and Limbaugh, respectively. Both were admirers but not without an ability to see serious flaws and contradictions, for example, O'Reilly's tendency to bully guests, to dissemble; Limbaugh's tendency to be a flack for the Republican Party. Mostly I have been hammering the class about the tone of the media jocks, the ways in which they violate basic tenets of conservatism, and, finally, the way their contempt for liberals parallels the claims of so many of my conservative students that they are disrespected by liberals. Mirror images if you will. The discussion heated up when I focused on Limbaugh's use of "feminazi" to describe feminists. As in my fairly ferocious comments on Ann Coulter's charge that liberals were traitors, I wanted to highlight the poisoning of discourse by such pejoratives. What I did was set off an explosion of anger, charges, and countercharges focusing on one student's comment comparing Abu Ghraib and Guantanamo to the Nazis. Marc just exploded from his chair to complain that any comparison to the Holocaust in terms of U.S. policies really drove him nuts and deeply angered him; Willie countered that he did not mean that our human rights violations were the same in scale as what the Nazis did, but that they were clearly forms of torture and, thus, comparable to other examples of human rights violations. This was clearly a sore point for many. Willie spoke of having trouble being clear-minded because of how upset he was with the discussion. I tried to make key distinctions—genocide as opposed to torture; that inside the military, especially among military attorneys, there was opposition to the circumvention of Geneva rules on torture; the issue of our use of torture techniques coming back to haunt us in terms of treatment of American prisoners. Darren mentioned Senator Durbin's controversial comments about Nazilike behavior as equivalent, but it seemed half-hearted.

What I increasingly conclude is that too much of conservative defense rests on a childish notion: "the other guy did it first, or did it much worse." In fact, it seems to me that the ideologizing of politics, the increasing ugliness of it, was driven by the Gingrich crowd who consciously went after moderates, who calculated inflammatory language to smear liberals and moderate Republicans, who have left us with a Congress in which the other party is rarely brought into decision making and in which there are rare friendships across the aisles. Unfortunately, this is also what left ideologues—myself included way back in the day—in some part hoped for: a more European-style politics, clearly defined conservative versus liberal parties, no corrupt fraternizing with the enemy, none of this Beltway intimacy that got in the way of principled policies.

Well, we have three more sessions to go. I'm going to miss this course and this group. Out in the hallway after class, the discussion continued for maybe ninety minutes, with several students actually going off to class and then returning to pick up the threads of the conversation. Remarkable.

COMPUTER CONFERENCING ON THE MEDIA JOCKS

Karl, from the Right, took them on:

> Coming from the right I believe these figureheads to be damaging to the conservative movement, Coulter is a "bitch," Limbaugh is a fat chump, and O'Reilly is a egomaniacal economic-driven conservative. I refuse to watch their shows because they do not gain support or shift the leftists to the right, rather it's the complete opposite. They only fuel the fire the Left has for the Right. I believe the neocons, on some levels, have a better time representing some key conservative agendas. The three aforementioned figureheads make outlandish remarks that warrant the attention of critics, and for that, they are nothing more then the "Howard Stern of conservative talk media." They should not be taken seriously because nothing they say or do is a quality representation of the conservative movement. They are in it for the money first, and politics second. Remember that and maybe you could laugh at the people who are diehards and cling to their every word, as i do (as a conservative). I laugh at Coulter's quotes, yet I also fail to find the importance or validity within them as well. She has a message, but underneath the joke and the outlandish slanderization of the left I fail to find any validity to her argument. In summation, I have a growing distaste for these three GREEDY MONEY TRAIN conservative media figureheads.

Janet, always astute:

> I really did expect most of the class to be at least distant from these figures as they do not seem to really add much integrity to conservatism. . . . I have to say though that I felt that this was a very interesting class. I think it was more honest in the sense that at first many were willing to say that they listened and enjoyed regardless of morals, standards, values, etc., but less honest that when challenged, no one wanted to step up and defend certain positions. And I'm sure someone is going to be mad at that, but sorry, that's how the class felt to me.

Neo–Social Darwinism

April 25

Reading students' electronic logs, I have been struck by Clark's comments in the last two entries. In the first instance, he asserted that those who were richer were smarter, in the second that he was comfortable with the rich getting richer and the poor poorer since anyone through hard work can be successful. He is not a mean kid, seems quite sincere and decent, and is usually quiet if attentive in seminar, yet there is a social Darwinian core to such beliefs. No compassion, no empathy for those who have had a difficult time, no awareness of how hard-working so many poor people are, how injury and illness and family circumstances and neighborhood dangers get in the way of making it.

I have been increasingly feeling that we need to restore the concept of neo–social Darwinism to describe some conservatives like Cheney and Rumsfeld, who are anti-ideological, wary of abstractions, certainly not religious right, clearly not libertarian in any principled way, and without any of the fanatical idealism of the neoconservatives. When I imagine them at the country club, after nine holes, sipping their scotch, I assume that in the inner sanctum of corporate power and privilege they are willing to assert a belief that might makes right, that the successful deserve their successes and fuck the rest who only deserve one's contempt for failing to work the system as they have. This doesn't mean that they are without human qualities with their loved ones or their friends, but it does mean that they are hard and essentially cruel elitists, smug, righteous, arrogant. There's the risk that I am stereotyping, but we have been around these men for some time and I see so much evidence that they consider themselves superior, justified in keeping secrets, justified in going after their enemies with all the weapons at hand. W. has a lot of this in him, although it's tempered by his religious faith, his good-old-boy sociability, and his pride in being ignorant. But one feels it in that incident when he mocked that newly born-again woman on death row, making fun of her appeal. One feels it in his use of humor, nicknames to infantilize those around him; one feels it in all of the stories of his temper, his explosions at aides. W. is a complicated man—aren't we all?—but at base, he remains a Deke, a Skull and Bones elitist, coarsened by Texas.

As some of the following essays suggest, I have been struggling with my dissatisfactions about the designation of neoconservative to describe key Bush figures like Dick Cheney and Donald Rumsfeld. I remain unconvinced that there is any value in thinking of them as neoconservatives or, more pointedly, as people who take thought seriously. They are, indeed, men of action—and, quintessentially, men of reaction.

Pat Buchanan and David Horowitz: Provocateurs

Class was excellent. Kristen reported on Pat Buchanan; interestingly, few of my students really cared about him. To them he's clearly a figure of the past, even though I anticipate that his anti-immigrant views may become more salient in the present environment. We discussed his presidential aspirations, especially his culture war rhetoric in 1992, his isolationism—I reminded them that the conservatism we began the term with, up until World War 2 was isolationist à la America First—but we spent more time than I anticipated discussing his alleged anti-Semitism, his criticisms of the neocon association with Israel, and his Holocaust denial/defense of pro-Nazi war criminal suspects.

Then Karl spoke of David Horowitz. His presentation was very thorough with the surprising exception of Horowitz's break with the Left. Horowitz interests me insofar as he is an example of the turn from the Left to the Right—the "God That Failed" phenomenon—that includes Whittaker Chambers and Frank Meyer. I told the seminar about how Horowitz recommended a woman as a bookkeeper for the Black Panthers only to be horrified when she disappeared, apparently murdered by the Panthers when she discovered that they were engaged in such criminal activities as drugs and extortion. That local leftists advised him to keep quiet to protect the Panthers (or in fear of the same) traumatized Horowitz. If that was all, I'd be much more sympathetic to him. But he became as intolerant a rightist as he was a leftist without so much as a gulp, no humility, no sense that perhaps he should be more modest in his claims, no ability to think of the world as complex, nuanced, contradictory. I once saw him speak and felt that if in his text we substituted the leftist definitions with rightist ones and vice versa, there would be no difference in his essential dogmatism, his arrogance.

Karl spoke of Horowitz's public campaign against black reparations. I suggested that there was a real issue about what the nation owed to blacks with regard to slavery and racism but that white guilt was rarely a useful vehicle for policy. Given the recent comments by a few of my libertarians about hard work always being the solution to poverty, I perhaps not so subtly suggested some of the factors that made it difficult for minority youth to transcend hypersegregated neighborhoods and for hard-working poor people to climb into the lower-middle class. Jack, sitting in the back, suggested that the solution was for poor people to move out of the neighborhoods to get to where the jobs were; it was a wonderfully naive observation seemingly oblivious to the barriers that keep poor black people out of the 'burbs.

Most of our discussion focused on Horowitz's efforts to persuade state legislatures to intervene in colleges and universities in order to impose his own version of academic freedom, a version that is a response to his claim that liberals enforce political correctness in hiring, promotion, and firing of colleagues and in the classroom, especially stilling conservative voices. Indeed, this has a piece of truth in it, but remains essentially mischievous and dangerous. First of all, most academics, most of whom are left of center, especially in the humanities, sciences, and social sciences, especially at the better institutions, are committed to genuine notions of academic freedom. Interestingly, my own seminarians, when speaking of their experiences in their majors, speak glowingly of the open-mindedness of their mostly liberal to radical teachers. So there was consensus among most of the students in the room that there wasn't a major problem, at least here at Stockton. I added that it seems likely that many bright conservatives choose not to become academics in part because they have interests in greater rewards within the business community. Most of my conservative students thought this to be so.

What too often sustains conservative critiques of higher education is a myth of a golden age in the period between World War II and the Berkeley Free Speech Movement, roughly what is conveniently called the "fifties." There is some truth to this myth, otherwise it would lack the power to persuade. For one, the GI Bill was indeed the most significant piece of legislation increasing social mobility; it made the United States the first nation to democratize higher education. Veterans poured into colleges and universities with generous subsidies; they were our first nontraditional students—older, more focused on learning, and more diverse. Southern and Eastern European Catholics and Jews and working-class white Protestants helped to transform our colleges into more meritocratic institutions. After all, prior to 1945, college campuses were dominated by sons of the elite often satisfied with gentlemen's Cs.

But it is hardly the case that academic freedom flourished in this postwar, McCarthyite era. At the same time, there was much of what conservative critic Allan Bloom evokes when describing his presixties students at the University of Chicago and at Cornell. A friend of mine took a seminar with Bloom when he was a visiting professor at Yale in the early sixties. He recalls a warm, charismatic figure, inspired by his eager and competitive seminar students. I was in college at that time; most of my classmates were more knowledgeable about Mickey Mantle and West Side Story *than about the great books that we began to absorb and cherish. And cherish we did; at least many of us. Most of us were "pre"—prelaw, premed, predental; quite practical, career-oriented. But we were also in awe at what our professors offered to us, even, perhaps especially, as we seemed to reject it for ourselves. We assumed that culture was of value, that it mattered that one come to grips with Shakespeare and Aristotle and Freud and Newton, that we should learn about Beethoven and Raphael and T. S. Eliot. In between our touch football games and drunken parties and Frisbee tosses, we discussed, passionately, the meaning of life, the existence of God, the value of abstract expressionism, of existentialism, of behaviorism. We bought into the life of the mind.*

Our students, at least those not attending the most competitive colleges, live in a different and more difficult environment. Much of the patina of the life of the mind has been worn down by vocationalism and, sadly, by the subversion of notions of objectivity coming from both the Left and the Right. And so many of our nonelite students work twenty to forty hours a week; they lack the time, the leisure, to engage in the out-of-classroom intellectual bullshit sessions that so characterized college experience fifty years ago.

David Horowitz does not understand that most students are quite oblivious to whatever politically correct messages they encounter in American classrooms. Such liberal to radical points of view are limited to that part of the curriculum most harried and career-oriented students barely tolerate—the liberal arts requirements in the humanities and social sciences. Their eyes are on the prizes of getting their degrees and focusing on their majors. Certainly there are faculty who abuse their charge, although Horowitz's "101 most dangerous academics" hardly offers any confidence that he can distinguish between polemics and the legitimate assertion of point of view. Equally telling, Horowitz is one-sided, focusing all of his moral outrage at those left of center, seemingly oblivious to the ways in which more conservative, often sectarian institutions violate academic freedom regarding the teaching of evolution, biblical analysis, or situational ethics.

This discussion shifted to what's wrong with our schools, K through 12, where there was a vigorous set of comments about excessive socialization, boredom, an admission that deviant opinions are more likely to face retribution from school boards and up-in-arms parents—and that the sports teams were considered more important to most parents and kids than the classrooms. I did suggest that the further up one went on the educational ladder, toward the elite colleges and most of our grad schools, the better American education looked in comparison with that of Europe and East Asia.

I can feel the class beginning to close in on wrap-up. I once had a psychoanalysis teacher who told the class that it was important to bury a class, to offer a funeral service so that a proper good-bye, closure could be experienced and processed. He actually would draw a cemetery gravestone with "R.I.P." on it to symbolize the ending of a class. So I'm beginning to think about how to end this seminar. Thursday we will have our visiting prof talk about being a conservative on a liberal campus; then Frank will talk about the aptly named Charles Krauthammer (no time today) and then we'll do the student evaluation forms. I'm hoping they all show up next Tuesday, our last day, when papers are due, so we can discuss the present Bush and the future, and try to sum up what we have explored and considered these last few months. I'm going to miss this crew.

Toward the end of the seminar, our discussion of what's wrong in our K–12 schools led to another opportunity for me to make what has been one of my hopefully not-too-righteous sermons on objectivity. My seminarians seemed to agree that whether a professor or teacher was liberal or conservative or radical, whether he or she was open or discreet about his or her point of view, what matters, as it did in scholarship and journalism, was whether they took seriously evidence that tended to subvert their own position or whether they blew it off, denigrated it, reduced it to the enemy's biased view, and so on. I used the example of the allegations of rape by Duke lacrosse players. My experience plus my biases lead me to assume, even wish that the evidence proves guilt. But my experience also tells me to be wary of what I assume to be so. They seemed to recognize this dilemma; the class seemed focused and fully there. It's so dangerous within our culture that the respective sides seem to only listen to "their own" and to immediately and arrogantly blow off anything the other position claims. If I accomplish anything in this course it should be that my students reexamine what they read, that they take seriously other points of view, that they not commit what I learned as the genetic fallacy, that the source of information defines the legitimacy of that data.

COMPUTER CONFERENCING: THE LIBERTARIAN'S GOOD SOCIETY

Dave's utopia:

> Wow, I'm not really sure I want to answer this question. Oh wait, yeah I am. The best society is one damn near anarchistic. One that is truly market based. One where people earn wages based on their skill level and job instead of how long they've been in the union. We should get rid of any restrictions placed on business. Maybe then companies wouldn't be so quick to move overseas or outsource. There should be no minimum wage or any price controls. Here's a great quote on the idea of the free market by Milton Friedman: "A major source of objection to a free economy is precisely that it gives people what they want instead of what a particular group thinks they ought to want. Underlying most arguments against the free market is a lack of belief in freedom itself."
>
> The government should be reduced to about the size it was at the turn of the century. That being from 1800s to 1900s. There is absolutely no reason in hell that the government should be the largest employer in the damn country. We could get rid of the Dept's of Education, Homeland Security, Environmental Protection, HHS, HUD. Did I forget any? Oh yeah, we should get rid of the Federal Reserve as well. Any government

interference in the economy is a bad thing. You only have to look at the Great Depression to see that.

I would like to abolish Social Security but I would settle for making it voluntary. Hell, I'd give up every dime I've put into it so far, if I could get out. I would love to see the abolition of the Welfare State. Nobody has a right to have their lifestyle subsidized by the more wealthy individuals in the country. You can talk about the morality of that but since when is it moral to steal money from somebody to give it to somebody else. I just finished reading Sir Walter Scott's *Ivanhoe*. That book has Robin Hood as one of the characters. You remember Robin Hood, right, steal from the rich to give to the poor? Yeah, makes a great story but that's about it. I would also include corporate welfare in that, as well. If a company can't compete in a free market then they deserve to go under.

Another way to make society better would be to actually teach about the U.S. Constitution. That way we'd get past this whole "living document" crap. The words mean the same thing now that they did two hundred years ago. The "people" still refers to the people. The "States" still refers to the states, although there are more of them now. It's really pretty simple and it's one area where the Left really fails the reading comprehension section of the test. There's a process to change the Constitution and it doesn't include a lack of reading comprehension skills. It would really be nice to see people respect all ten amendments of the Bill of Rights, instead of picking and choosing which ones are relevant.

I would also love to see a flat tax or a consumption tax, where you pay a tax on what you buy or use. That way, everybody pays their fair share. A much better idea, in my opinion, than making the top 5 percent pay 50 percent of the tax bill. Considering they pay the majority of the taxes, I think the rich deserve tax breaks. The idea of punishing people because they have the audacity to make $100K/year or more [is] sickening.

Finally, I would end the War on Some Drugs. That has been the biggest government failure in the history of the Unites States. Evidently, many people still think the Eighteenth Amendment was a resounding success. Yeah, so successful that they repealed it fourteen years later. The very idea of prohibition is repugnant to the ideals of liberty. How many hundreds of billions of dollars have been spent pursuing this disastrous policy, and for what reason? To keep people from engaging in activities that harm only themselves. That's it. Breaking and entering is illegal, no matter if the person did it for drug money or anything else. Murder is also illegal. Killing someone over drugs doesn't make them more dead than killing them because they were banging your wife, husband, etc. Another great quote from Milton Friedman. "Every friend of freedom . . . must be as revolted as I am by the prospect of turning the United States into an armed camp, by the vision of jails filled with casual drug users and of an army of enforcers empowered to invade the liberty of citizens on slight evidence." You know, that reminds me, I didn't even mention the Constitutional violations that the War on Drugs has spawned. Asset forfeiture? Clearly a violation of the "Due process" clause of the Fifth Amendment. Get nervous when you get pulled over by the cops? Don't show it, or they can have drug sniffing dogs running around your car. Can you imagine going to jail and losing your car because the idea of armed men treating you like a criminal because of a traffic violation made you nervous?

OK, I think I'm done now. Almost forgot. The healthcare issue. Somebody please show me where in the Constitution it says that you are entitled to healthcare on someone else's dime. As Milton Friedman said, "There's no such thing as a free lunch." Yes, I am a big fan of Milton Friedman. Damn, I could just go on and on and on and on, ad infinitum. I'd like to add one more thing. Going back to getting rid of the Federal Reserve, I think we should also go back to the gold standard. Worthless money isn't really money.

Conservative in Academe

April 27

Casey Rizzo was our guest today; we had talked weeks ago about her telling the seminar about her experiences as a conservative, Republican colleague. She's a good teacher as far as I can tell—forceful, funny, knowledgeable, relaxed. She spoke of her background, a Jersey girl, an ethnic Catholic, from a conservative Republican family. She told of how uncomfortable she has often felt being at Stockton—incidents that made her feel invisible, some sense that her tenure would be threatened by her politics, some issues over her initial refusal to join the union, concerns about the union's endorsement of Democrats, lunchroom conversations that presupposed everyone was a Democrat. Mostly she described the sense of being the outsider. But given that Casey is very stubborn, my sense is that she has a perverse kind of pride in being different, and in not only surviving but in flourishing, earning tenure and promotion. The class was very interested in her observations—lots of questions and comments, some on their own analogous experiences, some on her area of expertise in criminal justice. It is intriguing to me that no one knows what percentage of our faculty is Republican and/or conservative. The prevailing commonsense wisdom is that most, except in the business departments, are liberal to radical. That the most active faculty—those who come to assembly meetings, those who are deeply involved in general education, those who hold offices with the assembly and the union—are left of center is certainly true; those in business and preprofessional areas seem more likely to have other off-campus activities, consulting, and so on. As such, the assumption about political perspectives may be skewed by levels and intensities of activity.

Most interesting to me was our discussion of nonfaculty—staff-people, from fairly high-level people to janitors and secretaries. I've sometimes thought that approaching a liberal college from the vantage point of a conservative secretary or maintenance man would make for a great novel. This idea came to me from my experiences over the years taking a run during lunchtime. I almost never run with colleagues; most of my companions have been in athletics, maintenance, buildings and grounds, and so on. Many are more conservative than me. How they saw the college differed so much from the way most of my colleagues saw the college. And I enjoyed my running companions immensely—lively, full of mischief, iconoclastic, wicked in their ability to search out one's vulnerabilities. And I could give it back and then some. Isn't that what we all should do in the classroom and faculty seminars?

Closings: Reflections

May 1

I'm spending a lot of time trying to shape our last session tomorrow. I have to sufficiently address the present Bush administration and still have time for a summing up of themes. In the latter regard, I want to offer an honest appraisal of what I see as the conservative dilemma: essentially that there is still no discernible conservatism but rather conventional procorporate interest—for example, the K Street project, antiregulation, and so forth—best described as neo–social Darwinist. As such, I see the more-discussed ideologies as sincere but abused idealisms inexorably slapped around and manipulated to provide cover for the survival-of-the-richest views of such as Cheney and Rumsfeld and, with the caveat of his religiosity, G. W. Bush. I would have to add that there is a right-wing populism, with roots in McCarthyism and Wallace, often built on resentment of the challenges from blacks, Latinos, women, and gays; resentment at the snobbery of the liberal and radical intelligentsia; and a scary dose of authoritarianism, vigilantism, nativism. I know that this sounds too much like the trivialization of conservatism I have criticized on the Left, but what I'm trying to come up with is a more complex model for understanding the mix of idealism and opportunism, vision and rank interest that drive the Republican Party, especially, but also conservatism. We'll see how it goes tomorrow.

May 2

Quite a last seminar. I listed a wide range of issues and policies associated with the Bush administration on the board, hoping to spend the first hour on an overview of the present. Then I planned to shift to my own observations on the state of conservatism. We ended up focusing almost exclusively in the first part on 9/11 and Iraq. I had to work very hard in pushing some of my most conservative and hawkish students to make important distinctions—between terrorism and Al Qaeda and its related organizations; between 9/11 and Iraq, between Saddam and 9/11, between Afghanistan and Iraq. There was to me a surprising tenacity in holding to the notion that following the 9/11 attacks we had the right to go after any and all enemies, potential threats to us, with little sense of distinctions, not to speak of consequences. I pushed the class to understand that there were problems in the very notion of a "global war on terrorism." At the same time, especially when Willie articulated the pacifist take that violence never solves anything, I wanted to be as fair-minded as possible. As such, I forced the class to begin with the dilemma of post–Persian Gulf—Saddam still in power, no-fly zones protecting the Kurdish north, an economic boycott hurting the Iraqi economy, some erosion of that boycott. Most liberals and especially radicals were arguing pre-9/11 that the boycott was killing possibly half a million Iraqi children and must end. The logic of that position was to free Saddam up for a return to legitimacy and full oil revenues and possible regional mischief. Bush's invasion has allowed the Left to run away from this moral dilemma, but it remains—what, short of more of the same, with likely diminishing returns, should the United States have done regarding Saddam?

My conservatives tend to praise Bush by offering a simplistic critique of Clinton as a do-nothing commander-in-chief, especially regarding Al Qaeda. The truth seems to be that Bush I, Clinton, and Bush II shared an underestimation of Al Qaeda, with W. being the most negligent, at least in the months leading up to 9/11. We got to the issue of whether our national security interests have been strengthened or weakened by the war in Iraq. And I pushed them on the question of diverting attention from Al Qaeda and bin Laden with the Iraqi war. Curiously, several of my conservatives suggested that capturing or killing bin Laden was not important since it wouldn't affect the strength of terrorism. I felt that this was coming from an ideological defense of W. and asked them if Clinton were in office and hadn't captured bin Laden, whether the radio and TV shock jocks would have given him any slack for not accomplishing that task, to use W.'s terms, dead or alive. I think we clarified some of the categories but whether it affected how folks view things, well, I haven't had expectations in that regard, so why have them now? My task is to push them, to help them think more clearly, more consistently. For example to recognize that you can make pragmatic arguments to defend the tacit alliance with Saddam in the 1980s but cannot then switch to an absolutist moral approach to his overthrow. That's too easy and makes it possible to defend any and all inconsistencies in policy.

Then I closed off the foreign-policy debate to offer the seminar my thoughts on the state of American conservatism. I wanted to consider the ways in which libertarianism, the religious right, and neoconservatism had inherent limitations in shaping policy. I argued that libertarianism is an attractive ideal useful in challenging all threats to individual liberties but that it had limitations insofar as it was so out of sync with the social realities of the past century—corporatization, bureaucratization, globalization, environment threats, nuclear power, immigration policies, the very interdependence which so defines the world we inhabit. Maggie, who seems to have become one of my most astute conservatives despite speaking so rarely, argued in favor of the rights of small business; Karl argued for Wal-Mart's successes. I tried to frame the issue as one of coming to grips with a new economy of scale that could not be addressed by ideas grounded in a world based on small farms and shops. This is an old argument for me, but I laid it out clearly—the invention of the corporate form, its legal status as a person, was a recognition that we had moved to an age within which we needed to redefine how to protect individual rights and how to preserve democratic participation.

I suggested that the religious right was both empowered and limited by its constituency of about 25 percent—fiercely active but always prone to antagonize the other 75 percent who don't want moralists telling them what to do in the bedroom and other arenas of privacy. I also suggested that they were losing the culture war and their intensities reflected the panic over that reality—given the secular trend toward inclusion, tolerance, more education, a belief in the value of science. Gays would be considered legitimate and we would continue to teach evolution no matter how many short-term victories the religious right achieved. And they knew it.

I suggested that the neoconservatives reflected a tragedy of immense proportion. They began with the notion of a sobered liberalism, fully cognizant of the law of unintended consequences. But as their disenchantment with liberal Democrats turned churlish and furious, and as they succumbed to the romance with Reaganism, their Burkean conservatism turned toward conventional free-market ideology and they became less distinctive. Moreoever, they became captured by their foreign-policy critiques, initially in terms of the Cold War and then in terms of the right-wing Wilsonianism that provided the rationale for invading Iraq. In the final analysis they were consumed by the rage they felt toward their adversaries.

As the above suggests, there had never been a full-bodied, robust conservatism along the lines suggested by Burke, Weaver, Viereck, and Kirk. The neocons came closest and, therefore, their descent remains the most tragic.

Instead, what we have in the name but not the spirit of conservatism is a right-wing populism, fueled by frustration, resentment, and rage. Its spirit is that of Joe McCarthy and George Wallace, a gut politics exploited by the Rush Limbaughs and Bill O'Reillys and worse, which wages culture war and embodies nativism, forms of vigilantism, and a deep xenophobia. They fear globalization, the scientific method, human difference, all forms of the questioning of the status quo except when liberals are either in fact or presumed to be in the saddle. These, along with the religious right, with which they overlap in important regards, are the troops of the conservative movement and the GOP.

Finally, there are the true and ongoing movers and shakers, those representing corporate self-interest, big business at its worst, truly believing, at least in the privacy of their country clubs and gated communities, especially after a few belts of Scotch, that the rich are rich because they are better, smarter—and screw everyone else. They drink at the fountain of the libertarians when it's convenient, but only then. As such they are dependent on the idealism of others to sustain their essentially cynical agenda. I consider them to be neo–social Darwinists, survival of the corporate and national fittest. They drive fiscal policies, they shape the K Street Project, they are wedded to oil, they, not the neocons or the Israel lobby, drove our invasion of Iraq.

The class seemed attentive during this short monologue. We then returned to the issue of how successful businessmen deserve what they earn. I tried to frame things in terms of the sometime liberal contempt for the accomplishments of entrepreneurs, but suggested that it was not a question of the decency or venality of an individual CEO but rather how concentrated forms of power were always a threat to both liberty and democracy—Fortune 500, the feds, communist parties—any monopoly or near-monopoly of power put our best traditions at risk.

COMPUTER CONFERENCING: FINAL THOUGHTS FROM SOME SEMINARIANS

Clark:

> I thought this class was very interesting. I did not know what to think at first with a liberal professor teaching the course but I don't think I would have wanted any other teacher teaching it. I learned a lot about the history which I had no clue about. Although it was tough understanding the material early on, as the class progressed it got much easier to understand. Hopefully if you teach it again next year or the year after you will have students that really care about the class as I think our class did. Only suggestion would be to save a little more time towards the last couple weeks for current issues that truly affect us in the present. Other than that, I had a lot of fun learning about different point of views and I'm glad you pushed us with the papers and I thought posting online was a unique feature that most teachers disregard.

And Willie, ever honest:

> To make an honest reflection, I was a bit disappointed with the class.
>
> The class was too historical. I understand the need for a historical understanding to reach the present, but I wish we would have covered

> the "historical" aspects in like three weeks and then gotten into contemporary American Conservatism. Within the last ten to fifteen years, there has been a huge rise in Conservatism, and I would have liked to spend more time on that time period.
>
> The class really needs to be two semesters long, and American Liberalism also needs to be studied, and it can't be done within the framework of one class. It seems a bit disingenuous to look at one side of the story, when another (or more) is also available.
>
> I think that some of the students on both sides of the political divide should be encouraged to challenge each other more often. I know on more than one occasion, I left class thinking how incredibly ignorant one person or another was. I also wish we had a sign that said "GET TO YOUR POINT AND MAKE IT." People, again on both sides, were too verbose. And also, one point per statement.

What I wanted to end with was the Federalist metaphor, my Madisonian view, which sees dialogue, argument, differences, different interests as the very epicenter of what needs to be cherished, not resolved. I suggested that we need a robust conservatism and suffer for its absence; we need a revitalized, confident liberalism and a radical utopian vision because they work best together—that's when we've made our greatest progress, for example, the Progressive Era, New Deal, sixties. And that my venom in criticizing Ann Coulter et al. was essentially because their model of behavior precludes any dialogue, any cherishing of our differences with a grand tradition. Warren Susman, my mentor, always argued that we understand culture in terms of its tensions, its contradictions, its arguments. This has always made sense to me; it still does, indeed, even more now than before. And I hope that I have communicated the value of such an approach to these lively, passionate, and intellectually curious seminarians who I will miss dearly.

Course Syllabus

GIS 4628 **American Conservatism (V)**
Paul Lyons C140 x4627

Introduction

This course seeks to assist students in understanding the roots of modern American conservatism, its ideological, philosophical and political groundings, and its history. The premises of the course include the following: that too little attention has been paid to the strengths of conservatism, that there is a need to understand the complexities and contradictions within a much disputed conservatism, and that one cannot understand modern American political culture without coming to grips with the revival of American conservatism.

Requirements and Grading

This is a senior seminar. As such, each session, students will be responsible for leading discussions of selected readings and themes. Class participation will cover one-quarter of your grade. There will also be short papers that will entail one-half of the evaluation. Finally, there will be electronic conferencing through Web Board, with required weekly entries, which will equal one-quarter of the evaluation.

Readings

Edwards, Lee. *The Conservative Revolution: The Movement That Remade America.* New York: Free Press, 2002.

Schneider, Gregory, ed. *Conservatism in America since 1930: A Reader.* New York: New York University Press, 2003.

Assignments

January 17, 19

1. **The Roots of European Conservatism: Burke, de Maistre, Tocqueville The Roots of American Conservatism: Hamilton, Adams, Federalism, Calhoun**

Read: handouts on Burke; Schneider, Part III (Weaver, Kirk)

We will consider the ways in which modern conservatism began as a set of responses to the revolutions of the eighteenth and nineteenth centuries: French Revolution, industrial revolution, Enlightenment/scientific revolution.

January 24, 26

2. **Conservatism by Another Name: 1865–1929 The Response to New Deal Liberalism: Hoover, Liberty League, Nock**

Read: Schneider, Part I (So. Agrarians, Nock, Human Events); Edwards, Introduction and chapter 1

We will examine the ways in which American conservatism appropriated elements of what was called liberalism in the nineteenth century, especially free-market, laissez-faire capitalism, and then was forced into a defensive posture by the twentieth-century liberalism of the New Deal.

January 31, February 2

---

3. Libertarianism: Hayek

Read: Schneider, Part II (Hayek, Mont Pelerin),
Part III (Meyer), and Part VII (all)

We will explore the influence of Friedrich von Hayek's 1944 classic critique of statism, *The Road to Serfdom*, in the rise of a more powerful assertion of the relationship between liberty and free-market capitalism.

February 7, 9

---

4. Conservatism in the Age of McCarthyism: William F. Buckley Jr. and Peter Viereck William F. Buckley Jr. and *National Review* Fusionism

Read: Schneider, Part IV (all), Part V (all);
Edwards, chapters 2, 3, and 4

We will discuss the remarkable rise of Buckley, beginning with his criticisms of Yale liberalism and his defense of Joseph McCarthy, his battles with historian and poet Viereck, and the ways in which the founding of *National Review* in 1955 was the first successful mobilization of what has come to be called American conservatism as defined by fusionism, that is, the linking of free-market libertarianism and Burkean traditionalism through a shared opposition of communism and other forms of statism.

February 14, 16

---

5. Ayn Rand and Objectivism

Read: Rand handout

We will examine how and why Rand was marginalized within the conservative movement, despite her extraordinary success as a popular novelist, because of her militant atheism.

February 21, 23

6. The Goldwater Movement

Read: Schneider, Part VI (all);
Edwards, chapters 5, 6, and 7

We will consider how the ideas discussed above translated into a political movement that launched what appeared at the time to be a catastrophic presidential electoral campaign in 1964, the Goldwater debacle. We will examine how that defeat planted the seeds for eventual triumph in the 1970s and 1980s.

February 28, March 2

7. The Building of a New Right

Read: Schneider, Part VIII (all);
Edwards, chapters 8 and 9

We will discuss the emergence of the organizational and institutional forces upon which American conservatism moved toward political power, including data banks, foundations, institutes, corporate funding, and a populist message.

March 7, 9

8. Neoconservatism

Read: Schneider, Part IX (Tonser);
Edwards, chapter 10 (Paper Due)

We will study the rise and evolution of this important group of ex-liberal, ex-socialist intellectuals who provided American conservatism with some intellectual ballast through their writings, journals, and op-ed pieces.

March 21, 23

9. The Religious Right

Read: handouts; Edwards, chapter 11

We will explore the politicization of evangelical and fundamentalist Protestant Christianity in response to the cultural challenges associated with the 1960s, for instance, prayer in the schools, abortion rights, feminism, gay rights, cultural relativism, the importance of the family, and profanity and obscenity issues.

March 30

10. The Economics of Conservatism: Monetarism, Laissez-faire, Supply-side

Read: Schneider, Part II (Friedman)

We will explore the range of options within conservatism regarding the appropriate role of government in the economy vis-à-vis such issues as the federal budget, the role of the Federal Reserve Bank, and attitudes toward inflation and unemployment.

April 4, 6

11. The Reagan Revolution

Read: Schneider, Part IX (all);
Edwards, chapters 12 and 13

We will focus on whether the two terms of Ronald Reagan marked a fundamental watershed in American politics comparable to the New Deal. Within this framework, we will explore Reagan as personality, the role of Reagan in the end of the Cold War, the controversies over his economic and social policies, and the role of the Moral Majority within the Reagan administration.

April 11, 13

12. The Crisis of the End of the Cold War

Read: Schneider, Part X (Buchanan); Edwards, chapter 14

We will discuss how fusionism's success was subverted by the collapse of the Soviet Union and how this moment seemed to threaten the alliance between libertarians and traditionalists. In addition, we will consider those contending to take on the mantle of Reagan and Reaganism.

April 18, 20

13. Popular Culture: Televangelists, Talk Show Hosts, and Fox News (Rush, O'Reilly, Coulter, Ollie)

Read: handouts; Edwards, chapter 15

We will discuss the emergence of a right-wing populism on the airwaves, which gave conservatism a popular temperament not there in the 1950s or earlier. We will discuss some of the newer themes, including a critique of mainstream media (MSM) and a particular animus directed to the Clintons, both Bill and Hillary.

April 25, 27

14. George W. Bush and Conservatism

Read: Schneider, Part X (Francis, Gingrich, Weyrich, *Policy Review*); Edwards, chapter 16

Finally, we will examine the policies, foreign and domestic, of the second Bush, including responses to 9/11, the war on terrorism, Afghanistan and Iraq, tax cuts, budget deficits, compassionate conservatism, No Child Left Behind, the role of neocons, Cheney, Rumsfeld, Rice, Powell, and more.

May 2

Conclusions (Paper Due)

Bibliography

J. Andrew, *The Other Side of the Sixties: The Young Americans for Freedom and the Rise of Conservative Politics* (1997)

W. Bennett, *The De-Valuing of America* (1992)

D. Boaz, ed., *Left, Right, and Babyboom: America's New Politics* (1986)

M. Brennan, *Turning Right in the Sixties* (1995)

J. Bunzel, ed., *Political Passages: Journeys of Change through Two Decades* (1988)

W. Chambers, *Witness* (1987)

P. Collier, *Destructive Generation* (1990)

P. Collier and D. Horowitz, *Second Thoughts: Former Radicals Look Back on the 60s* (1991)

A. Crawford, *Thunder on the Right* (1980)

S. Drury, *Leo Strauss and the American Right* (1999)

L. Edwards, *The Conservative Revolution* (1999)

E. Fox-Genovese, *Feminism without Illusions* (1991)

M. Friedman, *Capitalism and Freedom* (2002)

M. Gerson, *The Neoconservative Vision* (1999) and *The Essential Neoconservative Reader* (1996)

N. Gingrich, *Winning the Future: A 21st Century Contract with America* (2005)

R. Goldberg, *Barry Goldwater* (1997)

B. Goldwater, *The Conscience of a Conservative* (1990)

P. Gottfried and T. Fleming, *The Conservative Movement* (1988)

F. Hayek, *The Road to Serfdom* (1967)

J. Himmelstein, *To the Right: The Transformation of American Conservatism* (1990)

G. Hodgson, *The World Turned Right Side Up: A History of the Conservative Ascendancy in America* (1997)

D. Hoeveler, *Watch on the Right: Conservative Intellectuals in the Reagan Era* (1991)

J. Judis, *William F. Buckley, Jr.: Patron Saint of the Conservatives* (1988)

R. Kirk, *The Conservative Mind* (2001)

J. Kirkpatrick, *Dictatorships and Double Standards* (1982)

I. Kristol, *Neoconservatism* (1995)

P. Lyons, *New Left, New Right and the Legacy of the Sixties* (1996)

L. McGirr, *Suburban Warriors: The Origins of the New American Right* (2002)

M. Magnet, *The Dream and the Nightmare: The Sixties' Legacy to the Underclass* (1993)

J. Micklethwait and A. Woolridge, *The Right Nation: Conservative Power in America* (2004)

M. Miles, *The Odyssey of the American Right* (1980)

C. Murray, *Losing Ground* (1984)

G. Nash, *The Conservative Intellectual Movement in America since 1945* (1998)

P. Noonan, *What I Saw at the Revolution* (1990)

D. Patai and N. Koertge, *Professing Feminism* (1994)

R. Perlstein, *Before the Storm: Barry Goldwater and the Unmaking of the American Consensus* (2002)

N. Podhoretz, *Breaking Ranks* (1980)

W. Rusher, *The Rise of the Right* (1984)

J. Schoenwald, *A Time of Choosing: The Rise of Modern Conservatism* (2000)

C. Sommers, *Who Stole Feminism?* (1994)

P. Steinfels, *Neoconservatives* (1980)

T. Teachout, ed., *Beyond the Boom* (1990)

M. Thorne, *American Conservative Thought since World War II* (1990)

P. Viereck, *Conservatism Revisited* (1949)

R. Weaver, *Ideas Have Consequences* (1984)

J. Wilson, *The Moral Sense* (1997) and *Thinking about Crime* (1985)

T. Wolfe, *Radical Chic and Mau-Mauing the Flak Catchers* (1971)

American Conservatism Defined

My students have occasionally asked for my definition of conservatism. I begin with a historical framework. Conservatism emerged as a response to what was perceived as the destructive nature of the French Revolution, New Deal–type welfare states, and the totalitarian threats—fascism and communism—of the mid-twentieth century. At its most decisive, American conservatives, in the spirit of Edmund Burke, were profoundly anti-utopian and in opposition to all revolutionary creeds with the exception of what conservatives perceived as the more traditional dimensions of the American Revolution. As such, American conservatives found themselves engaged in a sometimes fruitful but often acrimonious argument with those identified with the Enlightenment project but deeply antagonistic to totalitarianisms of the right and left.

Perhaps it would help if I shamelessly stole from Russell Kirk's well-known six canons of conservative thought, albeit with my own significant revisions:

1. Conservatives believe that there need to be some moral and ethical anchors and ballasts such that we are not adrift in a sea of postmodernist iconoclasm, a shallow relativism, or, worse, nihilism. As such, there is a tilt toward understanding and learning from historical experience, including a respect although not a veneration of tradition. Such beliefs need not be transcendent, nor be based on universal truths, for instance, natural law or natural rights.

2 Conservatives believe that utopian ideologies pose inherent threats to the thin veneer that sustains civilized societies. As such, conservatives mistrust all forms of rationalism, positivism, and any assertion that suggests the perfectibility of human beings. Conservatives are always respectful of the human capacity to descend toward the abyss, whether one calls this human frailty evil or sin or aggression. They also begin with a skepticism rooted in what some have called the law of unintended consequences, the possibility that good intentions can yield destructive ends.
3 Conservatives believe that ideological fixations on societal ideals—whether socialism/communism or laissez-faire, free-market capitalism—subvert the necessary ad hoc, piecemeal, and situational responses necessary within any particular social order. There needs to be an element of pragmatism within any thoughtful conservatism that asks: Does it work?
4 Conservatives believe that social change is both necessary and inevitable but must be approached with sobriety and caution. Conservatives are to be distinguished from reactionaries and radicals because they hold that what was and what is have greater weight than what ought to be.
5 Conservatives hold a proper respect for the diversity, variety, and perversity of human existence. Indeed, conservatives embrace and seek to nurture such expressions of the human spirit.
6 Conservatives believe in Edmund Burke's notion that society is "a partnership not only between those who are living, but between those who are living, those who are dead, and those who are to be born." Conservatives believe that such an organic approach has profound implications for how one educates the young, treats the old, and respects the environment.

As the canons suggest, there is nothing that inherently links conservatism to any of the following: right-wing populism, libertarianism, laissez-faire capitalism, fundamentalist Protestant Christianity, or K Street cronyism.

PART II

Thinking Conservatism

In the following essays I seek to explore the nature of American conservatism through a number of themes. In Chapter 3, "From Camelot to Cowboy," I look at the curious unfolding and then the seeming decline of an American cosmopolitanism from the 1960s to the present. In the essay, I raise the question of how we understand that moment mythologized as Camelot during which it seemed that the United States, through the Kennedy administration, was moving toward a Europeanization of our culture. I highlight the symbolic significance of both the play and film *Inherit the Wind*, which, I argue, seemed to be looking backward at what was perceived to be firmly wedded to the past—nativism, fundamentalism, evangelical Protestantism. Yet within a few decades we had moved to the point of looking on all things European—especially French—as suspect. How did this come to pass?

In Chapter 4, "Cities on a Hill," I explore the multiple and at times contradictory ways in which this metaphor of American exceptionalism has played out in recent decades, especially in terms of the George W. Bush administration's "War on Terror."

Chapter 5, "Is There an American Conservatism?" returns to some of the themes of the initial essay and suggests that it might be useful to reconfigure what we mean by conservatism. For one, I argue that what is often called conservative—especially libertarianism, the Christian right, and right-wing populism—falls far short of the essentially Burkean mold. More pointedly, I urge readers to recognize that some of the astute conservative work has come from thinkers more characteristically defined as liberal, such as Hannah Arendt, Reinhold Niebuhr, and George Kennan.

In the postscript, I attempt to make admittedly tentative and brief commentary on the state of American conservatism as we move beyond the Bush administration.

CHAPTER 3

From Camelot to Cowboy

One can argue that much of American cultural history through the mid-twentieth century was a struggle to overcome feelings of inferiority vis-à-vis European culture. Of course, there has always been the counterpoint; some would call it a compensation. That notion argued that American culture, its national character, precisely because of its New World innocence and egalitarian authenticity, was at the least morally superior to that of the effete, decadent Europeans. We might be the "rubes," but we had a native shrewdness always able to outsmart European sophisticates. Indeed, this tension over our identity, this conversation, has shaped American identity: envy and contempt, imitation and defiance, pride and shame.[1]

Many of our most astute intellectuals during the first two decades of the twentieth century challenged what they called the Genteel Tradition, that is, the efforts to identify with and imitate mostly English norms of civility, manners, and refinement. The critic Van Wyck Brooks spoke of the tensions between highbrow and lowbrow, genteel and vulgar, as preventing the United States from moving toward its own distinctive cultural renaissance. Folklorist Constance Rourke was one of the first to discover ways in which American humor, that is, an indigenous folk tradition of tall stories and comedic scenes, offered a path toward an American culture of note. Within this set of critiques, Mark Twain stood as the first truly American voice. Indeed, those like Brooks argued that Twain's authentic art was stymied if not crushed by a tragic desire to succeed within the term of the Anglophilic Genteel Tradition.[2]

One could argue that what Ann Douglas called Mongrel Manhattan, the mixing and matching of immigrant, Jewish, African American, and gay voices during the 1920s, reflects another stage in the working through of this tension.[3] Compare for example the speaking styles of Franklin Delano Roosevelt and his fireside chats with that of Clark Gable in *It Happened One Night.* Already seventy years old, the film's dialogue sounds strikingly modern. Just recall the wonderful road scene when Gable and his spunky traveling companion Claudette Colbert spar in slangy repartee and loosey-goosey body language over hitchhiking techniques. Or consider Louis Armstrong's and then Frank Sinatra's ways of telling stories within their music—conversational, colloquial, mischievous, American. FDR did lead what historian Michael Denning appropriately calls the Popular Fronting of American culture, but he did it as a personification of the past, of a still-Anglophilic style: "The only thing we have to fea-uh is fea-uh itself."[4] Very Groton. Gable, on the other hand, speaks machine-gun fast, in your face and in what we clearly recognize and applaud as an American idiom. And of course Satchmo pioneered the blackening—and whitening—of that idiom, as Sinatra voiced the coming together of ethnic streams of conversational prose—"It's quartah t' three; there's no one in the place, except you and me. So set 'em up Joe, I've got a little story you oughta know." They were drinkin', my friend, in a manner no longer Anglophilic, but fully confident, thoroughly indigenous.

During the postwar years, Eisenhower and Truman stand as Midwestern American voices, flat and nasal. "Give 'em hell" Harry's was punchier; Ike's more shaped by a lifetime in the military. But consider how in the movie *Patton*, Eisenhower's plainness is set off against the stereotypical British fussiness of Viscount Montgomery; Constance Rourke would have immediately recognized the continuity in this game. But neither Truman nor Eisenhower moved this particular cultural trope forward. To many postwar intellectuals, both were embarrassing reinforcements of the genus Americanus—parochial, middlebrow, intellectually sterile.

Much of 1950s cultural criticism lamented the presumed gap between highbrow and lowbrow, genteel and gritty. It worried about the hegemony of the middlebrow, of kitsch.[5] And one heard, resoundingly, complaints about a TV wasteland, of Ike's dowdy wife Mamie, of ketchup on everything, of an inferiority before our European cousins in London and Paris and Milan. Even in Moscow, where we feared that Ivan could outread Johnny, where subways had paintings and chandeliers, where the poetry of Yevtushenko sold to a mass market of cultivated if impoverished Russians. This, despite the glaring fact of Soviet repression of jazz, nonrepresentational art, and psychoanalysis.

The existence of the twice-defeated Adlai Stevenson only reinforced the notion of an inferior American culture. Our prototypical egghead, the butt of jokes, admired if feminized, suspect as alien, foreign. Perhaps Joe McCarthy reached deeper into the muck to mischievously call him "Alger," but others shared at least the more benign—and more damaging—aspects of the "pink" portrait. While Arthur Schlesinger Jr. argued for a tough-minded "vital center" liberalism, it seemed that the Democrats remained caught between the suspect folksiness of Estes Kefauver and the masculinity-deficient Stevenson.[6]

Thus the rise of John Fitzgerald Kennedy meant many things, but certainly it was taken to mark the final emergence of a proud, even imperial American culture, of a virile movie-star handsome leader, of what Jacqueline Kennedy later christened as Camelot. Pablo Casals, Robert Frost, the best and the brightest, the Harvards mixing with the Hollywoods and the Broadways, the pool parties, the seminars at Hickory Hill, the tours of the White House by the First Lady, her triumphant conquests of de Gaulle and the French people. Damon Runyon meets John Kenneth Galbraith. It seemed as if the United States had finally arrived, had finally achieved status as a cultural as well as a political and economic and technological power. We were, *at long last*, as good, nay, better than the Europeans. And at their own game! We had Saul Bellow and Jackson Pollock and MOMA and Frank Lloyd Wright and Einstein and Duke Ellington and Ella Fitzgerald and Tennessee Williams. We seemed to have transcended the seemingly unbridgeable gap between popular and elite, high and low, commercial and arty in this graceful, witty, and debonair president without a hat. Norman Mailer, in his laudatory "Superman Comes to the Supermarket," saw "the deep orange-brown tan of a ski instructor," "the matinee idol, the movie star," comparing JFK to Marlon Brando in his existential loneliness.[7]

Significantly, Kennedy's religion was effectively addressed with the rejoinder that it had no relevance to how he would preside over the nation. This was truly a secular moment, at which time Will Herberg's Protestant-Catholic-Jew seemed to blur into a kind of Judeo-Christian mush of surface piety and erupting eros.[8] Kennedy, our first Keynesian president, embodied much of the ongoing secularization predicted by many scholars, not the least of which in his dry wit and cool demeanor. The end of ideology, indeed. Many understood Daniel Bell to mean the collapse of Marxist utopian visions, but a deeper interpretation might include the secularization of religious faith, the end of millennial expectations.[9]

It is now more than forty years since, and it is difficult to understand what actually happened in the intervening years such that we now have as chief executive a man who prides himself on not reading newspapers, not to speak of novels, poetry, or philosophy. We have a president from a distinguished patrician family who mangles the language, cares more about NFL football than about the affairs of Europe, questions the validity of evolutionary theory, calls Jesus his most significant philosophical influence, and whose advisors think it is an effective campaign tactic to remind audiences that his opponent speaks French.

What has happened over these past forty years such that the promise of an American cultural arrival has turned back with a vengeance toward a dualism, a contention between middlebrow and highbrow, mainstream and "the chattering classes," NASCAR and Noam Chomsky? How are we to understand how and why this turn has taken place and why, circa 1960 to 1963, few if any anticipated that Camelot would turn into country and western?

Oh, where to begin? Perhaps we can start with an interrogation of those theories that proved strikingly false in their confident belief that Scopes and Billy Sunday and Joe McCarthy were atavistic and rapidly fading remnants of an increasingly buried past. It is fair to state that when most cultural observers watched either the theater or film versions of *Inherit the Wind*, they framed it as something of the past, almost quaint in its challenges to modernity. We were obviously past such reactionary nonsense outside, maybe, of a few Bible Belt enclaves reducible to images of Dogpatch.[10]

One chief culprit may be modernization theory, that is, the positivistic notion, with roots in Auguste Comte, that there was an inexorable movement in history from the sacred to the profane, from the charismatic and traditional to the bureaucratic. Although Max Weber worried that this process would yield an iron cage, the rationalization of everyday life, the American version of modernization characteristically saw hope and opportunity. It was the social science version of the Idea of Progress.[11]

Within this model, often shared by left-of-center ideologies, liberal to Marxist, there was a technological determinism which argued that in light of the industrial revolutions, the rise of the factory, the office, the communications revolution, quantification, the university as a knowledge industry—Clark Kerr's multiversity—reason was in the saddle and ride mankind. This was not translated universally as a benefit. To Weber, there was tragic loss and risk inherent within modernity. But the notion of an American century, of a Pax Americana, made it all seem like the GE slogan, "Progress is our most important product."

We have seen in what Eric Hobsbawm calls our short twentieth century from 1914 to 1991 the nightmares of totalitarianism, genocide, and total war. Some of the most astute cultural critiques resulted from apostles of reason honestly and painfully coming to grips with the brute facts of irrationality, human frailty, the banality of evil. When Hannah Arendt asserted the latter phrase, critics fixated on the issue of banality rather than the more remarkable attempt to come to grips with a pre-Enlightenment notion of evil.[12]

One might suggest that in the postwar environment, the central argument pitted those utopians still enamored with the Idea of Progress against those progressives, sobered by the nightmares of Auschwitz and Hiroshima, who sought to preserve the Enlightenment's most compelling hopes. It was here that theologians such as Reinhold Niebuhr challenged social gospel naïveté with a return to notions of sin, moral man and immoral society, while his brother Richard offered an existential, unresolvable tension between Christ and culture.[13] The best of post–World War II culture reflected this subdued, wiser liberalism, a decidedly cautious modernization. One finds it in many of the intellectual and cultural currents that helped to shape the Kennedy ascendancy, from Lionel Trilling's "liberal imagination" through Richard Hofstadter's liberal tradition, from the *Partisan Review*'s New York intellectuals through the best of the consensus school of historians. Ira Katznelson, in his brilliant *Desolation and Enlightenment*, suggests that a prominent and diverse group of political scientists sought ways to come to grips with the pervasiveness of evil, with the realities of total war, totalitarianism, and the Holocaust, to rethink a usable Enlightenment legacy. But others pursued a less chastened, more ambitious agenda.[14]

Consider the career of Walt Rostow with his still-utopian dreams of the ex-Marxist in his noncommunist stages of economic growth, modernization theory personified.[15] It is hardly a coincidence that Rostow was among those who became the most ideological of Cold Warriors during the Vietnam War era, never for a moment hesitating in his call for a Free World offensive. Those like Hans Morgenthau and George Kennan, scholars of the realist school, wary of the misplaced idealism of the Wilsonians, sought to anchor foreign policy in sober assessments of national security interests and understood that the weight of nationalism most often had greater staying power than any version of Marxism: tradition over reason.[16]

Consider how the most conservative voices—of a Burkean sensibility—of the 1960s were characterized as "liberal doves," for example, Morgenthau, Kennan, William J. Fulbright, Eugene McCarthy. They were public figures who worried about "the arrogance of power," who were suspicious of the rhetoric of Free World versus godless communism. All shared in the best of that Camelot moment, what might be called the Europeanization of American political culture.[17]

It is striking to recall how frightened so many Americans were in the heyday of the Cold War. Kennedy's inaugural speech was a generational call to arms. And yet, in retrospect, what should provoke our curiosity and wonder is the overwhelming fact that the United States was so much more powerful in every sense of the word than the Soviet Union. As an economy, we dominated the planet, our products defining our moment: GM, IBM, Ford, General Electric, Mobil. As a culture, we were becoming the trendsetter for all peoples. Recent revisionist studies point to the ways in which the State Department used artists such as Louis Armstrong and Ella Fitzgerald as emissaries to Third World countries.[18] Indeed. But this somewhat manipulative, disingenuous Cold War effort rested on the unquestionable influence of American culture, from film to jazz to nonrepresentational art, from high to popular culture, from Leonard Bernstein and Aaron Copland to Duke Ellington and Billie Holiday and Chuck Berry and Elvis and even the British invasion of the sixties, essentially an homage to the great rhythm-and-blues artists that groups like the Beatles and Stones worshipped. On this terrain, the Soviets could not compete; indeed, they weren't even on the playbill.

At the time of Camelot, our institutions of higher learning, measurably improved by the fresh talent spawned by the GI Bill and the National Defense Education Act, were the envy of all. And yet in the late 1950s, there was a wail, a lament of our decline. Some of it was rooted in the quest to complete the Europeanization of our culture, much of which would come with the rise of the great American auteurs—Scorsese, Woody Allen, Altman, Coppola; the restaurant renaissance that began in virtually every American city by the 1970s; the emergence of quality coffee, quality beers. Soon critics would refer to this as the "yuppification" of America. But despite its foolish qualities, well lampooned by such as Tom Wolfe and David Brooks, the rise of the Yuppie, at best, was the cutting edge of this Europeanization—no ketchup on everything, learning to bake grained breads, a plethora of arts-and-crafts stores and fairs.[19]

And yet, back in the late 1950s, there was a national panic over American education: "Soviets produce more engineers than U.S.," "Sputnik marks crisis of American education." Somehow, in the late 1950s and through much of the 1960s and even extending into the 1970s, lots of Americans, including our most educated and powerful, came to believe that the Soviets, as Khrushchev boasted, would bury us. Khrushchev's claim was that communism would outproduce capitalism, that the USSR would finally make better and cheaper commodities, sustain higher rates of economic growth, indeed, beat capitalism at its own game.

Now, it is absolutely clear that such claims were preposterous. There was no point at which the Soviet Union was even on the same playing field as the United States in any area other than military. Yes, the AK-47 of Mr. Kalashnikov was superior to our M-16. But what other Soviet products, especially those oriented to the consumer market, could compete against American or Western European or East Asian goods? I can recall an argument I had with some radical friends in the 1990s about the collapse of the Soviet empire. They argued that there was a myth about the collapse being caused by Soviet economic incompetence and failures. I looked at them with astonishment and said, "Just think: Hyundai versus Yugo." That defines the nub of the collapse of communism. The Soviet bloc could never produce a toothpick or a shoe or a suit or a clothes washer or a TV that anyone in their right mind would freely purchase, given alternatives.

Even militarily, we know that the famous "missile gap" proclaimed by JFK was actually one in our favor, that part of the reason Khrushchev blinked during the Cuban missile crisis was that he knew that *we* knew—through our U-2 flights—that we had the overwhelming edge in nuclear arsenals. That's why he recklessly sought to install intermediate-range ballistic missiles (IRBMs) in Cuba in the first place, to at least give the appearance of equity.[20]

So, given our economic, cultural, and military superiority circa 1960, why did so many of our leaders at least half-believe Khrushchev's boastings? Liberal critics made fun of Vice President Nixon's kitchen debate with Khrushchev, but in fact he was marking the most decisive ways in which communism was failing and in which capitalism, at least that tempered by welfare-state interventions, was flourishing. Somehow, despite the Camelot moment, despite our global dominance, we anticipated a decline, a softening, a defeat at the hands of a "youthful," more determined rival.

The de facto conservatives—Kennan et al.—were less taken in. They were so confident of the superiority of our system, maybe more, in the inferiority of the Soviets, they believed that if they could wisely if firmly contain communism, it would inevitably collapse of its own contradictions. That was what the strategy of containment promised.[21] Talk of hoisting Marx, or at least Lenin, on his own petard! It was with such confidence that the misnamed liberal doves saw Vietnam as unwise, marginal to our security interests, more manageable through diplomacy, and ultimately seduction and bribery, than through disproportionate force. They understood that the war made us look foolish to our neighbors and allies, unable to recognize long-term trends, unable to use time to our advantage. After all, the Vietminh saw the war as a pre–Marquis of Queensbury match in which they simply had "not to lose," whereas we had to win. If they did the rope-a-dope, if they "stayed close to our belts," if they survived, we would eventually get tired and go home. They *assumed* what historian Niall Ferguson has recently described as our refusal to take empire seriously; they saw us as essentially immature. And they were right.[22]

So what can we learn from the obviously fragile ascendancy of a liberal cosmopolitanism in the thousand days of Camelot? For one, we can recognize that underneath that triumph were resistant and resentful forces, never far from the surface, awaiting an opportunity to strike in the name of an insular nativism. Sometimes harkening backward to Joe McCarthy and Martin Dies, more successfully anticipating Ronald Reagan and George W. Bush, anticosmopolitans engaged in their initial forays through the Barry Goldwater and George Wallace presidential campaigns.

In both cases, the voice was populist. In both cases, it identified as the silent majority of the nation, the heartland, Middle America, mostly white, Christian, mainstream, traditionalist. It challenged the Popular Front ideology that dominated since FDR, the notion that the people—workers, farmers, minorities—stood against the plutocrats, the economic royalists. Instead, in its right-wing reformulation, we had the people—the silent majority—against the decadent poor and the decadent educated, the welfare cheats and the talking heads, the ghetto rioters and the pointy-headed intellectuals, the bra-burning feminists, immoral homosexuals, the tree-hugging environmentalists, the secular humanists, the yuppies, the hippies. This new conservative populism attacked what it defined as the cultural, rather than the economic, elite, Dan Rather instead of Donald Trump. It identified with the Indy 500 to obscure the responsibilities of the Fortune 500. We experienced it first in the remarkable image of Barry Goldwater, child of Jewish immigrants morphed into Western hero in the spirit of those Hollywood dream merchants who sold the romance of the West out of their shtetl hopes. The cowboy—first Goldwater, then a truly Tinseltown hero Ronald Reagan. Such populist imagery led the patrician George H. W. Bush to play up his love of country and western music, not to speak of pork rinds, as well as trade in his support of population control for an opposition to abortion. And it led his son, born and bred in gated suburban communities, to sell himself as a cowboy rancher only happy when clearing brush.[23]

Perhaps Bush Sr.'s devolution—his attack on the ACLU-card-carrying Michael Dukakis, the Willie Horton ads—offers some hint of another dimension of this return to a proud parochialism. And it worked up to a point: the Greek immigrant, workaholic Dukakis became the Massachusetts elite liberal, whereas the Kennebunkport Bush sought to morph into a man of the people. Of course, that he didn't know how a grocery-store scanner worked, that he remained a transplanted New Englander, that he fell back on his noblesse oblige to responsibly reread his lips about no new taxes, brought him down before the folksy charm of that Arkansas traveler Joe Willie Clinton. But his Texas-raised older son would prove better able to play at being the brush-cutting "regular guy," the voice of the people.

Some argue that we have seen the decline of the WASP elite that Digby Baltzell sought to diversify with a meritocracy open to Catholics, Jews, and minorities.[24] There no longer seems to be the kind of "best and the brightest" savaged by David Halberstam. Perhaps the Vietnam War debacle destroyed the notion of such an elite, perched high above in the State Department, running the Council on Foreign Relations, the key foundations, and the elite investment and law firms—George Ball, Douglas Dillon, Dean Acheson, the Bundys, Cyrus Vance, Averell and Pamela Harriman. Harvard, Georgetown, the Cape. All gone.

If they are gone. Yet certainly they have lost some of the unchallenged hegemony that was once their birthright. Part of the reason may have to do with their own ambivalence, their own contradictoriness, their own lack of confidence. Recall how facilely so many of them bought into a Cold War, Manichean worldview. More tellingly, how many came to doubt the eventual triumph of the United States in that Cold War? How could these well-educated, sophisticated men have been so taken in by the notion that the Soviet Union, not to speak of the People's Republic of China, was in any way a significant threat to American predominance? It is now more than ten years since the collapse of the Soviet bloc, the crumbling of the Berlin Wall, the marginalization of communism to the basket cases of North Korea and Cuba plus the capitalist-party dictatorships of China and Vietnam. Isn't it apparent that to credit Ronald Reagan with winning the Cold War is at best a partial truth, at worst, an avoidance of coming to grips with the demonstrable and inherent weakness of the USSR and its satellites?

One must conclude that the cosmopolitan elite of the Kennedy era showed a remarkable lack of confidence in the system they embodied. They dreaded that perhaps communism *would* bury us economically. Why else the space race? Why else the absurdity of Vietnam? Why else the exaggerated fear of Fidel Castro? A wise and confident elite, a cosmopolitan elite would have listened to its best voices—Kennan, Morgenthau, Fulbright, Ball—and extricated itself from the Vietnam quagmire.

Moreover, those wisest voices lacked the style with which to challenge a range of populist voices, which initially included the "participatory democracy" of the New Left, but which, over time, was shaped by those Reagan Democrats in Macomb County, Michigan, those who shifted their Popular Front egalitarianism from the New Deal to Reaganomics. That Reagan himself began as a New Dealer speaks to this transformation. Peggy Noonan, the Great Communicator's chief speechwriter, has always portrayed herself as the child of blue-collar, ethnic Democrats, betrayed by a more elitist liberalism characterized by identity politics and anti-Americanism.[25] Those who were actually the best and the brightest, such as Kennan, remained fundamentally ambivalent about democracy at best, contemptuous of it in their worst striped-pants moments.

The emerging right-wing populism, in addition to standing as a measure of deep reservations within the heartland about a kind of Europeanization of America, rested on the internal reservations of a cosmopolitan elite, still unsure of itself, still more boastful than confident. The Kennedy moment came and went. We still await a cosmopolitan ascendancy that is able to bring together the best of aristocratic and democratic traditions, wisdom and earthiness, patience and daring, taste and grit. And one that understands how deeply religious, how fundamentally Protestant this nation has always been.

We have yet to come to grips with the deeply religious, Protestant core of our city on a hill, even as we become more multicultural and multireligious. What must all the world see in our works and in our visions? Recent political decisions suggest that our city on a hill is not yet a cosmopolitan and blue-state American city. It also does not seem to be a city chastened by the horrors of this century, nor by the lessons of capitalism's limitations and blind sides. Instead, it seems to be an evangelical, literalist place where biblical truths miraculously correspond with corporate greed, where deeper veins of American innocence and European venality still yield gold, where intelligent design stalks our schools but is absent from our foreign policy. And it is indisputably a place that can energize its congregation to turn out at the polling sites.

Camelot seemed a moment when this American political culture of ours was finally growing up, coming of age. Yet, both within the Kennedy mystique and shadowing it in the hinterlands, there were hesitancies and qualms, even a rising rage. In a strange but not tongue-in-cheek manner, Karl Marx offers insight: "Religious feeling is, at one and the same time, the expression of real suffering and a protest against real suffering. Religion is the sigh of the oppressed creature, the heart of a heartless world, and the soul of soulless conditions. It is the opium of the people." Those who understood the implications of the horrors of the twentieth century responded with deep spiritual anguish—existential, tragic, stoic. But the voices of Kennan and Arendt, of Morgenthau and Niebuhr, remained fundamentally austere, suspicious of populist voices, even antidemocratic. They could not temper the soaring idealism of Camelot as it stumbled into the Deep Muddy; they could hardly understand the ways in which Weber's iron cage lay upon a deeply evangelical and ambivalent people. Camelot remains a kind of peek, a dress rehearsal if you will, of possible resolutions. Only now the challenge of reconciling our quintessential American voice with our European roots, the challenge of respecting our religious heart without insulting our secular brain, the challenge of reconciling our elite wisdom with our populist common sense, must be truly global.

CHAPTER 4

Cities on a Hill

When President Bush proclaims that the United States has made the pursuit of democracy and liberty the basis of our foreign policy, what exactly does he mean? Anti-Bush critics tend to simply write off such rhetoric as cover for less-attractive goals, including maintaining global hegemony, U.S. access and control of critical resources, and maximization of the interests of American multinational corporations. Perhaps some would highlight the evangelical aspiration to make fundamentalist Christian values dominant throughout the world. Others would argue for a neoconservative hand in transforming the Middle East to strengthen a Likud-dominated Israel.[1]

Those defending the president, on the contrary, not only take his liberating rhetoric at face value, but also contend that it is consistent with a long-term American idealism going back to the notion of a city on a hill for all the world to see—and emulate. His supporters challenge those who see Bush policy as a violation of long-term American views of our role in the world. Still, critics counter that those parts of the American experience, from Dollar Diplomacy to Gunboat Diplomacy; from Marines being sent to the Dominican Republic to United Fruit–influenced interventions in Guatemala; from CIA coups in Iran to U.S. support for apartheid in South Africa, reveal our less idealistic, more bullying past.[2]

It might be useful to consider the ways in which main currents within the history of both American foreign policy and, more broadly, America's responses to the rest of the world have shaped the particular initiatives and goals of the present Bush administration. There has been an ongoing and inherently contradictory set of questions and issues that have driven U.S. foreign policy from the outset of the nation's history.

One way to approach these questions and issues is to investigate what I will suggest are the multiple meanings of the notion of a city on a hill, their respective purposes, their varied audiences, their essential logics. Indeed, there is more than one version of that city, more than one notion of topography, and more than one target for more than one message.

One version, consistent from the beginning, is that humankind has been placed upon this earth to labor and make it plentiful to the greater glory of God and that the United States has taken on this covenant with greater success and with more consistency than any other nation. This essentially Protestant version fuses with an economic and technological emphasis that claims an American mission to bring the benefits of our sacred accomplishments to the rest of the world. In brief, this version evokes the notion of a redeemer nation, an America called to transform the earth in its own image. The most eloquent embodiment of this vision has been Ronald Reagan: "I in my own mind have thought of America as a place in the divine scheme of things that was set aside as a promised land. . . . I believe that God in shedding his grace on this country has always in this divine scheme of things kept an eye on our land and guided it as a promised land." It was at the close of Reagan's concession speech of 1976 that he evoked "a shining city on a hill."[3]

There are obvious connections with nineteenth-century notions of Manifest Destiny. Aware of such providential history, Lincoln referred to the United States as "the last best hope for mankind." More recently, neoconservative Ben Wattenberg extended this claim after the collapse of the Soviet empire, proclaiming America as "the first universal nation," the single and benevolent model for the entire world.[4] Lincoln's quote evokes the political dimension of American specialness, our constitution, our republican institutions, our democratic and egalitarian culture, a nation "of the people, by the people, and for the people." The religious, economic, and political dimensions of this claim, however, contain deep and powerful contradictions and fissures. The emphasis on productivity promotes the turning of a wilderness into a garden of plenty, but it concomitantly can justify imperial, even genocidal policies directed toward those less productive, less enamored with the Protestant version of a work ethic and with the compulsion to accumulate. Native American claims to this continent were denied, in part, by such a logic. Such a justification is consistent with social Darwinism—those who flourish in the ruthless marketplace, including that of wilderness development, are deserving of survival and celebration; those who falter, those who offer no value added to their lands, can be pushed aside and be marginalized, be absorbed, or simply disappear from the historical record. Indeed, such a narrative incorporates biblical notions of chosenness.[5]

This American city on a hill is not only democratic and egalitarian, albeit contemptuous of lesser peoples, it is also grounded in liberty. Nevertheless, there are tensions between liberty and democracy on several fronts. Who rules this city on a hill? How are decisions to be made in its name? For example, the libertarian commitment to the First Amendment, to the protection of minority rights, clashes with more populist notions concerning the will of the majority. In the name of the people, the Jacksonians denied the Supreme Court its charge to protect the minority rights of Native Americans and crushed Nicholas Biddle's Bank of the United States. Yet such a populist majoritarianism can swing right or left, depending on the setting. And it can join with a libertarian commitment to the free market to denounce an elitist monopoly.[6]

In a post–September 11 environment, as in previous moments when people's safety seemed at stake, individual and minority rights are threatened. From the Alien and Sedition Act to the Patriot Act, one finds a willingness to sacrifice constitutional safeguards to sustain various claims to insure homeland security. Our increasingly partisan politics extends these challenges to minority rights. The Bush administration's demand for "a vote, up or down" insists that all nominees be confirmed, with no consideration of the rights of the minority. When they control Congress, Republicans increasingly demand that legislation be passed only if there is no need for Democratic votes. When the Democrats control but lack a veto-proof majority, the Republicans have, for the most part, resisted all efforts at bipartisan compromise. Following his 2004 victory, George W. Bush claimed that the results settled the issue of the legitimacy of the Iraq war.

Nevertheless, Americans remain wary when such democratic principles yield results that alarm us. For example, when Islamic fundamentalist parties win elections, as in Algeria in the early 1990s, we seem willing and able to deny them the fruits of their victories. We may face such dilemmas in the future regarding Hezbollah in Lebanon, as we already gave regarding Hamas in Palestine. Of course, in the past, we subverted popularly elected governments in Chile and were unwilling to risk allowing such elections in Vietnam.[7]

Many believe that a democratic city on a hill rests on a moral essence, an assumption that whether one privileges elections or constitutional protections, it all falls apart without the cultivation of virtue and character.[8] This is so whether one relies on Jonathan Edwards's "Sinners in the Hands of an Angry God" or on the Roman republicanism of our founders. Without virtue, democracy sours into mob rule, the free market descends to piracy, liberty turns into libertinism. What sustains the American character? To some, it is rebirth, becoming a visible saint, to others it is a life of stoic resistance to the temptations of selfishness and indulgence. In addressing the sinfulness of all children of God, in recognizing the frailties of all human beings and their capacity for self-deception, the issue is how to build a commonwealth that reconciles such limitations with the capacity of humans to build that city. This is an issue fraught with difficulties for both conservatives and liberals. The former tend to shy away from addressing the antisocial and selfish dimensions of free-market capitalism; the latter seem to have difficulty coming to grips with the consequences of allowing that free market to drive the culture.

That liberal ambivalence suggests the most recent version of the city, resting on a different notion of liberty, the liberty to consume, to enjoy, to, indeed, pursue happiness in ways Jefferson could hardly have anticipated. To much of the world, this is the most visceral and prevalent sense of the American city on a hill, a city of popular music, of Westerns and madcap comedies; of a slangy informality; of a hedonism within which, as Cole Porter noted, anything goes, within which, if you can't be with the one you love, you can love the one you're with. This is a city that even those angry youth in the Third World burning American flags and effigies of George W. Bush emblematically claim. What else is one to make of their New York Yankee baseball caps, turned backwards, their Chicago Bull or Oakland Raider jerseys, their Nikes, their styles so shaped by *Desperate Housewives* and *Friends* and MTV and 50 Cent and Eminem? And, of course, it is within this city—Broadway, Hollywood, Motown—that questions of virtue and character most arise.[9]

When George W. Bush evokes his own version of the city on a hill, proclaiming that the United States embodies and, as such, must necessarily bring the gospel of liberty and free markets to the rest of the world's peoples for their own good, it is clear that he assumes that most of them welcome his efforts and cannot but assume his virtue and character. In addition, he has to presuppose that only the terrorists, the evil ones, the America-haters, the "blame America" crowd resist his idealistic proselytizing. Indeed, most Americans, at the least, want to believe, *choose* to believe, that Bush's version, which is simply a more ambitious and comprehensive version of those that preceded him, is an accurate portrait of our nation, our city on a hill.

Bush's set of assumptions was perhaps most acutely expressed in

Stanley Kubrick's *Full Metal Jacket*, when a senior officer instructs Private Joker that "inside every gook there is an American trying to get out."[10] Such national narcissism, however grounded in slices of reality, inevitably suggests a Herrenvolk version of the city on a hill, a racist vision of an Anglo or Nordic America, a white nation standing over colored peoples, whether red, yellow, brown, or black. Certainly there is an ugly history within this vision, worse in the past, but still powerful today.[11] Those like George W. Bush and his neoconservative advisors, who share a belief in America as universal nation, tend either to deny that ugliness or to place it in a distant past no longer relevant. Indeed, they tend to respond to all reminders of such moments as evidence of un-American sentiments, of mere political correctness. Recent battles over museum exhibits at the Smithsonian suggest the intensity of those seeking to whitewash the past, to protect their own mythic version of atomic diplomacy or the treatment of Native Americans.[12]

It would be most illuminating for those who share some benevolent version of the city on a hill vision to honestly engage in a rigorous examination of how these less-attractive and more-shameful moments make it more difficult for the case to be made about American exceptionalism. At the same time, those more critical of the United States, who charge gross hypocrisy, make their case along several fault lines, most particularly capitalism/imperialism and racism. In the first case, they see the United States as a dominant capitalist power, with ideals of liberty and democracy mere window dressing for the basics of profit maximization. As such, our policies in the Middle East, for example, are perceived as driven by our desire and our need to control oil, as our policies in Central America were once driven by the interests of United Fruit. Such critics see globalization as an instrument of American hegemony through the instrumentality of such organizations as the World Trade Organization (WTO), the International Monetary Fund (IMF), and the World Bank.[13]

The charges of racism can scarcely be denied in assessing the American response to Native Americans and African Americans throughout most of our history. Until the 1960s, until the implementation of the *Brown* decision and the passage of the Civil Rights Act of 1964 and the Voting Rights Act of 1965, the United States was an openly and legally racist political order. Critics note that the only time we have used nuclear weapons was against a nonwhite adversary. The pejorative "gook" used against the Vietnamese began during the imperialist occupation of the Philippines in the early part of this century. GIs called the boonies

"Indian country." From such a perspective the past weighs heavily on contemporary claims of a uniquely virtuous nation. One can either deny these blots on our heritage or claim that they are merely the past. In the latter case, one is reminded of that all-too-American tendency toward ahistorical thinking; recall Henry Ford's declaration that "History is more or less bunk." Whatever the benefits of Operation Iraqi Freedom, one winces at how our troops characteristically refer to Arab Muslims as ragheads, towelheads, Jihadis, sand niggers, and hajis.[14] Certainly there has been considerable progress toward inclusion and pluralism since the civil rights revolution of the 1960s, but it wouldn't be realistic to assume that several hundred years of bigotry has been wiped out in a few decades. Despite Colin Powell and Condi Rice and Barack Obama and Oprah, we still live in an environment in which African Americans encounter racial prejudice from someone white on a regular basis. That does not mean that most or all white people are racist; as sociologist Orlando Patterson once suggested, if only one in four whites is a bigot, that means that there remain two bigots for every black person.[15] If the Left tends to deny progress in race relations, the Right too often succumbs to a self-serving celebration of a proclaimed color-blind society. The rest of the world, especially the Third World, with its own imperialist and colonialist experience not so far in the distant past, is hardly likely to forget our Herrenvolk legacies in such matters.

Does the United States sometimes get beaten up unfairly over our contradictory past? Of course. In fact, one can make a reasonable argument, particularly given the difficulties Europeans have been experiencing with their non-Western immigrant populations in the past several decades, that the United States may be the *least* racist of Western societies insofar as Americans have had the most experience in fashioning an inclusive, diverse society. Indeed, part of an American advantage in global competition has been our welcoming of immigrants, something yet to be accomplished in Europe or Japan. But it nevertheless remains the case that the party making the most extensive nonracist and postracist claims is also the party least able to attract people of color to its standard. Genuine conservatives and loyal Republicans should be uncomfortable with the ways in which their forces consistently seek to minimize the African American vote through legal maneuvers, restrictions on former convicts, and techniques of harassment and deceit. Our gated suburbs make an uneasy fit with any vision of a pluralist, inclusive city on a hill.

Finally, some critics interrogate precisely that multicultural vision in terms of the essentially liberal core of the American political order. By liberal, I mean a constitutional structure and set of processes that translate democracy and liberty into such procedures as regularized elections, First Amendment freedoms, and a spirit of tolerance. Left-wing critics see such "bourgeois" liberties as veneer, as cover for the underlying power of capital, what Herbert Marcuse once called "repressive tolerance."[16] They still long for some kind of communitarian cooperative commonwealth; they too often romanticize and apologize for the Castro dictatorship in Cuba, as they once did for Mao's China. Or, in a less morally compromised way, they anticipate a more decentralized, less technocratic, more green society from whose vantage point the United States, as well as most of Europe, appears to be destructive of the environment and incapable of scaling down to something one might call the good life. More conservative critics challenge liberalism as a weak version of socialism within which, as Ronald Reagan proclaimed, government is the problem, not the solution. They also target liberalism's tolerance for varieties of decadence, in brief, its absence of standards to sustain virtue and character.[17]

Where does this leave the question of America's sense of self as reflected in the metaphor of a city on the hill for all the world to see? Perhaps it is best examined in terms of President George W. Bush's neo-Wilsonian proclamations concerning the American foreign policy objective to actively and forcefully seek the democratization of the entire world.

This is certainly not what anyone anticipated from President Bush, based on his track record and his 2000 campaign, which included particular attacks on Clintonian nation-building. But conservative commentators argue that the events associated with the Al Qaeda attacks of September 11, 2001, changed everything. Their argument is that 9/11 forced the United States to recognize that terrorism rested on dictatorships and their consequent instabilities. As such, democratization became a tough-minded necessity in a world threatened by nuclear, chemical, biological, and more conventional terrorist attacks.[18]

The dilemma is that the Bush doctrine requires either that one view the essence of the American foreign-policy experience as benevolent, a difficult case to make indeed, or that, despite the contradictory track record of generosity and venality, liberation and exploitation, one believe contemporary dynamics have moved the nation past such shameful moments to a trustworthy and deep goodness of intentions.

Let us examine this conservative Wilsonian doctrine and its implementation in terms of the very complicated legacy of a city on a hill. There is certainly some historical truth in the American commitment to the rule of law, constitutional governance, liberty, and democracy. In addition, there is the undeniable fact, all things being equal, that it is better to be dominated by an economically productive and efficient political economy such as the United States than by a backward Portugal (think Angola) or a reactionary France (think Indochina). Cuba before Castro was distorted by American interests that found expression in the Batista dictatorship, but, at the same time, Cuban literacy and health indices suggest comparative advantage. Of course, the cases of Guatemala and the Philippines are less compelling in terms of the advantages derived from American domination.[19]

With Afghanistan and, more particularly, Iraq, the Bush administration makes a case for the progressive outcome of American occupation. It is not unequivocal given the continuing violence wracking both of these societies. Here one can juxtapose the most salient of those cities on a hill. There remains resistance in the traditionalist Arab and Muslim world to the influences coming from American culture in the form of women's rights, sexuality, and popular culture including film, TV, and music. But these influences do not require American military occupation or presence, only a porous global environment within which fax, e-mail, the World Wide Web, satellite TV, CDs, and DVDs all cross borders despite the best intentions of ayatollahs and televangelists to block them.[20]

The evangelical Christian city on a hill perhaps most subverts more inclusive versions. It remains problematic to reconcile the dogmatic imposition by fundamentalists and right-wing evangelicals of moral standards regarding birth control and HIV/AIDS treatment and prevention with commitments to liberty, not to speak of the scientific method. Bush administration nation-building ambitions run smack into the zealotry of some of their core supporters. One recalls the still deputy undersecretary of defense, Lieutenant General Jerry Boykin, who declared that radical Islamists hated America "because we're a Christian nation," concluding in regard to a Somali Muslim warlord, "I knew my God was bigger than his. I knew that my God was a real God and his was an idol." Even the progressive interventions to stymie the government of Sudan from genocidal acts rest on a particular sensitivity to the persecution of Christians.[21]

More telling is the Bush complicity with the multinational energy corporations in stubbornly refusing to come to grips with the finitude of resources. Instead of investing in alternative sources of energy, the Bush administration not only spurns the Kyoto agreements on global warming, not only seeks to open the very limited oil fields of Alaska, but aggressively carries out oil and natural gas company interests in Iraq.[22] For those who opposed the U.S. invasion of Iraq but who agree that eliminating the Saddam Hussein regime was a positive outcome, there is a deep ethical dilemma in assessing what is to be done presently. For one, critics of the war have an obligation to challenge the Bush administration on its oil policies. A reasonable challenge might begin by insisting on consistency in our policies. For example, much of the Arab and Muslim world mistrusts our claims to altruism, arguing that we say democracy but mean oil. Given all of the reports of the special relationship between the administration and companies like Halliburton, it would make sense to state, as policy, now and into the future, that the United States has no interest whatsoever in profiting from Iraqi oil, either through direct purchases and ownership or through special sweetheart deals privileging American corporations.

In addition, critics, home and abroad, worry that the American desire to spread democracy and freedom is tarnished by the development of U.S. military bases and facilities in so many of the nations of Central Asia and Iraq itself. Wouldn't it be persuasive to those critics and skeptics for the president to assert, again as policy now and into the future, that the United States intends to leave Iraq and that our leaving speaks to our disinterest in the establishment of any military bases or facilities in that nation?[23]

Perhaps the best way to approach the question is within the framework of what even many conservative critics view as the catastrophic second term of George W. Bush. Following his defeat of John Kerry in 2004, Bush proclaimed a mandate for a variety of right-wing goals, including privatization of Social Security. Pundits anticipated another step in the unfolding of Karl Rove's strategy of a century of Republican conservative domination. Liberals concurred, albeit with some fury directed at the inept Kerry campaign and some hapless efforts to challenge the election results by an investigation of the voting irregularities in Ohio.

But, for the most part, it seemed as if conservatism was in the saddle and likely to remain there for some time, especially bolstered by the national security fears stimulated by the events of September 11, 2001. Those events gave conservative Republicans the illusion that they were the national security party as far as the eye could see. It gave them a distorted sense of what the public sought. And, most essentially, it brought out all of the inherent and contradictory weaknesses within conservatism and the Republican Party that had been obscured by electoral successes. It also highlighted the contradictions of the city on a hill.

Let us recall how united the nation was in the months following 9/11. Indeed, let us recall how united most of the world was in rallying behind the United States in recognizing the threats posed by Al Qaeda. The George W. Bush administration was able to take advantage of that international support in mobilizing forces to try to drive Al Qaeda out of Taliban Afghanistan. But, as many critics have suggested, in the aftermath the Bush administration wasted an opportunity to cement that support and, before the task was completed, placed Afghanistan on a back burner. Instead, James Mann's "vulcans" decided that it was the grand opportunity to reconstruct American foreign policy along lines suggested in the early 1990s, the post–Cold War moment, and invade Iraq.[24]

My own inclination is to distinguish two key elements in the new, consciously imperial policy of unilateralism and preemption. On the one hand, there are key players such as Vice President Dick Cheney and Secretary of Defense Donald Rumsfeld, both of whom were seeking a repudiation of the constraints placed on the imperial presidency in the Watergate era, both of whom seemed to believe that the United States needed to claim and then impose a uniquely dominant position among nations. They were attracted to war against Saddam's Iraq as a demonstration of the ability of the United States to impose its will on any nation that did not yield to American direction. Among the vulcans, that hawkish circle including Colin Powell, Condoleezza Rice, Richard Armitage, and Paul Wolfowitz, I see significant differences, especially between neocon Wolfowitz, pragmatists like Powell and Armitage, and Cheney and Rumsfeld, who in some ways I would prefer to call neo–social Darwinists or neoimperialists. The latter believed in power, were comfortable with hierarchy, had no difficulty in focusing on geopolitical interests, including control of oil, and had contempt for any and all who were reluctant to unleash American military power. These are not idealists; they are hard-headed men, secure in the notion that those at the top deserve to be there, those at the bottom, the same. Unlike Powell and Wolfowitz, they have not an iota of interest in issues of poverty or social justice. Finally, these are men who, in the context of the end of the Cold War, saw neither moral nor strategic dilemmas in the forceful assertion of a supreme and unchallenged American empire. Their city was truly imperial.

The neoconservatives, most particularly Paul Wolfowitz, Elliott Abrams, the *Weekly Standard*'s William Kristol, Robert Kagan, and David Brooks, allied with Cheney-Rumsfeld but had more idealistic, even utopian aspirations. They saw 9/11 as offering the United States the opportunity to implement the "national greatness" approach they associated with Theodore Roosevelt, albeit with rhetorical support from Woodrow Wilson. They anticipated the U.S.-generated democratization movement throughout the world, making the world safe for democracy, beginning with Iraq. In brief, the neo–social Darwinists/neoimperialists were cynics; the neoconservatives were fools.[25]

The latter's foolishness tells us much about the tragedy of neoconservatism. How could a movement initiated to inject some caution and skepticism into the body politic—Glazer's law of unintended consequences—descend into the most telling example of what happens when one pays no attention to consequences? Colin Powell's State Department clumsily tried to play the grown-up in the march to invading Iraq, but he was too much the company man, too much the insider unwilling to risk his position and his influence in the face of the tsunami of martial spirits. The neoconservatives joined with Cheney and Rumsfeld to run over all doubts, especially those coming from the senior military and intelligence communities. In that regard, George Tenet provided interference; Condoleezza Rice simply waved the warriors through without appropriate checks and balances.

Without reviewing what has become increasingly apparent, that the invasion of Iraq will go down as the most catastrophic foreign-policy decision and implementation in American history, I wish to consider why such experienced leaders succumbed to utopianism. For the neoconservatives, I believe that their shift away from a sobered New Dealism to a dogmatic and self-righteous internationalism rested on their contempt for their adversaries, domestic and foreign. From the very outset, neoconservatism was driven by its belief that the problems facing the United States could be reduced to the moral flabbiness of what they called "the new class," that is, the liberal to radical "blame America crowd" of formerly New Left, SDS academics, voices of the mainstream media, Hollywood. They, like Cheney and Rumsfeld, were haunted by the sixties, by Vietnam syndrome, by the notion that the American metanarrative of a vibrant golden age has been subverted by radicals, feminists, black power advocates, gays and lesbians, identity-politics activists, McGovernites—all those who, not even secretly, hated American culture and sought its comeuppance. It was the neoconservatives who rallied to Henry "Scoop" Jackson in 1972, who created the CIA's Team B, who created the Committee on the Present Danger, the Committee for the Free World, who saw the United States as "the universal nation."[26]

I believe that it was this deep, raw resentment brewing for thirty years, taking different form, neo–social Darwinist or neoconservative, which crystallized at the moment of 9/11 and the unilateralist and preemptive policies that followed in its wake. Of course, those policies were anything but conservative in a Burkean sense. They reflected a single-mindedness, an obliviousness to challenge, which could, incredibly, believe that there was a latent secular democracy just waiting to be born, under Ahmed Chalabi's leadership, in post-Saddam Iraq. And for the neo–social Darwinists, there was less an idealism than an overestimation of the consequences of military supremacy.

The George W. Bush administration did not believe in nation-building, either in domestic or foreign policy. In Iraq, the assumption was that once the mighty U.S. military shocked and awed the Iraqis, there would be no need for an American-directed reconstruction. The best accounts indicate that all efforts to prepare for a postwar reconstruction were denied; instead, the Bush administration filled its diplomatic positions in Iraq with party hacks and youthful conservatives whose only experiences seem to have been as officers in their school's chapters of College Republicans or Young Americans for Freedom.[27] And it is here that one discovers a key to the collapse of the George W. Bush administration and to the crisis of conservatism.

At the heart of the crisis of both the Republican Party and its dominant conservative factions is their contempt for government. At the very least, this contempt belies any adherence to conservative principles of moderation, restraint, skepticism, or respect for tradition. It runs through virtually all but the "greatness" *Weekly Standard* intellectuals who have some commitment to what Bush called "compassionate conservatism" and what Fred Barnes has called "big government conservatism."[28] Those who are essentially lobbyists for big business, the K Street Project legislators such as Tom DeLay and Rick Santorum, those who seek a Christian nation with legislative interventions in citizens' personal lives, those with free-market, Manchester liberal beliefs—all demonstrate a contempt for government, especially for administrative experience and staff expertise. It is in this sense that one can begin to understand the unmitigating political incompetence demonstrated by the George W. Bush administration since the 2004 election. Hiring to fill positions, whether in the Justice Department or Homeland Security or the Coalition Provisional Authority, seems to have been reduced to strictly ideological criteria. Their city on a hill is a brew of laissez-faire mixed with shameless lobbying and favors for the privileged, plus a dose of dogmatic righteousness.

Consider the Terri Schiavo fiasco. Legislators, including the physician and then Senate Majority Leader Bill Frist, were making medical claims without the slightest consideration for the views of those experts with direct, empirical knowledge. Consider the denials of global warming, the resistance to stem cell research, the responses to Hurricane Katrina, the scandals at Walter Reed, the firing of federal prosecutors. In each and every case, one discovers individuals promoted because of political considerations, policies promoted because of political advantage. Brownie, Inc. Those who have contempt for government are unlikely to govern effectively or efficiently. And at the very top, the president embodies all of these flaws. It is not that he is a stupid man; there is considerable intelligence in his development of a brush-clearing, Reaganesque persona. He possesses leadership qualities, some of which were already visible during his college years at Yale. But he is arrogant, dogmatic, and, most critically, intellectually incurious and lazy. He shares some of the Cheney-Rumsfeld corporate elitism; he is a born-again Christian redeemed from his most immature and self-destructive years; and he is shallow enough to at least have been attracted to the fantasies of the neocons.

My sense is that President Bush must be bewildered by his descent. By all accounts, he persuades himself that if he models himself on Harry Truman, a figure about whose policies he remains diametrically opposed, and Winston Churchill, someone whose eloquence makes any such identification somewhat farcical, he will be triumphant, at least among those writing the historical accounts in decades to come. But he does not seem to understand that his former popularity and successes rested on the undeserved support resulting from 9/11 and from the disarray of his Democratic opponents.

I would not offer any predictions about what is to come in the months and years following the 2008 presidential and congressional elections. But I do think that we as a nation are at another crossroads in our history. On one side, we have a conservative movement which seems to have shot itself so many times in the foot and other more sensitive parts of the body that it is in critical condition. I do not expect there to be a serious reconsideration of the nature of conservatism, although that would be the very best outcome both for self-styled conservatives and for the nation as a whole. Most likely they will bicker among themselves over who is to blame for their troubles—the religious right will blame the country club sophisticates, the neocon militants will blame incompetent Republicans and Colin Powell, the Buchananite isolationists will blame the neocons, the anti-immigrant nativists will blame selfish business interests—and all will blame the Bush administration. They seem to have been forced to choose leadership—John McCain—for purely opportunistic reasons, hoping to temporarily hold together disparate elements to defeat Barack Obama. But American conservatism will not recover so easily from the debacles and scandals of George W. Bush's two terms in office. Paradoxically, the hopes for conservatism are at least as likely to come from the Democrats.

Too often critics left of center focus on the contradictions of American global performance, on the hypocrisies that shatter our noble sentiments. Such criticism is essential but not sufficient in offering an alternative short of revolutionary transformation. Given that the United States is likely to remain a middle-class or bourgeois capitalist democracy as far as the eye can see, critics need to emphasize what can be done within such parameters. They can be more consistent in terms of the best of American visions, the most inhabitable of our cities on a hill.

But those compelled by the ideals associated with the city on a hill metaphor need to recognize that there are reasons why much of the world questions our right to present ourselves as on a higher plane for a less-worthy world to emulate. Minimally, they can begin to accept that there may be other compelling cities in the world we might find worthy of emulation. Haven't we all, in our travels abroad, seen ways of managing pollution, ways of facilitating urban space, ways of minimizing traffic, ways of becoming pedestrian-friendly, ways of becoming child-friendly that we wish were adopted in our own nation? Minimally, we can separate out those versions of our city on a hill that get us into trouble, that contradict the best we have to offer in terms of our constitutional system, our diversity, our economic dynamism, our vibrant culture, from those strands of that ideal that have tended toward arrogance and self-righteousness.

Those seeking to make the best of what has been a reckless and irresponsible set of military adventures, in addition to those pressing for specific steps toward withdrawal, could have challenged the Bush administration to live up to its most idealistic rhetoric of self-determination, liberty, and democracy. Indeed, what is most useful and effective is to subject such rhetoric to a historical analysis that neither demonizes nor whitewashes our contradictory past. Perhaps we might recall the wise reflections of George Kennan, who evoked "the continued and undiminished relevance in the modern world of Gibbon's assertion that 'there is nothing more contrary to nature than the attempt to hold in obedience distant provinces.'" The architect of containment concluded, "No people is great enough to establish a world hegemony."[29] If we come to an understanding of such limitations, perhaps our own journey toward democracy, toward a reconstructed and more self-reflective city on a hill, can come closer to our best aspirations. As such, we might become more the America that even most critics, domestic and global, recognize as the freest, among the more diverse, and the most economically successful nation in human history.

CHAPTER 5

Is There an American Conservatism?

In the October 24, 2005, issue of the *New Yorker*, Tom Reiss argued that "the first conservative," the historian and poet Peter Viereck, deserved to be lifted out of the relative obscurity that has been his experience since the mid-1950s. Viereck has always been credited in the literature with framing the revival of an American conservatism with his 1949 *Conservatism Revisited.* Yet Viereck's contributions to conservatism remain strangely understated; in most accounts, he is viewed as, in effect, a closet liberal who was out of sync with the conservatism associated with William F. Buckley Jr.'s *National Review.*[1]

Reiss attempted to rekindle interest in the Pulitzer Prize–winning Viereck by highlighting his Burkean approach, which framed his defense of the New Deal and his opposition to McCarthyism. Perhaps the last straw for the fusionists of the *National Review* was Viereck's conservative defense of his endorsement of Democratic presidential candidate Adlai Stevenson in 1956.[2]

It did not take long for today's conservatives to respond to Reiss's efforts at resurrection and revision. John J. Miller, national political reporter for *National Review*, suggested that Reiss was engaged in "a transparent attempt to attack 'the radicalism of the George W. Bush Presidency' by suggesting that the conservative movement, in its infancy, betrayed its founding father." Miller claimed that the "fundamental weakness of Viereck's conservatism . . . was its disdain of capitalism," which seems to translate as a repudiation of its laissez-faire version.[3]

In denying Reiss's claim that Viereck's adversaries were incensed by his criticisms of Joseph McCarthy, Miller defends as Buckley's "most significant accomplishments" the driving out of the conservative movement a variety of extremists, including the John Birch Society, pro-Nazis, and anti-Semites. And he concludes that liberals such as Viereck exaggerated the damage done by McCarthy, a mere "blowhard."[4]

Finally, Miller takes issue with Viereck's 1962 claim that conservatism had become "a movement infiltrated by religious fundamentalists, paranoid patriotic groups, and big business leaders, united in their loathing of the cosmopolitan elites on the nation's coasts." In his closing line, Miller, perhaps unintentionally evoking the ugliest spirit of the Second Red Scare, castigated "the liberals at *The New Yorker*" for using "a crude tactic that would do any Bolshevik proud."[5]

Miller's responses reinforce my own sense that there is value in reconsidering the nature and emergence of conservatism within the American polity and culture over the past half century. What is American conservatism? How did it come to be defined in certain ways to the exclusion of others? What are the implications and consequences of these categorizations? Are there ways in which the framing of American conservatism obscures and distorts political and cultural realities more than offering illumination and clarity? Would it be fruitful to engage in an interrogation of what historian Leo P. Ribuffo calls "the certification narrative" of American conservatism? Ribuffo offers one path toward a revised history of American conservatism through a reconsideration of the ways in which supposedly liberal administrations rested on seemingly conservative premises and vice versa.[6]

During the 1960s, those labeled as revisionists of what was characteristically called the consensus school of American historiography developed the notion of "corporate liberalism" to anchor a narrative that was oblivious to a seemingly weak and archaic conservatism and that sought to discover a radical tradition of participatory democracy and the beloved community. This New Left school was inspired by scholars such as William Appleman Williams, Gabriel Kolko, and Robert Wiebe, all of whom saw conservative ideas and consequences within the liberalism associated with the Progressive Era, the New Deal, and post–New Deal liberalism. Indeed some of the New Left historians, such as Williams and Eugene V. Genovese, offered surprisingly empathetic accounts of what was characterized as conservatism, for instance, Southern proslavery apologists and the administration of Herbert Hoover.[7]

Although the revisions of New Left historians are marred by their disparagement of this more conservative, corporate liberalism, it may be useful to reconsider their approach, in part stimulated by the revived interest in Peter Viereck. Lionel Trilling's much-cited laments that "liberalism is not only the dominant but even the sole intellectual tradition" and that "there are no conservative or reactionary ideas in general circulation" but merely what he denigrated as "irritable mental gestures which seek to resemble ideas," may serve as a starting point.[8] Indeed, I would not be the first commentator to note that Trilling himself was at the very least a spokesperson for an emerging neoconservatism. What I would like to do in this essay is to explore those of Trilling's generation, the postwar intellectuals usually defined as liberal but, to my mind, as least as accurately perceived as conservative. In that sense John Miller is certainly correct in arguing that Peter Viereck was closer to the liberal establishment of the 1950s than he was to Buckley's fusionist circle.[9] However, if one seeks to tease out the conservative within the liberal, and the liberal within the conservative, or even to explore the possibility that neither of these terms offer much assistance in understanding postwar American political culture, then perhaps a path can be found toward new insights.[10]

The work of Warren I. Susman and Leo P. Ribuffo point in the right direction. Susman recognized much of post–World War II cultural criticism as essentially conservative, including notions of "the organic society, the need for order, for roots, for place," as well as an emphasis on "paradox, irony, and tragedy," and worries "about excessive egalitarianism and its effects on culture." In Susman's analysis, American conservatism focuses on the idea of civilization, an institutional perspective, as opposed to what he calls "the liberal-radical tradition," which tends to emphasize the idea of culture, gemeinschaft, an interest in "the maximization of individual pleasure and the achievement of individual grace and fulfillment." As such, Susman, like Lionel Trilling several decades earlier, argued that "there is no effective conservatism, in my sense, operating in America today."[11]

His student Leo Ribuffo challenges what he calls "the certification narrative" of American conservatism as grounded in, "not the absence of good scholarship but the [historical] profession's failure . . . to 'mainstream' the copious good scholarship that already exists." His most astute analysis points to the complexities of labeling, suggesting, for example, that "there is much evidence to support Warren Susman's contention that American culture grew more conservative during the Depression." Ribuffo adds that the post–World War II environment continued that conservatizing trend. Indeed, during the 1950s both liberals and conservatives purged themselves of their problematic allies, Popular Fronters from the left, John Birchers and anti-Semites from the right, in what one might call the search for vital centers. Ribuffo delights in pointing to the need for scholars to recognize the often contradictory and situationally shaped expressions of both liberalism and conservatism, but he especially calls for skepticism toward a narrative that inherently marginalizes, and therefore trivializes, conservatism.[12]

Historian Alan Brinkley, in his influential *The End of Reform: New Deal Liberalism in Recession and War*, argues that what emerged in the postwar era was "a new kind of liberalism: a liberalism less inclined to challenge corporate behavior than some of the reform ideas of the 1930s had done, a liberalism more reconciled to the existing structure of the economy, and a liberalism strongly committed to the use of more 'compensatory' tools—a combination of Keynesian fiscal measures and enhanced welfare-state mechanisms—in the struggle to ensure prosperity."[13] He adds, "It was not just conservative opposition that caused those changes. Liberals caused them too."[14] Brinkley does highlight the development of strategies to expand notions of individual and group rights, but for the most part laments what "detached liberalism from its earlier emphasis on reform": a class-based politics, an emphasis on democracy as grounded in real economic self-determination, and a suspicion of the concentration of economic power.[15] Alan Wolfe labeled this "The Politics of Growth"; Robert M. Collins called it "Growth Liberalism"; in both metaphors, there is the implication of quantity trumping quality, of a narrowing of vision, of the abandonment of a more robust and populist liberalism.[16]

I don't wish to challenge these interpretations but rather to suggest that they are necessary but not sufficient explanations of the conservative turn within liberalism in the postwar decades. During this period, the accumulation of the horrors of what Eric Hobsbawm calls "the age of catastrophe"[17]—to George Steiner it was a "season in hell," 1914–1945[18]—two bloody world wars, the rise of the rival totalitarian systems of Bolshevism and fascism, the Holocaust, the use of nuclear weapons—had perhaps a larger influence on a wide variety of thinkers, all of whom can be defined as essentially liberal, all of whom developed significantly conservative strains and caveats. The political scientist Ira Katznelson best captures the struggle of some of these intellectuals, such as Hannah Arendt and Karl Polanyi, to temper Enlightenment ideas in the shadow of total war, totalitarianism, and the Holocaust: "[they] sought to understand the origins of dark times, not as a means to overcome humankind's cruelty and potential for harm, for this they knew to be impossible, nor was it to devise an ideal state and its rules . . . but to learn how to live with the now-widened spectrum of ugly possibility, by first discerning how the collapse of the best elements in the western tradition could have been conceivable."[19]

A number of intellectuals, often considered conservative, responded to a season in hell by challenging the operating assumptions of Enlightenment thought. Steiner, T. S. Eliot, Leo Strauss, Friedrich Hayek—each in his fashion castigated liberalism's denial of transcendence, its reliance on reason, its relativism, its inability to recognize evil. Several schools of what came to be viewed as conservative thought emerged from this profound moral crisis, as did several more radical traditions: Straussians and the Frankfurt School perhaps best embody these antiliberal approaches. To traditionalist conservatives, there was a line that began with either William of Occam or Machiavelli or Rousseau, but in all cases to an investment in reason; to those more radically inclined, there had to be some qualities within modern bourgeois culture, within capitalist political economy, that allowed the irrational to flourish, be it an escape from freedom, sexual repression, one-dimensionality, or instrumental reasoning.[20]

This moment remains a critical point of departure for understanding the contradictory unfoldings of postwar liberalism, conservatism, and neo-Marxism. In that sense, perhaps less so for the Marxists, the age of catastrophe marked an abiding turn toward conservatism, a recognition that things could not continue without fundamental repair. Certainly there are dress rehearsals in the lead-up to this moment: the responses to our own Civil War from Oliver Wendell Holmes Jr. and others of the Metaphysical Club so well described by Louis Menand;[21] the disillusion resulting from the Great War within the lost generation of Erich Maria Remarque, Robert Graves, and Ernest Hemingway. But the building up of horror seems to have grabbed the throats of those who saw themselves as consciously carrying the mantle of the Enlightenment, knowing that they had to come to grips with stubborn and frightening facts that belied so much of the hopes and dreams of liberal ideals. Such thinkers may have come to reject redistributionist economics, but they were haunted by ghosts of a genocidal and very recent past.

One of the most influential such figures was Hannah Arendt who, as much as any postwar thinker, "achieved a major work in historical social science arraying total war, totalitarianism, and holocaust in a single historical constellation."[22] Historian Richard Pells concludes that Arendt's *The Origins of Totalitarianism* "is one of those books whose grandeur and brilliance are undiminished even when the battalion of revisionists later 'prove' the author wrong."[23] Political scientist Ira Katznelson argues that Arendt, along with Karl Polanyi, "aimed their efforts to comprehend the origins of the deep cleft between then and now as a contribution to putting an end to illusions, whether associated with liberal conceits about unfolding reason and liberty, Marxist conceits about class struggle producing progress, conservative conceits about the bulwarks of tradition, or imperial conceits mapping the West as a zone of civilization at the top of the globe's hierarchy of cultural difference, achievement, and privilege."[24] Arendt, reflecting on first learning about Auschwitz in 1943, understood how this marked a fundamental breach in history, a Before and an After:

> at first we didn't believe it . . . because militarily it was unnecessary and uncalled for. . . . Before we had said: Well, one has enemies. That is entirely natural. Why shouldn't a people have enemies? But this was different. It was really as if an abyss had opened. Because we had the idea that amends could somehow be made for everything else, as amends can be made for just about everything at some point in politics. But not for this. *This ought not to have happened.* And I don't mean just the numbers of victims. I mean the method, the fabrication of corpses and so on—I don't need to go into that. This should not have happened. Something happened there to which we cannot reconcile ourselves. None of us can. . . . This was something completely different.[25]

Arendt struggled with the issue of evil as manifested in both the rise of totalitarianism and in the Holocaust. She initially defined it as "radical evil," a Kantian notion suggesting an intention to do evil, including both Auschwitz and the Soviet gulag. But, as her biographer Elizabeth Young-Bruehl argues, Arendt came to see a different kind of evil in figures such as Adolph Eichmann, a "banality of evil" that resulted from a bureaucratic thoughtlessness, "the headless recklessness or hopeless confusion or complacent repetition of 'truths' which have become trivial and empty."[26]

She most was disturbed by the underlying assumption that perceived human beings as being superfluous. To Arendt, all of the great traditions were ill-equipped to come to grips with this frightful break with the past; as such, she pointed the way to the necessity for a radical interrogation of liberalism, conservatism, and Marxism: "An insight into the nature of totalitarian rule, directed by our fear of the concentration camp, might serve to devaluate all outmoded political shadings from left to right, and, beside and above them, to introduce the most essential political criterion for judging the events of our time: will it lead to totalitarian rule or will it not?"[27]

As such, Peter Baehr is correct to see Arendt as "a deeply paradoxical figure." Her good friend, the political scientist Hans Morgenthau once asked her, "What are you? Are you a conservative? Are you a liberal? Where is your position within the contemporary possibilities?" Her response was quite consistent with her life's work: "I don't know. I really don't know and I've never known. And I suppose I never had any such position. You know the left think I am conservative, and the conservatives sometimes think I am left or a maverick or God knows what. And I must say I couldn't care less. I don't really think the real questions of this century will get any kind of illumination by this kind of thing."[28] And to Arendt, the real questions led her to an admiration for the American Revolution and to what she emphasized as its republicanism, which she linked to a council model of grassroots participation, which she saw in the early stages of all revolutionary movements. Despite the horrors of this short twentieth century, Arendt opted for what she called the *vita activa*, an affirmation of a love of the world, *amor mundi*. Although influenced by the great German sociologist Max Weber, she resisted the notion of an "iron cage" of bureaucracy with her belief in the capacity of human beings to find ways outside the control of oppressive states or party apparatuses to assert what she defined as action, the involvement of citizens in public spaces that they create. It is part of Arendt's paradox that she admired both John Adams and Rosa Luxemburg.[29] So it is not surprising to find that she stands closer to Edmund Burke in her criticisms of the French and admiration for the American Revolution.[30] But this strand of traditionalist conservatism did not align her with Eric Voegelin, who sought to link the rise of totalitarianism to what he perceived as the consequences of liberalism. As Arendt pointedly concluded, "liberals are clearly not totalitarians."[31] She had no sympathy with arguments that called for a return to transcendence, for a revival of religion and authority. The rise of totalitarianism requires a recognition that there had been a radical rupture in history. Arendt refused to fall back on essences—about history or nature—because she saw them as more integral to the elements that brought forth totalitarian nightmares.

Reinhold Niebuhr was a less elusive thinker, less daunting than Arendt; as such, his influence was more apparent and, perhaps, broader.

Niebuhr is clearly the intellectual figure most mentioned by that group of postwar liberals, including Arthur Schlesinger Jr., Richard Hofstadter, and George Kennan, seeking to reframe the Enlightenment project.

Biographer Richard Wightman Fox concludes that Niebuhr's "prime intellectual contribution was to weld together the tragic sense of life and the quest for justice."[32] His abandonment of the effort to blend a Christian realism with a pragmatic Marxism in *Moral Man and Immoral Society* led Niebuhr, by the late 1930s, to his role in the 1941 founding of the Union for Democratic Action and, later, Americans for Democratic Action, the most important liberal anticommunist organization of the postwar era.[33]

By the time he wrote *The Nature and Destiny of Man* in 1943, Niebuhr had come to a more Kierkegaardian view of the human dilemma, the paradoxical intertwining of sinfulness and free will within the divided self. As Fox notes, "he was a religious modernist devoted to Biblical symbols; a political democrat infatuated with Burkean traditionalism; a skeptical relativist committed like William James to the life of passionate belief and moral struggle."[34] In *The Children of Light and the Children of Darkness*, Niebuhr asserted, "Man's capacity for justice makes democracy possible; but man's inclination to injustice makes democracy necessary."[35]

Niebuhr played a central role in mobilizing liberals in the Cold War, but it must be made clear that he sought an approach which recognized that beneath Soviet belligerence was weakness and that Americans had to be on guard against our own immaturity, our tendencies to respond in moral abstractions, and, worse, our inclination to externalize all problems; in brief, to deny our own flaws.

The diplomat and historian George Kennan was less influenced by the Holocaust and the rise of totalitarianism than Arendt or Niebuhr. Indeed, he was, according to historian Anders Stephanson, "a conservative of organicist orientation." He was "at the outset of the second World War . . . a radically conservative man, bordering on the reactionary."[36] In contrast to Niebuhr, who developed his hard-headed realism from encounters with, indeed the embrace of Marxism, and to Arendt, whose rejection of Marx did not preclude her admiration for Rosa Luxemburg, Kennan began and remained in his own mind, "a conservative by deepest conviction."[37]

Kennan's association with the containment strategy during the Cold War rested on both his realist policy framework and his analysis of the nature of Soviet dynamics. It is clear that Kennan's initial proposals and arguments did not sufficiently distinguish between the military and the political/diplomatic dimensions of containment, something Kennan worked very hard to correct during the 1950s and after. His conservatism informed his analysis of all empires: "I was brought up to recognize the continued and undiminished relevance in the modern world of Gibbon's assertion that 'there is nothing more contrary to nature than the attempt to hold in obedience distant provinces.' Out of this grew my feeling that one must not be too frightened of those who aspire to domination. Not one people is great enough to establish a world hegemony."[38] Kennan, fully aware of Soviet strengths and weaknesses, called for American diplomats to eschew moralistic and dogmatic righteousness for, instead "keeping cool nerves, and maintaining it consistently, not in a provocative way but in a polite way, a calm way, preserving at all times our strength and our firmness, but never blustering or threatening, always keeping the door open for them when they finally do decide to come in—I personally am quite convinced that they will not be able to withstand."[39] The emergence of a rival Communist power in China, the success of Tito in creating an independent Yugoslavia, and the glimmering of what came to be called polycentrism, all deepened Kennan's belief that a realist diplomacy could bear fruit in limiting Soviet ambitions. As he often urged, "The primary quality must be patience. We must neither expect too much nor despair of getting anything at all. We must be as steady in our attitudes as Russia is fickle in hers. We must take what we can get when the atmosphere is favorable, and do our best to hold on to it when the wind blows the other way. We must remain as unperturbed in the face of expansive professions of friendliness as in the face of underhand opposition. We must make the weight of our influence felt steadily over a long period of time, in the direction which best suits our interests."[40] Kennan, who worried that the "very word 'diplomacy' has been semantically discredited in our American vocabulary," embodies all that one means in calling a mode of thought Burkean.[41] Indeed, how was it possible that those who claimed the label of conservative, who defended Joe McCarthy, and who advocated a moralistic and dogmatic approach to the Cold War could possibly be considered anything but "pseudo-conservatives"?[42]

Of course it was a liberal cluster of intellectuals, many of them social scientists such as Daniel Bell, who refused to grant the term "conservatism" to those beginning to claim that designation. I would argue that in addition to Arendt, Niebuhr, and Kennan, many of what were called the "New York intellectuals" associated with influential journals like *Parti-*

san Review as well as the social scientists like Bell, Seymour Martin Lipset, and Nathan Glazer, who were involved in the anthology *The Radical Right*, shared in the conservatizing of liberalism and liberalizing of conservatism sought by Peter Viereck. Daniel Bell conversed often with Richard Hofstadter about the traumatic impact of both the Holocaust and Stalinism, leading them to ask: "What happens when a mass gets out of hand and becomes a mob? . . . [T]here was a great suspicion and fear of mass action of a particular kind, and fear of those situations which in a sense tear down the very fragile bonds of society."[43] As such, liberals such as Hofstadter, Niebuhr, Arendt, and the sociologist David Reisman, according to Bell, "in this sense . . . became somewhat conservative."[44] Historian Neil Jumonville argues, in his study of the New York intellectuals, that "even in the 1930s these intellectuals had clear tendencies toward what later became neoconservatism" in their commitment to elite culture, their wariness of the mass.[45]

Indeed, there is something of a consensus from multiple points of view of this more conservative liberalism of the late 1940s and 1950s. Those who would be the inspirations for the New Left, especially the sociologist C. Wright Mills, deplored what they perceived as careerism. Those who rallied around Bill Buckley's *National Review* bridled at the suggestion by Viereck that liberals and conservatives should join forces against the totalitarians. And those arguing that there was, alas, only a liberal tradition in America—Lionel Trilling and Louis Hartz—fervently believed that the culture suffered from the absence of a conservative challenge.

Why did Viereck's call for a different kind of "fusion," or at least productive discourse, between liberal and conservative traditions fail? Why did American conservatism become the fusionism of Frank Meyer, an awkward truce between its libertarian and traditionalist wings, negotiated through a shared anticommunism? The historian George Nash makes the best case for this emergence and, in the process, gives full weight to how improbable and illogical it could often be. After all, Friedrich Hayek, the Manchester liberal, never called himself a conservative; Russell Kirk could never accommodate himself to a worship of the free market. One of the problems with Nash's analysis is that he too facilely allows the notion of anticommunism to define both wings of conservatism, but by omission denies what is clear and overwhelmingly the case regarding what leftists called Cold War liberals.[46]

To be precise, conservative fusionism did not rest on anticommunism since that approach pervaded both policy makers and liberal intellectuals in the postwar era, without exception.

I am trying to get at how what we call conservatism came to pass and how what we call liberalism came to be so thoroughly separated from conservatism. The libertarians are relatively easy to place within this history: at their best, they held to a logically consistent set of beliefs and policy parameters that privileged the individual, private property rights, the inviolability of the market, and profit maximization, and they mistrusted to the point of pathology government, especially federal government, interventions claiming to speak in the public interest. One can criticize the libertarians, as one can the anarchists, by pointing to the realities of interdependence since the communications and transportation revolutions of the nineteenth century, not to speak of the rise of the corporation, a legal fiction that inherently recognizes the inadequacy of individualism. But that is not the point I wish to make. What I wish to emphasize is simply that this ideology valorizing the individual cannot claim, on its own, to be conservative. That doesn't necessarily make it irrelevant or without use; it does heighten one's interest in how it became "conservative." After all, when Milton Friedman called for the legalization, with no public health inspections, of prostitution on free-market principles, suggesting that if one was infected with a venereal disease from a prostitute one could engage in a tort suit, a violation of contract, he could be called many things but not a conservative.

The traditionalist conservatives often stood on the six canons delineated by Russell Kirk. One can understand why this type of conservatism believed it was perhaps permanently a "remnant," a voice in the wilderness. The first canon, a "belief in a transcendent order, or a body of natural law, which rules society as well as conscience," is not limited to conservatives. In fact, it was at the core of the African American civil rights revolution. The canon affirming "the proliferating variety and mystery of human existence" seems to allow for adherence by romantics, bohemians, and hippies. The fourth, which links freedom and property and which opposes leveling, is shared by virtually all liberals as long as there is a caveat about hugely disproportionate ownership of property having the capacity to threaten liberty. The fifth, which mistrusts abstract design and seeks checks on "man's anarchic impulse," and the sixth, which calls for prudent, not precipitous, change, wouldn't be difficult for most nonconservatives to affirm. It is the third canon that undermines traditionalist conservatism and renders it politically unacceptable:

the notion that "civilized society requires orders and classes." Kirk does juxtapose this Burkean view with Marx's classless utopia, but almost all those who follow Kirk include the redistributionist welfare state as equally dangerous. Indeed, Kirk allows for a limited franchise: "In good government, the object of voting is not to enable every man to express his ego, but to represent his interests, whether or not he casts his vote personally or directly."[47] So, in a very real sense, the Burkean conservatism of Russell Kirk, as well as that of so many other traditionalists, for example, Richard Weaver, Eric Voegelin, and Leo Strauss, was incapable of becoming politically serious in an egalitarian and free society. In that sense, Louis Hartz was correct in marginalizing conservatism from the liberal tradition.

But, nevertheless, there were recognitions of the ways in which conservatism could bridge to liberalism and vice versa. Kirk stated that "Burke was liberal because he was conservative," noting that "conservatism never is more admirable than when it accepts changes that it disapproves, with good grace, for the sake of general conciliation; and the impetuous Burke, of all men, did most to establish that principle."[48] One might ask why such wisdom was inapplicable to the New Deal. It wasn't only Peter Viereck who made such a case. The historian Clinton Rossiter, in *Conservatism in America*, according to George Nash, "chided such conservatives as Kirk, Richard Weaver, and Anthony Harrigan for their profound, and in his view intemperate, hostility to liberalism."[49]

Finally, fusionist conservatism could not flourish on either its libertarian or traditionalist arguments, however insightful both could be about the contradictory realities of modern, industrial society. Nor could it bridge its own contradictions with an anticommunism already integral to a bipartisan policy dominated by the Democrats. It positioned itself for challenging the liberal consensus, which ran from the New Deal through the Great Society, by discovering a populist appeal, neither libertarian nor traditionalist, which began with an aggressive, unilateralist, and Manichean kind of anticommunism and which then tapped into frustrations and resentments generated by the social movements of the 1960s—civil rights and black power, the Vietnam War, the New Left student movement, the counterculture, rising crime rates, feminism, gay rights, environmentalism.

The right-wing populism that fueled McCarthyism, a politics of resentment and envy, a phenomenon skeptical liberals like the historian Richard Hofstadter called status politics, was the beginning of a turn among conservatives that would lead to political success. McCarthy fed at the trough of nativism, although he never indulged in either anti-Semitism or racism. But he was strikingly successful in using as his ongoing foil the cosmopolitan, the urbane, sophisticated liberal—Adlai (or is it Alger?) Stevenson, Dean Acheson, mocked for his Connecticut Anglicanism, his "phony British accent," being born with a silver spoon in his mouth. McCarthy was on to something that resonated with voters having difficulty making sense of the Cold War. How was it that the most powerful nation in the world—economically and militarily—could not prevent the Communists from seizing Eastern and Central Europe and China, and from threatening more gains? McCarthy could target that segment of the Democratic Party—indeed that part of the GOP—that represented educated, white, and affluent voters, future yuppies. His message was essentially nativist—Acheson and Stevenson were not red-blooded Americans—and homophobic—they were not really men.[50]

The limits of McCarthyism, of the Second Red Scare, was rooted in the extraordinary accomplishments of what most economists call the golden age of American capitalism, driven by the Keynesian-defined politics of growth that kept the Democrats in power through the late 1960s. McCarthy and his conservative supporters could not compete with the GI Bill, with the impact of Social Security and union wages and benefits, with rising home ownership, suburbanization, a car in every garage and a mall on every interstate highway. Americans were unlikely to invest in a good-time-Charley demagogue when the times were so hopeful. And the bipartisan foreign policy followed by Truman, Eisenhower, and Kennedy seemed, if not to dissolve all fears, to give a sense that the grown-ups were effectively in charge.

In brief, the construction of modern American conservatism during the 1950s and 1960s ran smack into the realities of liberal success, except among little old ladies in tennis sneakers, U.S.-out-of-the-UN isolationists, and cranky fusionists.[51]

The 1960s set the table for conservative success, in many ways building more on the populism of McCarthyism than on either the free-market libertarianism of Milton Friedman or the traditionalism of Russell Kirk. Lots of attention has been paid to both the Goldwater campaign of 1964 and the ominous primary showing of then-Democrat George Wallace.[52] The Goldwater campaign indicated the success of conservatives in building constituencies in the South and West, backed by corporate wealth able to compete with the Rockefeller internationalist wing of the party. But the Wallace votes in Democratic primaries in Wisconsin, Indiana, and Maryland were more telling. Yes, Goldwater's campaign was an indication of the marked shift of white Southerners from the Democratic Party to the Republican Party, driven by resentment at the former's support of the civil rights revolution. But Wallace was marking the birth of what would later be called Reagan Democrats—Northern, immigrant-stock, "blue-collar ethnics"—a more significant attrition of Democratic Party strength. Such voters in smokestack regions suffering from the beginnings of deindustrialization, prone to white backlash, fearful of the erosion of their unions' leverage, began to turn to those offering them solidarity. Paradoxically, the quite cosmopolitan, urbane William F. Buckley Jr. was able to tap into this rising resentment in his landmark campaign for the New York City mayoralty of 1965, when he won a surprising 13 percent of the vote as a candidate on the Conservative Party ticket against John Lindsay and Abe Beame.[53] The riots, on campuses and in black urban neighborhoods, were building a constituency for a right-wing populism.

It is here that the McCarthyite assault on liberals as wimpy cosmopolitans began to morph into Wallace's legions and, later, Nixon's great silent majority. Indeed, those of the New Left mounted their own campaigns to delegitimate the corporate liberals, the best and the brightest, the Clark Kerrs and Robert McNamaras, in the name of participatory democracy and, unfortunately, later a utopian and Third Worldist revolutionary communism.

What does any of the above have to do with the question of a legitimate conservatism? Certainly it would be difficult to define the Alabama bantamweight governor as a conservative, as, to their credit, many conservatives refused to do.[54] Indeed, Buckley had gone to incredible and impressive lengths to marginalize the right-wing kooks, the John Birchers, within the conservative movement. But it *was* now a movement; the Goldwater campaign relied on the organizational structures of both Birchers and Wallaceites to reach voters.[55] Libertarians may have opposed Social Security and the progressive income tax, traditionalists may have blanched at the violations of states' rights, but the rising constituencies of the Republican Party, especially its now-dominant conservative base, was a counterattack on the movements of the 1960s. When Ronald Reagan ran his successful campaign for governor of California in 1966, he attacked the black rioters in Watts and the free speech movement and Vietnam Day student activists at Berkeley.[56]

It is at this point that another moment occurred that offered the possibilities of a genuine conservatism, what might be called a skeptical, tempered liberalism, comparable to that which I have identified in the postwar decade with Arendt, Niebuhr, and Kennan, as well as with, for the most part, the New York intellectuals associated with *Partisan Review*, *Commentary*, and the Congress of Cultural Freedom. It is, of course, the emergence of the neoconservatives in response to what they perceived as the disruptive and threatening challenges to authority associated with the 1960s. Wallace may have provided the troops, but the neocons offered, for the first time, a substantial intellectual heft to conservatism.

I consider the emergence of neoconservatism as both a promise and a tragedy in American intellectual life. This movement of ex-liberals and ex-radicals in many ways promised to fulfill the hopes of those like Lionel Trilling—himself sometimes described as a neocon—for a compelling conservative tradition to challenge the complacencies of a dominant liberalism.[57] During the 1950s there was some complacency among what was called the consensus school of historians about the liberal essence of the American experience. Some called it a celebration. But the most astute and able of those historians, Richard Hofstadter and Louis Hartz, were distinctly uneasy with the absence of a deeply rooted conservative intellectual tradition. They worried about American parochialism, about how the United States would be able to engage effectively with an increasingly global environment without having the experience of political and philosophical differences.[58]

In Hofstadter's case, this discomfort rested on a response to the traumas of totalitarianism, Holocaust, and total war similar to that of Arendt. But whereas Arendt's conservative sensibility was framed by a deep identification with republicanism, by a fierce belief that the only life was as citizen in the public sphere, Hofstadter tended to fear anything that hinted at mass movements. Much of the body of his work subjected abolitionists, progressives, and what he called pseudo-conservatives to psychological analysis. He worried about the paranoid style left and right, the anti-intellectualism left and right. Only the New Deal seemed to escape his iconoclastic jabs, and even there it was FDR's style rather than its Popular Front populism that attracted him. As such, Hofstadter embodied all of the qualities many observers ascribe to the skeptical, conservative liberalism of the postwar era: "irony, ambiguity, paradox, complexity."[59]

These were exactly the qualities eschewed by both New Left and New Right during the 1960s. Each sought commitment, ideological purity, clear-cut choices, authenticity.[60] Consider the similarities—and, of course, the sharp differences—between the Democratic and Republican conventions of 1964—the moral purity of the Mississippi Freedom Democrats refusing the deal offered by LBJ and the scorn directed at those liberals—didn't it become a dirty word within the movement?—and the venom tossed at Nelson Rockefeller by the Goldwaterites—didn't liberal become a dirty word there as well? In both cases a politics of ultimate ends denied legitimacy to a politics of responsibility, that is, winning an election. "In your heart you know he's right" seemed to me to parallel the cult of authenticity that so pervaded both the New Left and the counterculture.

Those who became the neoconservatives reserved most of their criticisms for those on the left, but it is clear that they also were discomforted by the intolerance within the Goldwaterite movement, not to speak of its racist shadings. It is in that sense that the civil rights revolution, climaxed by the passage of the Civil Rights Act of 1964 and the Voting Rights Act of 1965, liberated them and, eventually, all conservatives. To their credit, virtually all those identified as neocons supported the civil rights revolution through the mid-1960s. But the shifts in the post–civil rights period—the rise of black power, the romanticizing of ghetto riots, affirmative action, busing, uncritical calls for expansions of welfare—that sparked much of the shift from a skeptical liberalism to neoconservatism.

In 1965, at an early stage when the term neoconservative did not yet exist, Irving Kristol and Daniel Bell inaugurated the policy journal *Public Interest* to mark their concerns as "realistic meliorists, skeptical of government programs that ignored history and experience in favor of then-fashionable left-wing ideas spawned by the academy. . . . One forgets just how frothy this climate was. The centerpiece of the War on Poverty was the sociological fantasy that if one gave political power to the poor, by sponsoring 'community action,' they would lift themselves out of poverty at the expense of the rich and the powerful."[61] Kristol, clearly more conservative than Bell, Seymour Martin Lipset, or Nathan Glazer, was nevertheless expressing a concern among self-defined liberal intellectual–cum–social scientists that something was seriously wrong with Johnson's Great Society.

The responses to Daniel Patrick Moynihan's *The Crisis of the Negro Family* only compounded the concern.[62] And what followed included the New York City teachers' strike against community control, the Columbia SDS building takeovers, and a host of other challenges to authority that brought neoconservatism to the fore. In the initial years of the *Public Interest*, specifically limited to domestic policy issues, one finds a sober, cautious, ironic voice, not at all strident or righteous, open to a range of thinkers from James Q. Wilson to Robert Solow. The temperament, if not the ideology, of the journal was conservative, in the sense that it was wary of abstractions, focused on empirical analysis, and skeptical about transformative claims. Perhaps the most emblematical voice was that of Nathan Glazer, whose "The Limits of Social Policy" established a most Burkean guideline, the law of unintended consequences, the notion that, presumably, liberal and radical good intentions were insufficient to insure beneficial outcomes. In many ways, Glazer's warning was at the heart of the neoconservative sensibility, a sobered liberalism, still committed to a defense of governmental interventions in the spirit of the New Deal—regulatory, fiscal, safety net, even planning—but increasingly wary of the liberal reforms associated with the Great Society, especially the War on Poverty and affirmative action.[63]

What happened to this promising development? How did the beginnings of a conservatism accepting of a mixed economy, supportive of racial equality, and loyal to an alliance of liberals and organized labor, transform itself into a neoconservatism that joined the Reagan Revolution of the 1980s and became identified with an ideologically combative foreign policy asserting the thoroughly anticonservative call for a unilateral war to make an entire region of the world safe for democracy? Certainly there is a change of players, a generational shift that plays some role. But the continuities are also clear and not only those within families, for example, Irving and William Kristol.

Some would argue that neoconservatives like the elder Kristol, along with his ally Norman Podhoretz, thrived on a Trotskyist take-no-prisoners political culture that now saw the "new class" of liberal and radical academics and journalists as their enemies. The early neocons certainly were incensed with what they saw as the decadent cultural challenges of the 1960s; as such, they were important and powerful initiators of what has come to be called the "culture wars." This included old ex-leftists who had always been culturally conservative and Straussians like Allan Bloom who valued virtue over freedom. This dimension of neoconservatism has perhaps most visibly been personified by William Bennett, called by some a "virtucrat." But given the essentially modernist bent of most neoconservatives, their cultural sophistication, their very Europeanness, their role in the culture wars has always been limited by their discomfort with their more powerful religious right allies, the evangelicals and fundamentalists much more unequivocally hostile to "secular humanism."[64]

The neoconservatives also have been associated with the post–civil rights criticisms of affirmative action and other race-focused remedies to de facto segregation. In this instance, the neoconservatives have indeed played a significant role in legitimating opposition to the positions held by most African American intellectuals and activists. They have been able to effectively rebut the charge that they are motivated by racism. To a person, they had supported civil rights, equal opportunity before the law. Their very criticisms rested on this rupture in race policy. Nathan Glazer has even shifted away from his initial argument about reverse discrimination to reluctantly support affirmative action because of what he perceives as the devastating consequences regarding black college enrollment if it were eliminated.[65]

But the neoconservative policies regarding race and racism have lacked staying power. The most severe and telling burden the fusionist conservatives carried during the 1950s and 1960s was their opposition to the civil rights revolution. When one reads, for example, the *National Review* in those decades, one is overwhelmed by the assumptions of racial superiority that are laced through most pieces dealing not only with civil rights in the United States but also with independence struggles in the Third World. Certainly there was a genuine belief in states' rights and a conservative wariness of the demands for the elimination of legal segregation. But there was also a pervasive colonialist paternalism, an often smug response to the "wogs" of the world, not the least of which led to support for Ian Smith in Rhodesia and for apartheid in South Africa.[66]

The civil rights revolution liberated such conservatives from the burden of their own bigotries. Barry Goldwater, of course, embodied the early form of the contradiction—a man with generous responses to racial injustice in his personal and local life who could not but recognize that so much of the support he was gathering in the South and in some Northern backlash pockets was driven by racial resentments.[67] As late as 1980, Ronald Reagan, another conservative leader with no apparent racial animus, began his campaign in Philadelphia, Mississippi, the site of the murders of Goodman, Chaney, and Schwerner during Freedom Summer, a choice most commentators understood as a wink at Southern bigots.[68] But, nevertheless, the success of the civil rights movement in eliminating de jure segregation liberated conservatives to claim that their opposition to a race-based affirmative action was based on their unearned belief in equal opportunity. Even the moderate and opportunistic George H. W. Bush, as a Houston Republican Congressman, had voted against the Civil Rights Act of 1964.[69]

There have been a variety of factors that have subverted the initial promise of neoconservatism, not the least of which is simply responding to the seduction of Ronald Reagan, that is, to the coming to power of conservatives. But I would argue that domestic policies were always the caboose; foreign policy was always and ever the engine driving neoconservatives away from their beginnings as a fulfillment of Lionel Trilling's hopes for a genuine, that is, a traditionalist, cautious, sober conservatism.

The central thrust of neoconservatism, once its initial promise of a sobered liberalism sensitive to the law of unintended consequences was marginalized, became its assertion of the hegemonic destiny of the United States, its claim to be, as Ben Wattenberg so unabashedly put it, the "universal nation."[70] Ironically, it has been this hubristic claim that has most driven neoconservatives away from any legitimate claim to a traditionalist conservatism, including gross violations of its initial mantra—the law of unintended consequences.

The villain in the neoconservative narrative is what they call "the new class," what George Will refers to as "the chattering classes."[71] They are presumably those who initially rallied to the "new politics" associated with the McGovern campaign of 1972 and all of the left-liberal and new-leftist baggage the neocons associated with those elements. Many commentators have noted the irony that those castigating a new class seem to represent one of its important wings. If there is a difference over time, it would be that the neocons' nemesis was placed both in the elite institutions of higher education and within the mainstream media (the networks, the weeklies); the neocons have succeeded in inspiring their own institutional apparatus, for instance, foundations, journals like the *Weekly Standard*, media like the Fox News network, syndicated columns by writers such as Charles Krauthammer and David Brooks. In some instances they share influence with other conservative subgroups—paleoconservatives, religious conservatives, libertarian conservatives.

What seems to power this venom—shared by other conservatives—is the notion that the new class—the liberals—are the "hate America," "blame America" crowd. So the neoconservatives have, from the start, been responding to those who they blame for the defeat of the United States in Indochina. They rallied around the hawkish candidacy of Henry "Scoop" Jackson, the senator from Boeing, Washington, a liberal Democrat close to President Kennedy, who was alienated from the more dovish direction the party seemed to be taking in the early 1970s. A number of neoconservatives, most particularly Richard Perle but also the important former leftist Social Democrats USA faction, worked in Jackson's office and were discouraged by his inability to become his party's nominee for president.[72] Most of these neoconservative staffers for Jackson would soon reject the Democratic Party as hopelessly dominated by the new class and turn toward the hawkish Ronald Reagan and the Republican Party by 1980. During the 1970s, they were central to the efforts to combat what they perceived as "Vietnam syndrome," the unwillingness of the United States to risk the loss of significant GI lives for national security ends. As such, they were in the forefront in challenging intelligence reports —such as the well-known Team B report—that did not agree with their belief that the Soviet Union was aggressively marching forward in military spending and Third World interventions.[73]

The neoconservatives sought a reassertion of American power, including increased military spending, a greater nuclear arsenal, the implementation of what came to be called Star Wars, missile defense, and aggressive intelligence operations in the Third World. Indeed neoconservatives like Perle were aghast at Reagan's gestures toward the elimination of all nuclear weapons with Gorbachev at Reykjavik in 1987.[74] When the Soviet Union collapsed and the Cold War ended, the neoconservatives were the most forceful group asserting the appropriateness of American global hegemony and calling for military action, particularly against Saddam Hussein in Iraq. Without going into the contemporary controversies concerning the U.S. invasion and occupation of Iraq, it is abundantly clear that neoconservatives have been appropriately perceived as the driving force behind notions of unilateralism, preemptive war, contempt for the United Nations, resistance to accepting international treaty obligations, and the claim that the overthrow of the dictator Saddam Hussein would contribute to the democratization of the Middle East. If there is any case of the law of unintended consequences greater than this most egregious foreign-policy disaster, this author cannot think of one.[75]

The tragedy, beyond issues of foreign policy not central to the argument of this essay, is the collapse of the neoconservative promise to become a genuinely conservative voice, a conservative presence within American political culture. The pull of a highly ideological, militant foreign policy, an aggressive nationalism, the delusion of a benevolent imperialism—all subverted the initially tempered, sober, ironic contributions one could still discover in neoconservatism's domestic organ, the *Public Interest*. But that accomplishment, mostly the responsibility of the older generation of neoconservatives—Lipset, Bell, Moynihan, Glazer—is essentially gone or, more hopefully, incorporated into mainstream liberal social science and criticism. But neoconservatism has been sadly reduced to blaming the hapless George W. Bush for failing to implement the neoconservative fantasies about imposing democracy in conquered nations.

Over the past half century in foreign policy, an actual conservatism continues to function as a voice for caution: caution about messianic crusades, caution about the abstractions of universal rights, caution about military solutions to complex problems, caution about not paying attention to the facts on the ground, to the role of nationalism and local histories in understanding other peoples. During the Vietnam War era, such cautions came from Hans Morgenthau, who was a close friend of Hannah Arendt, George Kennan, Walter Lippmann, J. William Fulbright, and Eugene McCarthy. From my perspective, all of these important voices were shaped by essentially conservative themes about realism, about the arrogance of power, and about the imperial presidency. Our political culture seems unable to recognize that our binary labeling system often obscures more than it illuminates about the rationales of such critics. But in all of the above cases, it was an awareness of the risks of hubris, a humility before the tasks of national security in a globalized and at times threatening environment, which led these quite different figures to question the arguments that led the United States to Americanize the war in Vietnam and to remain there for more than eight years.[76]

All of this leads back to the question of definitions and, more significantly, the consequences of definitions. Historian Jennifer Burns offers one approach in her astute reconsideration of George Nash's most influential *The Conservative Intellectual Movement in America since 1945*. Burns suggests that Nash underplayed the significance of anticommunism in the fusionism of the Buckleyite conservatives, especially its "populist emphasis" and its focus on "a well defined enemy."[77] She notes Nash's resistance to clear-cut definition, his promotion of self-definition of conservatism à la fusionism, and his seeming obliviousness to historical and materialist considerations, from racism to the New Deal, and concludes that "conservative ideas have made little headway in universities, the traditional bastion of intellectuals." Burns's observations, despite a harsh criticism of what she calls the pluralist responses to conservatism, that is, the tendency of Hofstadter, Bell, et al. to reduce *National Review*–type conservatism to pathology, to status anxiety, suggest important directions for those seeking to build on Nash's pioneering work.[78]

For one, the emphasis on an enemy suggests that Nash's intellectualist approach plays down the ways in which the groups that identify as parts of a conservative movement—libertarians, traditionalists, neoconservatives, cultural or religious conservatives—share a common enemy. Here is where the significance of McCarthyism and the tragedy of neoconservatism come together to point to the centrality of that common enemy whose name is liberalism. The McCarthyites focused on the Soviet Communist threat; the neoconservatives shared that concern but have demonstrated the ability to shift focus to what many of them call "Islamo-fascism." The Cold War and the Global War on Terror both externalize what is essentially perceived as an internal threat from those on the other side of the barricades within the culture war. From sneering references to Dean Acheson's "phony British accent" to the same regarding John Kerry's Frenchness, the conservative movement—what calls itself, like the New Left, "the movement"—is fundamentally opposed to the array of cultural formations associated with secular humanism, pragmatism, postmodernism, social gospel Christianity, cultural relativism, multiculturalism, and what it calls identity politics.[79]

I want to argue that this movement makes it difficult for other dimensions of conservatism, traditionalist or libertarian, to sustain any intellectual consistency. I have not spent much time addressing the libertarian side. Indeed, I have great respect for its most accomplished practitioners—Hayek, Von Mises, Friedman. The work of organizations like the Cato Institute and the journalistic acumen of columnists like Cathy Young offer a thoughtful critique of state interventions that threaten market efficiencies and personal liberties. I am glad that the libertarians exist. However, I do not consider them to be conservatives in any meaningful sense, nor do I see how they offer a vision of a good society that can come to grips with the overwhelming realities of interdependence, from global warming to the threat of nuclear proliferation to the dangerous powers of multinational corporations.

The traditionalist, or Burkean, conservatives offer more to our polity and culture. As Peter Clecak has argued, "The conservative vision . . . is a corrective to the critical spirit of modern radicalism, though evidently not a replacement. It serves also as a ballast to the facile optimism of so much of the prevailing liberal rhetoric."[80] Indeed, Clecak suggests that "the conservative idea of balance informs all ecological visions."[81] These conservative traits, which Clecak calls "temperamental conservatism," are essential to all ideological formations.[82] In this sense, Lionel Trilling's call for a conservatism that keeps liberals honest remains relevant despite the apparent triumph of what passes for conservatism over the past half century.

The columnist and commentator George Will, at his best, has been one of the most influential voices for such a conservatism. In his impressive *Statecraft as Soulcraft: What Government Does*, Will called for an Augustinian project that involved "a core consensus of the Western political tradition as first defined by Aristotle, and as added to by Burke and others."[83] Will declared: "It is time to come up from individualism. We have had quite enough Leatherstocking Tales, thank you. We need a literature of cheerful sociability, novels of social 'thickness' that make society seem a complex but friendly place where social relationships facilitate rather than frustrate individualism and 'self-realization.' And we need a public philosophy that can rectify the current imbalance between the political order's meticulous concern for material well-being and its fastidious withdrawal from a concern for the inner lives and moral character of citizens."[84] Will recognized that "when conservatives begin regarding the market less as an expedient than as an ultimate value, or the ultimate arbiter of all values, their conservatism degenerates into the least conservative political impulse, which is populism."[85] He saw the central problem in this question: "How do you educate a comfortable, complacent society to do what is complicated, difficult, dangerous if done wrong and necessary only in the long run?"[86] Unfortunately, Will has fallen short of measuring up to such standards as a media pundit, too often succumbing to partisanship, too often becoming consumed by his loyalties and by his targets. Will's most egregious violations include his praising of Ronald Reagan's performance in his 1980 debate with Jimmy Carter without revealing that he had coached the California Republican in his preparations. His polemical arguments that money is speech with regard to campaign finance reform and that there is insufficient scientific evidence regarding global warming seem far from the kind of Burkean conservatism with which he most often identifies.[87]

An equally thought-provoking figure is the contentious historian Eugene V. Genovese, a giant among students of slavery, race, and the South, for many years an active and influential Marxist thinker, and over the past several decades someone who has sought to restore to moral and intellectual prominence the ideas and legacy of white Southerners, antebellum and postbellum. Genovese, at his best, offers a respectful approach to figures like John Randolph of Roanoke and John C. Calhoun, whom he associates with "transatlantic traditionalism" in its belief in a transcendent order, its acceptance of social stratification and hierarchy, and its suspicion of all efforts to level individuals and communities to a classless or radically egalitarian order.[88] Genovese recognizes the flaws of such a tradition, particularly its racism and antidemocratic qualities and, like Will, has nothing but scorn for the libertarian free-marketeers. But he suggests that there is much to learn from more modern Southern conservatives such as Richard Weaver and M. E. Bradford.[89]

But there seems to be little of either an intellectual or a social movement associated with either Will's or Genovese's call for a traditional conservatism. We instead face the prospects for the continuation of a conservatism consistent with the populist pugnacity of McCarthyism as transmuted through George Wallace and as presently articulated by Bill O'Reilly, Ann Coulter, Rush Limbaugh, Sean Hannity, and the take-no-prisoners electoral strategies of Karl Rove and the ghost of Lee Atwater.

And so long as forms of radicalism—Marxist, postmodern, identity politics, antiglobalization—remain oblivious to the insights of the best of conservative thinking, so long as liberalism avoids coming to grips with those moments within its own history which have been deeply and affirmatively colored by a conservative strain, for that long we will be frustrated in combating a populist conservatism that has had great success in tapping in to the unease of many Americans struggling to deal with a contradictory and sometimes frightening environment.

In the eighteenth century, alongside of the Enlightenment Founders of the American Republic, there were more numerous village preachers, mostly Calvinist, increasingly evangelical, caught up in the First Great Awakening, who told their congregants that they were sinners and that their sinful behavior was the cause of British oppression directed toward them. These pastors, in effect, argued that those filling their pews were *equally* sinners and, therefore, equal. This Calvinist egalitarianism, deeply democratic, thoroughly sober about the frailties of human beings, suggests something of the "crooked paths" perhaps required to move forward on a conversation between radical, liberal, and conservative traditions.[90]

It would be perhaps utopian to call for a blending of the best of these ideologies. Indeed, I would frame the issue by suggesting a conservative social or political movement may be a contradiction in terms; Burkean axioms, inherently elitist, cannot drive a movement with aspirations to electoral power. At best, one can hope for what Trilling sought: an intellectually vibrant conservatism, a voice within the life of the mind.

The social and political movements claiming to be conservative would be better defined as more broadly right-wing and containing contradictory elements of populism, Christian evangelical fundamentalism, libertarianism, and a never-to-be-underestimated defense of the corporation. None of these are consistent with traditionalism referencing Edmund Burke; most indeed subvert such a sober and skeptical approach.

As such, we would be well served by the infusion of the best *within* each tradition *into* each tradition: a conservatism cognizant of First Amendment protections, social solidarity, and global stewardship; a liberalism sensitive to the law of unintended consequences, aware of the limitations of possessive individualism; a radicalism sobered by the consequences of communist totalitarianism and willing to integrate some notion of evil not reducible to social forces within its vision of the good society. Within that set of models, we all could do worse than to return to the kinds of questions and the beginnings of answers brought forth by skeptical liberal thinkers like Hannah Arendt and Reinhold Niebuhr and that most remarkable liberal conservative Peter Viereck.

POSTSCRIPT

As We Approach the Future

I write in the immediate aftermath of the election of Barack Obama as president of the United States. The 2008 election reinforces my sense that there is a rising tide against American conservatism or, more accurately, against the Bush administration and its policies and performance. As such, it remains essential to keep in mind both the distinction between the conservative movement and the Republican Party and the differences among the various and often confusing claims on conservatism. It remains clear, however, that what we are experiencing seems more a crisis in conservatism than a resurgence of liberalism, more a collapse of the Republican Party than an embrace of the Democrats, despite some survey and electoral data suggesting a possible sea change, especially among young voters. The shelves are packed with books by disillusioned conservatives who feel betrayed by the Bush administration and by liberals hopeful of resurrecting the intellectual, moral, and political power of their own faith.[1]

For one, most conservatives, including the religious right, the paleo- or isolationist wing, and the neocons, have been trying desperately to separate themselves from George W. Bush. One hears, often, the lament that Bush betrayed conservatives, that he never really was a conservative, that he was a tax-and-spend big-government chief executive, that he lined up with the country club Republicans on the immigration issue, that he was seduced by nefarious neocons to violate traditional conservative principles in seeking war in Iraq, that he embraced liberal solutions in education and health care that were budget busters. All that seems left to praise are his court appointments, which are indeed quite a legacy from the point of view of right-wingers.

What one hears outside of conservative circles is that this has been the worst president, the worst administration in American history or, at least, in the twentieth century, that it has done more damage to the national interest—Iraq, the "war on terror," environmental neglect and abuse, corruption, cronyism, erosions of fundamental liberties, abuses of power, deepening gaps between the rich and everyone else.

All of the above will be debated for decades. What it will suggest about American conservatism will be determined more by what follows from the two terms of the Bush administration, not only in the narrow political sense, but perhaps more significantly in the sense of our national discourse. To return to the lament of Lionel Trilling, voiced more than a half century ago, does our political culture need a conservative voice, a conservative tradition? Are we diminished by the absence of ballast, a sobering perspective to temper our historical tendencies toward an ahistorical utopianism, an intolerant moralism, and a can-do spirit whose sunniness obscures an abiding immaturity?

One way to approach this issue is to ask what is rarely asked, either during the 2008 campaign or elsewhere: What does it mean to call proposals for huge tax cuts for the most privileged "conservative"? Why do we accept calls for the most draconian responses to undocumented immigrants "conservative"? Does it make sense to assume that opposition to stem cell research or abortion or affirmative action or gun control or environmental protection in terms of global warming is "conservative"? Why define Protestant fundamentalism as "conservative"? Yes, self-described conservatives take such positions, but in what ways are these stances consistent with conservative tradition and values? In the presidential campaign it has been striking to me that the discussions of whether John McCain is conservative rarely get past the level of assertion and denial. It is apparent that his nomination and candidacy for the presidency have exacerbated the fissures between the conservative movement and the Republican Party. Perhaps, if we are so fortunate, the nation will come out of this extraordinary campaign prepared for a conversation about what we mean by American conservatism.

Much within this volume suggests that we still suffer from the absence of a traditionalist, Burkean conservatism, that what operates in its name—libertarianism, big-business selfishness, politicized fundamentalism, neoconservatism—does not speak to, indeed, characteristically contradicts and subverts, conservative values. I have argued that whatever has emerged to articulate conservatism has come in liberal guise, a kind of conservative liberalism or liberal conservatism. Louis Hartz was certainly right to suggest that we have only a liberal tradition, but he did not sufficiently recognize the tensions, the conversation within that tradition that began with responses to the American and French revolutions of the eighteenth century. Paine and Burke, Locke and Hobbes, Emerson and Hawthorne all engaged in fundamental questions about human nature and history, about institutions and culture, about the individual and the community. Perhaps we need to consider how conservative truths can inform a revitalized liberalism or even a revived and finally indigenous radicalism.

I hope that such a revitalization of conservatism informs our foreign policy as we seek to repair the damages done to our reputation and standing in the world. One hears such voices, left to right, from such critics as Zbigniew Brzezinski, James Baker, and, especially, the Boston University military historian Andrew Bacevich, all of whom apply conservative principles in their often-scathing critiques of unilateralism, preemptive war, and utopian quests to Americanize the world.[2]

The future of our nation and of the world requires the insights of our great intellectual traditions. Conservatism forces all of us to consider the unintended consequences of radical change, especially the sad historical record of well-meaning revolutionaries descending to totalitarian nightmare. There are, after all, risks to big government. Liberalism is in need of infusions of many fresh ideas, but more than anything it needs to get its mojo back. Since the stagflation of the 1970s ended the quarter-century-long Keynesian run of prosperity for welfare states, liberals have lost faith in their own remedies and have too often been consumed with a politics more symbolic than substantive. Affirmative action, for example, remains worth defending, but does anyone really think that it is decisive in the emergence of a black middle class or, more critically, that it has any bearing on the deep and disgraceful state of that one-third of African Americans mired in hypersegregation, high unemployment, family dysfunction, and schooling failures?

Lastly, my own tradition, that of radicalism, seems most in need of revival. Presently it seems adrift, moored in hothouse academic environments that seem to reinforce its every pathological tendency, more a negative critique (for instance, antiglobalization) than any positive vision of the good society. Perhaps it is time for radicals, those within the Marxist tradition, to imagine the good society outside of expectations of the withering away of the state or the absolute elimination of capitalism. What is the best we can achieve, in terms of our liberties, our participation in an egalitarian, democratic order, our sense of ecological balance, our capacity to find meaning and beauty in our lives? I believe, utterly, that radicals need to listen to liberal and conservative truths to even begin to get there. Our Founders understood the centrality of conversation, dialogue, argument; that's why they provided all of us with the institutional protections of the First Amendment and a glorious history that allowed the people to reject leaders and see them replaced by new ones, without violence, without coups, without military dictators. If there is anything that worries me in today's environment, it is the ideologizing—mostly within what claim to be conservative circles—that denies legitimacy to other points of view. That is the most dangerous trend that we face, and American conservatives need to join with liberals and radicals in challenging it and in fashioning an ideologically, philosophically diverse culture.

To do that we need to resist the powerful pressures to extend the "war on terror" to other governments, most particularly Iran. There are powerful forces, mostly but not exclusively within the Republican Party, driven by a combination of neoconservative zealotry, imperial hubris, anachronistic fixations on Middle Eastern oil, and misplaced loyalties to Israel, that see the solution to Iraq in attacks on its Shi'a Persian neighbor. This would be absolutely disastrous insofar as it would pose a fundamental threat to our already fragile civil liberties and would deepen and broaden the hostility and rage directed against the United States by much of the world, especially that shaped by Islam and Arab culture.

What we need is a strong dose of the best of conservatism, a mature caution about reckless adventures. First we need our leaders to treat us like adults and tell us just how bad things are. For example, the situation in Iraq is much worse than what we faced in Indochina, where the consequences of our departure were negligible. This is a region of the world where there are significant risks of religious civil war, ethnic cleansing, genocidal rages, and suicidal urges to harm the United States in particular and the West in general. It is going to take a long time for the United States to reestablish any moral standing first among our potential allies and then with those who have reasons to respond to us with suspicion. This will require great patience; it takes time to see the effects of soft power. There will be bad moments, even horrific ones, including more terrorist attacks within our shores. Of course we will need to respond firmly and ferociously to any such attacks. But we will also have to begin to address longer-term problems, from our dependence on Middle Eastern oil and its related support for corrupt and dictatorial sheikdoms and military dictatorships to our role in helping to finally establish a Palestinian state capable of living in peace and security with Israel. How can we support forces that can deliver social services to the Arab masses without the ideological baggage of Hamas or Hezbollah? How can we assist the Middle East to use its oil riches to build the human capital, the schools, the decent housing, the sense of hopefulness that presently seem so out of reach in Cairo and Gaza and Baghdad? And how can we help our own people recognize that it is better to encourage the learning of Arabic than to call people "hajjis" or, worse, "sand niggers"?

If we are fortunate, we may be at that point in history when we can reconcile the sobriety of conservatism with the hopes of liberalism and radicalism. To do this we might consider that tradition, liberty, democracy, and justice must always exist in creative tension, that in the conversation between serious voices, as Jefferson told us at our national beginnings—between our roots and our love of the road, between our families and our selves, between our experience and our sense of adventure, between our sense of loyalty and our individual conscience, between our patriotism and our humanity, between our memories and our dreams—there is neither resolution nor closure but only creative and delirious tension.

Our new president seems to be a serious and disciplined thinker who may be the kind of liberal who will pay attention to the cautions of conservatives and yet be inspired by the mission of the radical community organizer. Obama is fundamentally a pragmatist committed to what works. Let us hope that he can move us forward in coming to grips with the serious crises desperately in need of the best of our intellectual and moral traditions.

Notes

PREFACE

1. Lage, "Interview with Lawrence W. Levine," 802.
2. Lyons, *New Left, New Right and the Legacy of the Sixties.*

INTRODUCTION

1. Hartz, *Liberal Tradition in America*, 50–66.
2. Williams, *Tragedy of American Diplomacy*; Williams, *Contours of American History*; Williams, *Great Evasion: An Essay on the Contemporary Relevance of Karl Marx and on the Wisdom of Admitting the Heretic into the Dialogue about America's Future*, one of the most wonderfully subtitled polemics in modern memory; Susman, "Nature of American Conservatism,"57–74; Genovese, *Southern Tradition*; Weinstein, *Corporate Ideal in the Liberal State.*
3. Bell, *Cultural Contradictions of Capitalism.*
4. Rawls, *Theory of Justice.*
5. Freud, *Civilization and Its Discontents*, 59–195.
6. Heimert, *Religion and the American Mind*; Heimert, *Great Awakening.*
7. Freud, *Civilization and Its Discontents*, 90.
8. Moore, "Utopian Themes in Marx and Mao."
9. Rainwater and Yancey, *Moynihan Report and the Politics of Controversy.*
10. Hayek, *Road to Serfdom.*
11. Jacobs, *Death and Life of American Cities*; Goodman, *Growing Up Absurd*; Nove, *Economics of Feasible Socialism.*
12. Hodgson, *America in Our Time.*
13. Trilling, *Liberal Imagination*, 5.

14. Nash, *Conservative Intellectual Movement in America since 1945*, chs. 6 and 7; Hodgson, *World Turned Right Side Up*, chs. 3–5.
15. Williams, *Contours*, 343–89.
16. Nock, *Memoirs of a Superfluous Man*; Ortega y Gasset, *Revolt of the Masses*; and the inaugural issue of the *National Review*, November 11, 1955, 5.
17. Kazin, *Populist Persuasion*, ch. 7.
18. Nash, *Conservative Intellectual Movement*, 142–46, 275–76.
19. Phillips, *Emerging Republican Majority.*
20. Lyons, *People of This Generation.*
21. Trilling, *Liberal Imagination*, vii.
22. Steinfels, *Neoconservatives*, 19.
23. Clecak, *Crooked Paths*, 103–4.
24. Goodman, *Growing Up Absurd.*

CHAPTER 3

1. Lewis, *American Adam*; Marx, *Machine in the Garden*; Rourke, *American Humor.*
2. Rourke, *American Humor*; Rourke, *Roots of American Culture*, esp. the preface by Van Wyck Brooks, v–xii, and "The Roots of American Culture," 3–59; Rourke, *Trumpets of Jubilee*, esp. the chapter on P. T. Barnum," 276–319; Brooks, *Early Years*, esp. "The Wine of the Puritans," 1–60, and "America's Coming of Age," 79–158; Rosenberg and White, eds., *Mass Culture*; Susman, *Culture as History*, esp. "Introduction: Toward a History of the Culture of Abundance," xix–xxx, and "Culture Heroes: Ford, Barton, Ruth," 105–21. For a more recent and perceptive analysis, Pells, *Not Like Us*, esp. ch. 1.
3. Douglas, *Terrible Honesty*; Stansell, *American Moderns.*
4. Denning, *Cultural Front.*
5. Reisman, *Lonely Crowd*; Whyte, *Organization Man*; Mills, *White Collar.*
6. Schlesinger, *Vital Center.*
7. Mailer, *Cannibals and Christians.*
8. Herberg, *Protestant-Catholic-Jew.*
9. Bell, *End of Ideology*; Waxman, ed., *End of Ideology Debate.*
10. Larson, *Summer for the Gods*; Wilson, ed., *Darwinism and the American Intellectual.*
11. Wilensky and Lebeaux, *Industrial Society and Social Welfare*; Rockefeller Foundation, ed., *Modernization and Cultural Values*; Berger, *Homeless Mind*; Eisenstadt, *Modernization*; Kahl, *Modernization, Exploitation and Dependency in Latin America*; Rostow, *Stages of Economic Growth.*

12. Katznelson, *Desolation and Enlightenment*, 84–88.
13. H. Richard Niebuhr, *Christ and Culture*; Brown, ed., *Essential Reinhold Niebuhr.*
14. Katznelson, *Desolation.*
15. Rostow, *Stages.*
16. Stephanson, *Kennan and the Art of Foreign Policy*, 177–79, 200–1; Morgenthau, *Vietnam and the United States.*
17. All of the noted figures introduced an element of skepticism, a sense of limits to their critiques of U.S. policy in Vietnam. For example, see Fulbright, *Arrogance of Power.*
18. Van Eschen, *Satchmo Blows Up the World.*
19. Wolfe, *Purple Decades*, esp. "Those Radical Chic Evenings," and "Mau-Mauing the Flak-Catchers," 181–234, and "The Me Decade and the Third Great Awakening," 265–296; Brooks, *Bobos in Paradise.*
20. Beschloss, *Crisis Years* and *Mayday.*
21. Stephanson, *Kennan*, 106.
22. Ferguson, *Colossus.*
23. Phillips, *Emerging Republican Majority*; Dionne, *Why Americans Hate Politics*; Edsall and Edsall, *Chain Reaction.*
24. Baltzell, *Protestant Establishment.*
25. Noonan, *What I Saw at the Revolution*; Lyons, *New Left, New Right and the Legacy of the Sixties*, 143–52.

CHAPTER 4

1. Ruppert, *Crossing the Rubicon*; Klare, *Blood and Oil*; Chomsky, *Hegemony or Survival*; Halper and Clarke, *America Alone*; Daalder and Lindsay, *America Unbound*; Cherry, ed., *God's New Israel.*
2. Hanson, *Between War and Peace* and *Autumn of War*; Boot, *Savage Wars of Peace*; Mead, *Power, Terror, Peace, and War* and *Special Providence*; Morley, *Imperial State and Revolution*; Paterson, *Contesting Castro*; Bonner, *Waltzing with a Dictator*; Schlesinger and Kinzer, *Bitter Fruit*; Kinzer, *All the Shah's Men*; Borstelmann, *Apartheid's Reluctant Uncle.*
3. Tuveson, *Redeemer Nation*; Cherry, *God's New Israel*; Hayward, *Greatness*, 89; Morris, *Dutch*, 401; Kengor, *Crusader*, 59–64; Roberts, ed., *City upon a Hill*, 31–33. At Reagan's memorial service, Justice Sandra Day O'Connor read from John Winthrop's sermon, "We shall be as a city on a hill" in evoking Reagan's vision, in Edwards, ed., *Essential Ronald Reagan*, xii.
4. Wattenberg, *First Universal Nation.*
5. Marx, *Machine in the Garden*; Drinnon, *Facing West*; Horsman, *Race and Manifest Destiny*; Stephanson, *Manifest Destiny*; Onuf, *Jefferson's*

Empire; also see Warrior, "Canaanites, Cowboys, and Indians: Deliverance, Conquest, and Liberation Theology," in Alpert, ed., *Voices of the Religious Left*, 51–57.

6. Hammond, *Banks and Politics in America*; Remini, *Andrew Jackson and the Bank War* and *Andrew Jackson and His Indian Wars*; Wallace, *Long, Bitter Trail*; Kazin, *Populist Persuasion*.
7. Willis, *Islamist Challenge in Algeria*; Davis, *Last Two Years of Salvador Allende*; Herring, *America's Longest War*, ch. 2.
8. For an example linked to foreign policy, see Bennett, *Why We Fight*.
9. DeGrazia, *Irresistible Empire*; Cohen, *Consumers' Republic*; Leach, *Land of Desire*; Douglas, *Terrible Honesty*.
10. *Full Metal Jacket* (1987), directed by Stanley Kubrick, a Warner Brothers film, was based on Gustav Hasford's short story "The Short-Timers."
11. Horsman, *Race and Manifest Destiny*; Stephanson, *Manifest Destiny*.
12. Bird and Lifschultz, eds., *Hiroshima's Shadow*. For Bush defenders, see Kagan, *Of Paradise and Power*; Mann, *Rise of the Vulcans*; and Daalder, *America Unbound*.
13. Hardt and Negri, *Multitude*; Klein, *Fences and Windows*; Roy, *Ordinary Person's Guide to Empire*; Goodman, *Exception to the Rulers*. For a more nuanced critique, see Stiglitz, *Globalization and Its Discontents* and Mandle, *Globalization and the Poor*.
14. Burlingame, *Henry Ford*, 7; Karnow, *In Our Image*; Herbert, "From 'Gook' to 'Raghead'"; Swofford, *Jarhead*.
15. Patterson, *Ordeal of Integration*, 61.
16. Marcuse, *One-Dimensional Man* and *Essay on Liberation*.
17. Albert and Hahnel, *Looking Forward*.
18. Mead, *Power*; Hanson, *Between War and Peace*; Kagan, *Of Paradise and Power*; Mann, *Rise*; Halper, *America Alone*; Daalder, *America Unbound*.
19. Schlesinger, *Bitter Fruit*; Bonner, *Waltzing*; Paterson, *Contesting Castro*.
20. Friedman, *Lexus and the Olive Branch*; Barber, *Jihad and McWorld*.
21. Cooper, "General Casts War in Religious Terms"; Hertzke, *Freeing God's Children*.
22. Klare, *Blood and Oil*; and Posner, *Secrets of the Kingdom*.
23. Johnson, "America's Empire of Bases," and *Sorrows of Empire*; Bacevich, *New American Militarism*.
24. Mann, *Rise of the Vulcans*.
25. I would consider Richard Perle, often identified as a key figure among neoconservatives, to be as cynical as Cheney and Rumsfeld, and less foolish than Wolfowitz. Recall that the early neocons attacked Jimmy Carter's human rights position and were exemplified by Jeane Kirkpatrick's "Dictatorships and Double Standards," *Commentary*, November 1979, which argued that the United States should support

pro–United States right-wing authoritarian regimes. Ronald Reagan should be credited with introducing the utopian, "foolish" strain in neoconservatism; see Diggins's intriguing *Ronald Reagan*, esp. ch. 1, "The Political Romantic," 19–54. The *Washington Post* four-part series "Angler: The Cheney Vice Presidency," June 24–27, 2007, offers extensive examples of the vice president's probusiness, antiregulation views, but does not attempt to explore Cheney's political philosophy. Cockburn's *Rumsfeld*, while excellent on Rumsfeld's arrogance and ambition, is similarly limited in addressing his broader vision. Also, Dubose and Bernstein, *Vice*, highlights the ways in which Watergate and the end of the Vietnam War shaped Cheney's monarchical views on federalism but offers little on underlying ideology.

26. Ehrman, *Neoconservatism*; Stelzer, ed., *Neocon Reader.*
27. Chandrasekaran, *Imperial Life in the Emerald City*, esp. ch. 5; Packer, *Assassin's Gate*, esp. chs. 4–6.
28. Barnes, *Rebel-in-Chief*; for a thoughtful conservative critique, see Garfinkle, "Toward National Greatness?"
29. Kennan, *Memoirs, 1925–1950*, 136.

CHAPTER 5

1. Reiss, "Life and Letters," 38–47.
2. Reiss, "Life and Letters," 45.
3. Miller, "Veering Off Course," 2.
4. Miller, "Veering Off Course," 3.
5. Miller, "Veering Off Course," p. 3.
6. Ribuffo, "Why There Is So Much Conservatism," 438–49.
7. Williams, *Contours of American History*; Kolko, *Triumph of Conservatism*; Wiebe, *Search for Order*; Genovese, *Southern Tradition.*
8. Trilling, *Liberal Imagination*, vii.
9. Miller, "Veering Off Course," 1.
10. Jumonville, *Critical Crossings*, 195.
11. Susman, "Nature of American Conservatism," 73.
12. Ribuffo, "So Much Conservatism."
13. Brinkley, *End of Reform*, 139.
14. Brinkley, *End of Reform*, 139.
15. Brinkley, *End of Reform*, 269.
16. Wolfe, *America's Impasse*; Collins, *More*, esp. ch. 2.
17. Hobsbawm, *Age of Extremes.*
18. Cited in Katznelson, *Desolation and Enlightenment*, x, from George Steiner, in *Bluebeard's Castle: Some Notes toward the Redefinition of Culture* (London: Faber, 1971), 13.
19. Katznelson, *Desolation and Enlightenment*, 49.

20. Katznelson, *Desolation and Enlightenment*, 36–43; also see Pells, *Liberal Mind in a Conservative Age*, 71–83.
21. Menand, *Metaphysical Club*, part 1.
22. Katznelson, *Desolation and Enlightenment*, 64.
23. Pells, *Liberal Mind*, 85.
24. Katznelson, *Desolation and Enlightenment*, 73.
25. Baehr, *Portable Hannah Arendt*, 13–14.
26. Young-Bruehl, *Why Arendt Matters*, 2, 4, 5.
27. Young-Bruehl, *Why Arendt Matters*, p. 39.
28. Young-Bruehl, *Hannah Arendt*, 451.
29. Young-Bruehl, *Hannah Arendt*, 403.
30. Baehr, *Portable Hannah Arendt*, esp. part 6, "Revolution and Preservation," and, within that, "The Revolutionary Tradition and Its Lost Treasures," 508–39.
31. Baehr, *Portable Hannah Arendt*, 160.
32. Fox, *Reinhold Niebuhr*, 247.
33. Fox, *Reinhold Niebuhr*, chs. 8–10.
34. Fox, *Reinhold Niebuhr*, 34.
35. Fox, *Reinhold Niebuhr*, 219.
36. Stephanson, *Kennan and the Art of Foreign Policy*, vii, 117.
37. Stephanson, *Kennan*, 221.
38. Kennan, *Memoirs*, 38.
39. Kennan, *Memoirs*, 319.
40. Stephanson, *Kennan*, 22–23.
41. Stephanson, *Kennan*, 108.
42. Bell, ed., *Radical Right*, esp. Richard Hofstadter, "The Pseudo-Conservative Revolt," 75–96.
43. Jumonville, *Critical Crossings*, 222.
44. Mills, *Sociological Imagination*; Mattson, *Intellectuals in Action*, ch. 2. James Pierson makes similar arguments in *Camelot and the Cultural Revolution*: "Liberalism, a doctrine of reform, thus began to absorb some of the intellectual characteristics of conservatism—a due regard for tradition and continuity, a sense that progress must be built on the solid achievements of the past, an awareness of the threat of Soviet totalitarianism, and a conviction that its domestic opponents were radicals at war with modernity" (3, 9, 11).
45. Pierson, *Camelot*, viii, p. 45.
46. Nash, *Conservative Intellectual Movement in America since 1945*, esp. 79–80.
47. Kirk, *Conservative Mind*, 8–11.
48. Kirk, *Conservative Mind*, 47.
49. Nash, *Conservative Intellectual Movement*, 197.
50. Kazin, *Populist Persuasion*, 183–90.

51. When I drove down in 1980 for my first interview at Stockton College along Route 30, I passed a well-known sign covering the entire side of an Egg Harbor City house, "U.S. Out of U.N."
52. Brennan, *Turning Right in the Sixties*; Carter, *The Politics of Rage.*
53. Judis, *William F. Buckley, Jr.*, chs. 14–16.
54. Nash, *Conservative Intellectual Movement*, 320–21.
55. Brennan, *Turning Right.*
56. Diggins, *Ronald Reagan*, 130–32.
57. Steinfels, *Neoconservatives*, 15.
58. Brown, *Richard Hofstadter*, 120–41; Hofstadter, *Anti-Intellectualism in American Life*; Hartz, *Liberal Tradition in America*; Pells, *Liberal Mind*, 151–62.
59. Steinfels, *Neoconservatives*, 27; Brown, *Richard Hofstadter*, 120–41.
60. Lyons, *New Left, New Right and the Legacy of the Sixties.*
61. Kristol, *Neoconservatism*, 29–31.
62. Rainwater and Yancey, *Moynihan Report and the Politics of Controversy.*
63. Glazer, "Limits of Social Policy"; the *Public Interest*, from its initial issues and well into the early 1970s, was decidedly social-democratic albeit iconoclastic, that is, open to more conservative voices such as Robert Nisbet, James Q. Wilson, and Milton Friedman, as well as the increasingly conservative Irving Kristol, the coeditor. The first issues included pieces by left-of-center thinkers such as Robert Heilbroner, Victor Fuchs, Christopher Jencks, Charles Reich, Kenneth Boulding, and Herbert Gans.
64. On Bennett, see my *New Left, New Right*, 149–52.
65. Glazer, *We Are All Multiculturalists Now*, compared with his earlier *Affirmative Discrimination.*
66. Nash, *Conservative Intellectual Movement*, 248; Hodgson, *World Turned Right Side Up*, 81.
67. Goldberg, *Barry Goldwater.*
68. Raspberry, "Reagan's Race Legacy," A17.
69. Edsall and Edsall, *Chain Reaction*; Micklethwait and Wooldridge, *Right Nation*, 29–34.
70. Wattenberg, *First Universal Nation.*
71. Although Will uses the term often, its origin, according to the Oxford English Dictionary, can be traced to the Australian critic Clive James in 1985.
72. Social Democrats USA, formed in 1973, was organized by those hawkish activists who supported Henry (Scoop) Jackson's campaign for the Democratic nomination for president in 1972. They were part of the emergence of neoconservatism. Leaders include Carl Gershman, Jeanne Kirkpatrick, Max Kampelman, and Sandra Feldman.

73. Hodgson, *World Turned Right Side Up*, 230–38.
74. Diggins, *Ronald Reagan*, 374–87.
75. Drew, "Neocons in Power"; Stelzer, *Neocon Reader*, for defensive responses to the disasters which followed the occupation of Iraq, see Rose, "Neo Culpa," 82–90, 144–46.
76. Morgenthau, *Vietnam and the United States*; Fulbright, *Arrogance of Power*; McCarthy, *Limits of Power*; Severeid, Severeid, and Lippmann, *Conservations with Eric Severeid*; Kennan, *Memoirs*; references to Arendt and Kennan above.
77. Burns, "In Retrospect: George Nash's *The Conservative Intellectual Movement in America Since 1945*," 448, 454.
78. Burns, "In Retrospect," 458–59.
79. Lyons, "From Camelot to Cowboy," ch. 3 in this book.
80. Clecak, *Crooked Paths*, 119.
81. Clecak, *Crooked Paths*, 114.
82. Clecak, *Crooked Paths*, 103.
83. Will, *Statecraft as Soulcraft*, 21.
84. Will, *Statecraft as Soulcraft*, 65.
85. Will, *Statecraft as Soulcraft*, 120.
86. Will, *Statecraft as Soulcraft*, 77.
87. Will has too often engaged in conventional Republican partisanship, including his morally dubious involvement in prepping Ronald Reagan for debate followed by commentary without mention of his involvement, his one-sided and often vitriolic criticisms of the Clinton administration, and his devotion to the notion that all forms of campaign finance restrictions are violations of free speech.
88. Genovese, *Southern Tradition*, 22.
89. Genovese, *Southern Tradition*, 88–91, 17–18.
90. Clecak, *Crooked Paths*, ch. 5.

POSTSCRIPT

1. Conservative reflections include Viguerie, *Conservatives Betrayed*; Sager, *Elephant in the Room*; Tanner, *Leviathan on the Right*; Bartlett, *Imposter*; Sullivan, *Conservative Soul*; Dean, *Conservatives without Conscience*. Among the efforts to revitalize liberalism: Krugman, *Conscience of a Liberal*; Reich, *Reason*; Dionne, Jumonville, and Mattson, *Liberalism for a New Century*; Starr, *Freedom's Power*.
2. Brzezinski, *Choice*; Iraq Study Group, Baker, and Hamilton, *Iraq Study Group Report*; Bacevich, *New American Militarism*.

Bibliography

Albert, Michael, and Robin Hahnel. *Looking Forward: Participatory Economics for the Twenty-First Century.* Boston: Beacon Press, 1991.

Bacevich, Andrew. *The New American Militarism: How Americans Are Seduced by War.* New York: Oxford University Press, 2005.

Baehr, Peter, ed. *The Portable Hannah Arendt.* New York: Penguin Books, 2003.

Baltzell, E. Digby. *The Protestant Establishment: Aristocracy and Caste in America.* New York: Vintage Books, 1964.

Barber, Benjamin. *Jihad and McWorld: How Globalization and Tribalism Are Reshaping the World.* New York: Ballantine Books, 1996.

Barnes, Fred. *Rebel-in-Chief: Inside the Bold and Controversial Presidency of George W. Bush.* New York: Crown Forum, 2006.

Bartlett, Bruce. *Imposter: How George W. Bush Bankrupted America and Betrayed the Reagan Legacy.* New York: Doubleday, 2006.

Bell, Daniel. *The Cultural Contradictions of Capitalism.* New York: HarperCollins, 1996.

———. *The End of Ideology.* New York: Free Press, 1960.

———, ed. *The Radical Right—Expanded and Updated.* Garden City: Anchor Books, Doubleday, 1964.

Bennett, William J. *Why We Fight: Moral Clarity and the War on Terrorism.* New York: Doubleday, 2002.

Berger, Peter L. *The Homeless Mind: Modernization and Consciousness.* New York: Random House, 1973.

Beschloss, Michael R. *The Crisis Years: Kennedy and Khrushchev, 1960–1963.* New York: Harper Collins, 1991.

———. *Mayday: The U-2 Affair, the Untold Story of the Greatest USSR Spy Scandal.* New York: HarperCollins, 1987.

Bird, Kai, and Lawrence Lifschultz, eds. *Hiroshima's Shadow: Writings on the*

Denial of History and the Smithsonian Controversy. Washington, DC: Pamphleteer's Press, 1998.

Bonner, Raymond. *Waltzing with a Dictator: The Marcoses and the Making of American Policy*. New York: Vintage Books, 1988.

Boot, Max. *The Savage Wars of Peace: Small Wars and the Rise of American Power*. New York: Basic Books, 2003.

Borstelmann, Thomas. *Apartheid's Reluctant Uncle: The United States and South Africa in the Early Cold War*. New York: Oxford University Press, 1993.

Brennan, Mary C. *Turning Right in the Sixties: The Conservative Capture of the GOP*. Chapel Hill: University of North Carolina Press, 1995.

Brinkley, Alan. *The End of Reform: New Deal Liberalism in Recession and War*. New York: Vintage Books, 1996.

Brooks, David. *Bobos in Paradise: The New Upper Classes and How They Got There*. New York: Simon and Schuster, 2001.

Brooks, Van Wyck. *The Early Years*. New York: Harper Torchbook, Harper and Row, 1968.

Brown, David S. *Richard Hofstadter: An Intellectual Biography*. Chicago: University of Chicago Press, 2006.

Brown, Robert McAfee, ed. *The Essential Reinhold Niebuhr*. New Haven: Yale University Press, 1986.

Brzezinski, Zbigniew. *The Choice: Global Domination or Global Leadership*. New York: Basic Books, 2005.

Burlingame, Roger. *Henry Ford*. Chicago: Quadrangle Books, 1954.

Burns, Jennifer. "In Retrospect: George Nash's *The Conservative Intellectual Movement in America Since 1945*," *Reviews in American History* 32 (2004): 448, 454.

Carter, Dan T. *The Politics of Rage: George Wallace, the Origins of the New Conservatism, and the Transformation of American Politics*. Baton Rouge: Louisiana State University Press, 2000.

Chandrasekaran, Rajiv. *Imperial Life in the Emerald City: Inside Iraq's Green Zone*. New York: Alfred A. Knopf, 2007.

Cherry, Conrad, ed. *God's New Israel: Religious Interpretations of American Destiny*. Chapel Hill: University of North Carolina Press, 1998.

Chomsky, Noam. *Hegemony or Survival: America's Quest for Global Dominance*. New York: Metropolitan Books, 2003.

Clecak, Peter. *Crooked Paths: Reflections on Socialism, Conservatism, and the Welfare State*. New York: Colophon Books, Harper and Row, 1978.

Cockburn, Andrew. *Rumsfeld: His Rise, Fall, and Catastrophic Legacy*. New York: Scribner, 2007.

Cohen, Lizabeth. *A Consumers' Republic: The Politics of Mass Consumption in Postwar America*. New York: Vintage Books, 2003.

Collins, Robert M. *More: The Politics of Economic Growth in Postwar America.* New York: Oxford University Press, 2000.
Cooper, Richard T. "General Casts War in Religious Terms." *Los Angeles Times*, October 16, 2003.
Daalder, Ivo H., and James M. Lindsay. *America Unbound: The Bush Revolution in Foreign Policy.* Washington, D.C.: Brookings Institution Press, 2003.
Davis, Nathaniel. *The Last Two Years of Salvador Allende.* Ithaca: Cornell University Press, 1985.
Dean, John W. *Conservatives without Conscience.* New York: Penguin, 2007.
DeGrazia, Victoria. *Irresistible Empire: America's Advance through Twentieth-Century Europe.* Cambridge: Belknap Press of Harvard University Press, 2005.
Denning, Michael. *The Cultural Front.* New York: Verso, 1998.
Diggins, John Patrick. *Ronald Reagan: Fate, Freedom, and the Making of History.* New York: W. W. Norton, 2007.
Dionne, E. J. *Why Americans Hate Politics.* New York: Simon and Schuster, 1992.
Dionne, E. J., Neil Jumonville, and Kevin Mattson. *Liberalism for a New Century.* Berkeley: University of California Press, 2007.
Douglas, Ann. *Terrible Honesty: Mongrel Manhattan in the 1920s.* New York: Farrar, Straus and Giroux, 1996.
Drew, Elizabeth. "The Neocons in Power." *New York Review of Books* 50, no. 10 (June 12, 2003).
Drinnon, Richard. *Facing West: The Metaphysics of Indian-hating and Empire-building.* Minneapolis: University of Minnesota Press, 1980.
Dubose, Lou, and Jake Bernstein. *Vice: Dick Cheney and the Hijacking of the American Presidency.* New York: Random House, 2006.
Edsall, Thomas Byrne, and Mary D. Edsall. *Chain Reaction: The Impact of Race, Rights, and Taxes on American Politics.* New York: W. W. Norton, 1992.
Edwards, Lee, ed. *The Essential Ronald Reagan: A Profile in Courage, Justice, and Wisdom.* Lanham, MD: Rowman and Littlefield, 2005.
Ehrman, John. *Neoconservatism: Intellectuals and Foreign Affairs, 1945–1994.* New Haven: Yale University Press, 1995.
Eisenstadt, S. N. *Modernization: Protest and Change.* Englewood Cliffs: Prentice-Hall, 1966.
Ferguson, Niall. *Colossus: The Rise and Fall of the American Empire.* New York: Penguin Books, 2005.
Fox, Richard Wrightman. *Reinhold Niebuhr: A Biography.* Ithaca: Cornell University Press, 1996.
Freud, Sigmund. *Civilization and Its Discontents*, in *The Complete*

Psychological Works of Sigmund Freud, vol. 21. London: Hogarth Press, 1973.

Friedman, Thomas L. *The Lexus and the Olive Branch: Understanding Globalization.* New York: Anchor Books, 2000.

Fulbright, J. William. *The Arrogance of Power.* New York: Random House, 1967.

Garfinkle, Adam. "Toward National Greatness? A July 4th Reflection." *Foreign Policy Research Institute* 1, no. 4 (July 1998).

Genovese, Eugene. *The Southern Tradition: The Achievements and Limitations of American Conservatism.* Reprint, Cambridge: Harvard University Press, 1996.

Glazer, Nathan. *Affirmative Discrimination: Ethnic Inequality and Public Policy.* Cambridge: Harvard University Press, 1987.

———. "The Limits of Social Policy." *Commentary*, September 1971.

———. *We Are All Multiculturalists Now.* Cambridge: Harvard University Press, 1998.

Goldberg, Robert Alan. *Barry Goldwater.* New Haven: Yale University Press, 1997.

Goodman, Amy. *The Exception to the Rulers: Exposing Oily Politicians, War Profiteers, and the Media That Love Them.* New York: Hyperion, 2004.

Goodman, Paul. *Growing Up Absurd.* New York: Random House, 1960.

Halper, Stefan, and Jonathan Clarke. *America Alone: The Neo-Conservatives and the Global Order.* Cambridge: Cambridge University Press, 2004.

Hammond, Bray. *Banks and Politics in America from the Revolution to the Civil War.* Princeton: Princeton University Press, 1991.

Hanson, Victor Davis. *An Autumn of War: What America Learned from September 11 and the War on Terrorism.* New York: Anchor Books, 2002.

———. *Between War and Peace: Lessons from Afghanistan to Iraq.* New York: Random House, 2004.

Hardt, Michael, and Antonio Negri. *Multitude: War and Democracy in the Age of Empire.* New York: Penguin/Putnam, 2004.

Hartz, Louis. *The Liberal Tradition in America.* New York: Harvest Book, Harcourt, Brace and World, 1955.

Hayek, Friedrich. *The Road to Serfdom.* Chicago: University of Chicago Press, 1944.

Hayward, Steven F. *Greatness: Reagan, Churchill, and the Making of Extraordinary Leaders.* New York: Crown Forum, 2005.

Heimert, Alan. *Documents to Illustrate the Crisis and Its Consequences.* Indianapolis: Bobbs-Merrill, 1967.

———. *Religion and the American Mind: From the Great Awakening to the Revolution.* Eugene, OR: Wipf and Stock, 2006.

Herberg, Will. *Protestant-Catholic-Jew: An Essay in American Religious Sociology.* Chicago: University of Chicago Press, 1983.

Herbert, Bob. "From 'Gook' to 'Raghead.'" *New York Times*, May 2, 2005.

Herring, George. *America's Longest War: The United States and Vietnam, 1950–1975*. 4th ed. New York: McGraw-Hill, 2002.

Hertzke, Allen D. *Freeing God's Children: The Unlikely Alliance for Global Human Rights*. London: Rowman and Littlefield, 2004.

Hobsbawm, Eric. *The Age of Extremes: A History of the World, 1914–1991*. New York: Vintage Books, 1996.

Hodgson, Godfrey. *America in Our Time: From World War II to Nixon—What Happened and Why*. New York: Vintage, 1976.

———. *The World Turned Right Side Up: A History of the Conservative Ascendancy in America*. New York: Houghton Mifflin, 1996.

Hofstadter, Richard. *Anti-Intellectualism in American Life*. New York: Vintage Books, 1963.

Horsman, Reginald. *Race and Manifest Destiny: The Origins of American Racial Anglo-Saxonism*. Cambridge: Harvard University Press, 1987.

The Iraq Study Group, James A. Baker, and Lee H. Hamilton. *The Iraq Study Group Report: The Way Forward—A New Approach*. Washington: Filiquarian, 2007.

Jacobs, Jane. *The Death and Life of American Cities*. New York: Random House, 1961.

Johnson, Chalmers. "America's Empire of Bases," *www.tomdispatch.com*, posted Jauary 15, 2004.

———. *The Sorrows of Empire: Militarism, Secrecy, and the End of the Republic*. New York: Metropolitan Books, 2004.

Judis, John B. *William F. Buckley, Jr.: Patron Saint of the Conservatives*. New York: Touchstone Books, 1990.

Jumonville, Neil. *Critical Crossings: The New York Intellectuals in Postwar America*. Berkeley: University of California Press, 1991.

Kagan, Robert. *Of Paradise and Power: America and Europe in the New World Order*. New York: Knopf, 2003.

Kahl, Joseph A. *Modernization, Exploitation, and Dependency in Latin America*. New Brunswick: Transaction Books, 1976.

Karnow, Stanley. *In Our Image: America's Empire in the Philippines*. New York: Random House, 1989.

Katznelson, Ira. *Desolation and Enlightenment: Political Knowledge after Total War, Totalitarianism, and the Holocaust*. New York: Columbia University Press, 2003.

Kazin, Michael. *The Populist Persuasion: An American History*. Ithaca, NY: Cornell University Press, 1998.

Kengor, Paul. *The Crusader: Ronald Reagan and the Fall of Communism*. New York: Regan/HarperCollins, 2006.

Kennan, George F. *Memoirs, 1925–1950*. New York: Bantam Books, 1969.

Kinzer, Stephan. *All the Shah's Men: An American Coup and the Roots of Middle East Terror.* New York: Wiley, 2003.

Kirk, Russell. *The Conservative Mind: From Burke to Eliot.* 7th rev. ed. Washington: Regnery Publishing, 1986.

Klare, Michael C. *Blood and Oil: The Dangers and Consequences of America's Growing Petroleum Dependency.* New York: Metropolitan Books/Henry Holt, 2004.

Klein, Naomi. *Fences and Windows: Dispatches from the Front Lines of the Globalization Debate.* London: Picador, 2002.

Kolko, Gabriel. *The Triumph of Conservatism: A Reinterpretation of American History, 1900–1916.* New York: Free Press, 1977.

Kristol, Irving. *Neoconservatism: The Autobiography of an Idea.* Chicago: Elephant Paperbacks, Ivan R. Dee, Publisher, 1999.

Krugman, Paul. *The Conscience of a Liberal.* New York: W. W. Norton, 2007.

Lage, Ann. "An Interview with Lawrence W. Levine." *American Historical Review* 93, no. 3 (December 2006).

Larson, Edward J. *Summer for the Gods: The Scopes Trial and America's Continuing Debate over Science and Religion.* New York: Basic Books, 2006.

Leach, William R. *Land of Desire: Merchants, Power, and the Rise of a New American Culture.* New York: Vintage Books, 1994.

Lewis, R. W. B. *The American Adam.* Chicago: University of Chicago Press, 1959.

Lyons, Paul. *New Left, New Right and the Legacy of the Sixties.* Philadelphia: Temple University Press, 1996.

———. *The People of This Generation: The Rise and Fall of the New Left in Philadelphia.* Philadelphia: University of Pennsylvania Press, 2004.

Mailer, Norman. *Cannibals and Christians.* New York: Pinnacle Books, 1981.

Mandle, Jay R. *Globalization and the Poor.* Cambridge: Cambridge University Press, 2002.

Mann, James. *The Rise of the Vulcans: The History of Bush's War Cabinet.* New York: Viking Press, 2004.

Marcuse, Herbert. *An Essay on Liberation.* Boston: Beacon Press, 1971.

———. *One-Dimensional Man: Studies in the Ideology of Advanced Industrial Society.* Boston: Beacon Press, 1964.

Marx, Leo. *The Machine in the Garden: Technology and the Pastoral Ideal in America.* New York: Oxford University Press, 1999.

Mattson, Kevin. *Intellectuals in Action: The Origins of the New Left and Radical Liberalism, 1945–1970.* University Park: Pennsylvania State University Press, 2002.

McCarthy, Eugene. *The Limits of Power: America's Role in the World.* New York: Dell, 1968.

Mead, Walter Russell. *Power, Terror, Peace, and War: America's Grand Strategy in a World at Risk*. New York: Knopf, 2004.

———. *Special Providence: American Foreign Policy and How It Changed the World*. New York: Routledge, 2002.

Menand, Louis. *The Metaphysical Club: A Story of Ideas in America*. New York: Farrar, Straus and Giroux, 2001.

Micklethwait, John, and Adrian Wooldridge. *The Right Nation: Conservative Power in America*. New York: Penguin, 2004.

Miller, John J. "Veering Off Course." *National Review Online*, October 26, 2005, *www.nationalreview.com*.

Mills, C. Wright. *The Sociological Imagination*. New York: Oxford University Press, 1959.

———. *White Collar: The American Middle Classes*. New York: Oxford University Press, 1951.

Moore, Stanley. "Utopian Themes in Marx and Mao," *Dissent*, March–April 1970.

Morgenthau, Hans. *Vietnam and the United States*. Washington, DC: Public Affairs Press, 1965.

Morley, Morris H. *Imperial State and Revolution: The United States and Cuba, 1952–1986*. Cambridge: Cambridge University Press, 1987.

Morris, Edmund. *Dutch: A Memoir of Ronald Reagan*. New York: Random House, 1999.

Nash, George H. *The Conservative Intellectual Movement in America since 1945*. Wilmington, DE: Intercollegiate Studies Institute, 1998.

Niebuhr, H. Richard. *Christ and Culture*. New York: Harper and Row, 1951.

Nock, Albert Jay. *The Memoirs of a Superfluous Man*. Tampa, FL: Hallberg, 1994.

Noonan, Peggy. *What I Saw at the Revolution*. New York: Random House, 1990.

Nove, Alec. *The Economics of Feasible Socialism*. London: G. Allen and Unwin, 1983.

Onuf, Peter S. *Jefferson's Empire: The Language of American Nationhood*. Charlottesville: University Press of Virginia, 2000.

Ortega y Gasset, José. *Revolt of the Masses*. New York: W. W. Norton, 1957.

Packer, George. *The Assassin's Gate: America in Iraq*. New York: Farrar, Straus and Giroux, 2006.

Paterson, Thomas G. *Contesting Castro: The United States and the Triumph of the Cuban Revolution*. New York: Oxford University Press, 1994.

Patterson, Orlando. *The Ordeal of Integration: Progress and Resentment in America's "Racial" Crisis*. Washington, DC: Civitas/Counterpoint, Publishers Group West, 1997.

Pells, Richard H. *The Liberal Mind in a Conservative Age: American*

Intellectuals in the 1940s. Middletown, CT: Wesleyan University Press, 1989.

———. *Not Like Us: How Europeans Have Loved, Hated, and Transformed American Culture since World War II.* New York: Basic Books, 1997.

Phillips, Kevin. *The Emerging Republican Majority.* New York: Anchor Books, 1970.

Pierson, James. *Camelot and the Cultural Revolution: How the Assassination of John F. Kennedy Shattered American Liberalism.* New York: Encounter Books, 2007.

Rainwater, Lee, and William L. Yancey. *The Moynihan Report and the Politics of Controversy.* Boston: M.I.T. Press, 1967.

Rand, Ayn. *The Virtue of Selfishness.* New York: Signet Books, 1964.

Raspberry, William. "Reagan's Race Legacy," *Washington Post*, June 14, 2004, A17.

Rawls, John. *A Theory of Justice.* Cambridge: Belknap, Harvard University Press, 1971.

Reich, Robert B. *Reason: Why Liberals Will Win the Battle for America.* New York: Vintage, 2005.

Reisman, David. *The Lonely Crowd.* New Haven: Yale University Press, 1995.

Reiss, Tom. "Life and Letters: The First Conservative," *New Yorker*, October 24, 2005.

Remini, Robert V. *Andrew Jackson and the Bank War: A Study in the Growth of Presidential Power.* New York: W. W. Norton, 1967.

———. *Jackson and His Indian Wars.* New York: Viking, 2001.

Ribuffo, Leo P. "Why There Is So Much Conservatism in the United States and Why Do So Few Historians Know Anything about It?" *American Historical Review* 99, no. 2 (April 1999).

Roberts, James C., ed. *A City upon a Hill: Speeches by Ronald Reagan before the Conservative Political Action Conference.* Washington, DC: American Studies Center, 1989.

Rockefeller Foundation, ed. *Modernization and Cultural Values, A Bellagio Conference, June 1978.* New York: Rockefeller Foundation, 1979.

Rose, David. "Neo Culpa." *Vanity Fair*, January 2007, 82–90, 144–46.

Rosenberg, Bernard, and David Manning White, eds. *Mass Culture: The Popular Arts in America.* New York: Free Press, 1957.

Rostow, W. W. *The Stages of Economic Growth: A Non-Communist Manifesto.* Cambridge: Cambridge University Press, 1960.

Rourke, Constance. *American Humor: A Study of National Character.* New York: Doubleday, 1953.

———. *The Roots of American Culture.* New York: Harvest Book, Harcourt, Brace and World, 1942.

———. *Trumpets of Jubilee.* New York: Harbinger Books, Harcourt, Brace and World, 1963.

Roy, Arundhati. *An Ordinary Person's Guide to Empire.* Boston: South End Press, 2004.

Ruppert, Michael C. *Crossing the Rubicon: The Decline of the American Empire and the End of the Age of Oil.* New York: New Society, 2004.

Sager, Ryan. *The Elephant in the Room: Evangelicals, Libertarians and the Battle to Control the Republican Party.* New York: Wiley, 2006.

Schlesinger, Arthur, Jr. *The Vital Center.* New York: Sentry Edition, Houghton Mifflin, 1962.

Schlesinger, Stephen C., and Stephan Kinzer, *Bitter Fruit: The Story of the American Coup in Guatemala.* Cambridge: Harvard University Press, 1999.

Severeid, Arnold Eric, Eric Severeid, and Walter Lippmann, *Conservations with Eric Severeid.* Washington, DC: Public Affairs Press, 1976.

Stansell, Christine. *American Moderns: Bohemian New York and the Creation of a New Century.* New York: Holt, 2001.

Starr, Paul. *Freedom's Power: The True Force of Liberalism.* New York: Perseus Books, 2007.

Steiner, George. *Bluebeard's Castle: Some Notes Toward the Redefinition of Culture.* London: Faber, 1971.

Steinfels, Peter. *The Neoconservatives: The Men Who Are Changing America's Politics.* New York: Touchstone Books, Simon and Schuster, 1979.

Stelzer, Irwin, ed. *The Neocon Reader.* New York: Grove Press, 2004.

Stephanson, Anders. *Kennan and the Art of Foreign Policy.* Cambridge: Harvard University Press, 1992.

———. *Manifest Destiny: American Expansionism and the Empire of Right.* New York: Hill and Wang, 1995.

Stiglitz, Joseph. *Globalization and Its Discontents.* New York: W. W. Norton, 2003

Sullivan, Andrew. *The Conservative Soul: Fundamentalism, Freedom and the Future of the Right.* New York: Harper, 2007.

Susman, Warren I. *Culture as History: The Transformation of American Society in the Twentieth Century.* New York: Pantheon Books, 1984.

Swofford, Anthony. *Jarhead: A Marine's Chronicle of the Gulf War and Other Battles.* New York: Scribner, 2003.

Tanner, Michael D. *Leviathan on the Right: How Big-Government Conservatism Brought Down the Republican Revolution.* Washington: CATO Institute, 2007.

Trilling, Lionel. *The Liberal Imagination.* New York: Viking Press, Anchor Books, 1953.

Tuveson, Ernest Lee. *Redeemer Nation: The Idea of America's Millennial Role.* Chicago: University of Chicago Press, 1980.

Van Eschen, Penny M. *Satchmo Blows Up the World: Jazz Ambassadors Play the Cold War.* Cambridge: Harvard University Press, 2004.

Viguerie, Richard A. *Conservatives Betrayed: How George W. Bush and Other Big Government Republicans Hijacked the Conservative Cause*. Los Angeles: Bonus Books, 2006.

Wallace, Anthony. *The Long, Bitter Trail: Andrew Jackson and the Indians*. New York: Hill and Wang, 1993.

Warrior, Robert Allan. "Canaanites, Cowboys, and Indians: Deliverance, Conquest, and Liberation Theology." In *Voices of the Religious Left: A Contemporary Sourcebook*, ed. Rebecca T. Alpert. Philadelphia: Temple University Press, 2000.

Wattenberg, Ben J. *The First Universal Nation*. New York: Touchstone Books, 1992.

Waxman, Chaim I., ed. *The End of Ideology Debate*. New York: Clarion Books, Simon and Schuster, 1968.

Weinstein, James. *The Corporate Ideal in the Liberal State*. Boston: Beacon Press, 1968.

Whyte, William H. *Organization Man*. Philadelphia: University of Pennsylvania Press, 2002.

Wiebe, Robert H. *The Search for Order*. New York: Hill and Wang, 1966.

Wilensky, Harold L., and Richard Lebeaux. *Industrial Society and Social Welfare: The Impact of Industrialization on the Supply and Organization of Social Welfare*. New York: Free Press, 1965.

Williams, William Appleman. *The Contours of American History*. Chicago: Quadrangle Books, 1966. Reprint, New York: W. W. Norton, 1989.

———. *The Great Evasion: An Essay on the Contemporary Relevance of Karl Marx and on the Wisdom of Admitting the Heretic into the Dialogue About America's Future*. Chicago: Quadrangle Books, 1964.

———. *The Tragedy of American Diplomacy*. New York: W. W. Norton, 1988.

Willis, Michael. *The Islamist Challenge in Algeria: A Political History*. New York: New York University Press, 1999.

Wilson, R. J., ed. *Darwinism and the American Intellectual: A Book of Readings*. Homewood: Dorsey Press, 1967.

Wolfe, Alan. *America's Impasse: The Rise and Fall of the Politics of Growth*. New York: Pantheon Books, 1981.

Wolfe, Tom. *The Purple Decades: A Reader*. New York: Berkley Books, 1987.

Young-Bruehl, Elizabeth, *Hannah Arendt: For Love of the World*. New Haven: Yale University Press, 1982.

———. *Why Arendt Matters*. New Haven: Yale University Press, 2006.

Index